P9-CJU-774

Guide to America's Outdoors

New England

Guide to America's Outdoors
New England

By Gary Ferguson
Photography by Michael Melford

NATIONAL
GEOGRAPHIC
WASHINGTON, D.C.

Contents

Cover: Paper birches, White Mountain National Forest, New Hampshire *Page 1:* Gulliver's Hole, Quoddy Head State Park, Maine *Pages 2-3:* Hikers on Mount Mansfield, Vermont *Opposite:* Polly Hill Arboretum, Martha's Vineyard, Massachusetts

Treading Lightly in the Wild

Chicken of the woods fungus

NATIONAL GEOGRAPHIC GUIDE TO AMER-ICA'S OUTDOORS: NEW ENGLAND takes you to some of the wildest and most beautiful natural areas in a region famous for its spectacular coastline, rocky mountainsides, woods of maple, aspen, and birch afire with autumn color, and remote lakes that ring with the antic call of the loon.

Visitors who care about this region know they must tread lightly on the land. Ecosystems can be damaged, even destroyed, by thoughtless misuse. Many have already suffered from the impact of tourism. The marks are clear: litter-strewn acres, polluted waters, trampled vegetation, and disturbed wildlife. You can do your part to preserve these places for yourself, your children, and all other nature travelers. Before embarking on a backcountry visit or a camping adventure, learn some basic conservation dos and don'ts. Leave No Trace, a national educational program, recommends the following:

Plan ahead and prepare for your trip. If you know what to expect in terms of climate, conditions, and hazards, you can pack for general needs, extreme weather, and emergencies. Do yourself and the land a favor by visiting if possible during off-peak months and limiting your group to no more than four to six people. To keep trash or litter to a minimum, repackage food into reusable containers or bags. And rather than using cairns, flags, or paint cues that mar the environment to mark your way, bring a map and compass.

Travel and camp on solid surfaces. In popular areas, stay within established trails and campsites. Travel single-file in the middle of the trail, even when it's wet or muddy, to avoid trampling vegetation. Be particularly sensitive in boggy or coastal areas, and avoid stepping on mussels, sea stars, and the like. When exploring off the trail in pristine, lightly traveled areas, have your group spread out to lessen impact. Good campsites are found, not made. Travel and camp on sand, gravel, or rock, or on dry grasses, pine needles, or snow. Remember to stay at least 200 feet from waterways. After you've broken camp, leave the site as you found it.

Pack out what you pack in—and that means *everything* except human waste, which should be deposited in a cathole dug away from water, camp, or trail, then covered and concealed. When washing dishes, clothes, or yourself, use small amounts of biodegradable soap and scatter the water away from lakes and streams.

Be sure to leave all items—plants, rocks, artifacts—as you find them. Avoid potential disaster by neither introducing nor transporting non-native species. Also, don't build or carve out structures that will alter the environment. A don't-touch policy not only preserves resources for future generations; it also gives the next guy a crack at the discovery experience.

Keep fires to a minimum. It may be unthinkable to camp without a campfire, but depletion of firewood harms the backcountry. When you can, try a gas-fueled camp stove and a candle lantern. If you choose to build a fire, first consider regulations, weather, skill, and firewood availability. At the beach, build your fire below the next high-tide line, where the traces will be washed away. Where possible, employ existing fire rings; elsewhere, use fire pans or mound fires. Keep your fire small, use only sticks from the ground, burn the fire down to ash, and don't leave the site until it's cold.

Respect wildlife. Watch animals from a distance (bring binoculars or a telephoto lens for close-ups), but never approach, feed, or follow them. Feeding weakens an animal's ability to fend for itself in the wild. If you can't keep your pets under control, leave them at home.

Finally, be mindful of other visitors. Yield to fellow travelers on the trail, and keep voices and noise levels low so that all the sounds of nature can be heard.

With these points in mind, you have only to chart your course. Enjoy your explorations. Let natural places quiet your mind, refresh your spirit, and remain as you found them. Just remember, leave behind no trace.

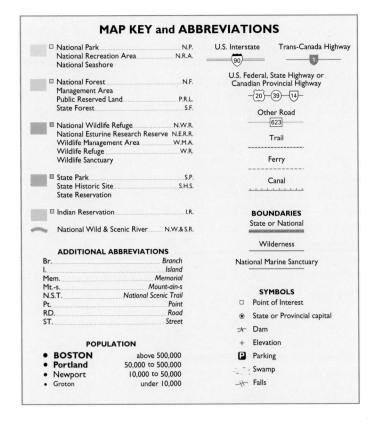

MAP KEY and ABBREVIATIONS

National Park .... N.P.
National Recreation Area .... N.R.A.
National Seashore

National Forest .... N.F.
Management Area
Public Reserved Land .... P.R.L.
State Forest .... S.F.

National Wildlife Refuge .... N.W.R.
National Esturine Research Reserve N.E.R.R.
Wildlife Management Area .... W.M.A.
Wildlife Refuge .... W.R.
Wildlife Sanctuary

State Park .... S.P.
State Historic Site .... S.H.S.
State Reservation

Indian Reservation .... I.R.

National Wild & Scenic River .... N.W.&S.R.

ADDITIONAL ABBREVIATIONS

Br.	Branch
I.	Island
Mem.	Memorial
Mt.-s.	Mount-ain-s
N.S.T.	National Scenic Trail
Pt.	Point
RD.	Road
ST.	Street

POPULATION

● **BOSTON**	above 500,000
● **Portland**	50,000 to 500,000
● Newport	10,000 to 50,000
• Groton	under 10,000

U.S. Interstate
90

Trans-Canada Highway
1

U.S. Federal, State Highway or
Canadian Provincial Highway
20   39   14

Other Road
623

Trail
- - - - - - - - - - -

Ferry
- - - - - - - - - - -

Canal

BOUNDARIES
State or National

Wilderness

National Marine Sanctuary

SYMBOLS

□   Point of Interest
⊛   State or Provincial capital
⋟   Dam
+   Elevation
🅿   Parking
      Swamp
      Falls

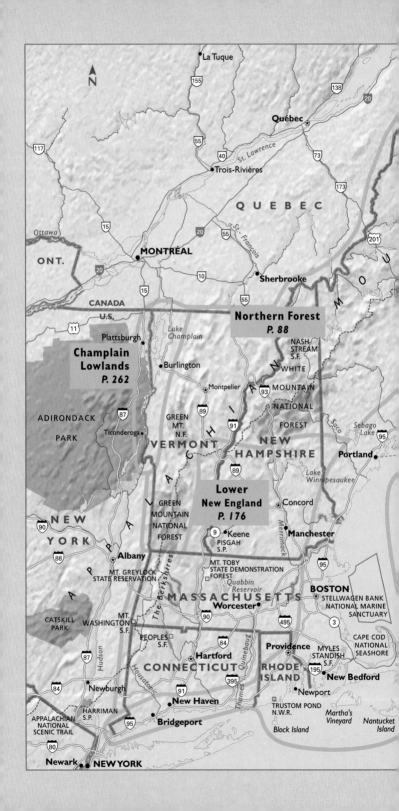

N

La Tuque

155

138

20

Québec

40

Trois-Rivières

73

117

55

173

201

15

20

55

St-François

Ottawa

QUÉBEC

ONT.

MONTRÉAL

10

Sherbrooke

15

55

CANADA

U.S.

11

Lake Champlain

Northern Forest
P. 88

Plattsburgh

Champlain Lowlands
P. 262

Burlington

NASH STREAM S.F.

WHITE

Montpelier

87

ADIRONDACK PARK

GREEN MT. N.F.

89

91

MOUNTAIN

93

NATIONAL

Ticonderoga

VERMONT

FOREST

NEW HAMPSHIRE

Saco

Sebago Lake

95

Portland

89

Lower New England
P. 176

Lake Winnipesaukee

Concord

NEW

90

YORK

88

GREEN MOUNTAIN NATIONAL FOREST

9

Keene

PISGAH S.P.

Manchester

Albany

MT. TOBY STATE DEMONSTRATION FOREST

Merrimack

MT. GREYLOCK STATE RESERVATION

Quabbin Reservoir

95

CATSKILL PARK

MASSACHUSETTS

BOSTON

STELLWAGEN BANK NATIONAL MARINE SANCTUARY

MT. WASHINGTON S.F.

The Berkshires

Worcester

90

495

3

Hudson

PEOPLES S.F.

84

Quinebaug

Providence

MYLES STANDISH S.F.

CAPE COD NATIONAL SEASHORE

87

Housatonic

Hartford

CONNECTICUT

195

New Bedford

84

Newburgh

91

395

RHODE ISLAND

Thames

TRUSTOM POND N.W.R.

Newport

95

New Haven

Martha's Vineyard

Nantucket Island

APPALACHIAN NATIONAL SCENIC TRAIL

HARRIMAN S.P.

Bridgeport

Block Island

80

Newark

NEW YORK

A P P A L A C H I A N

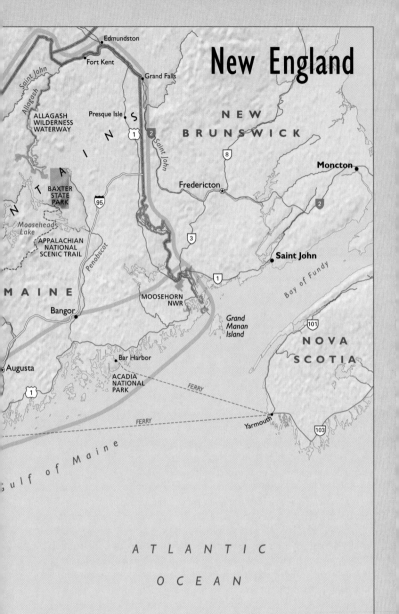

New England

Edmundston

Fort Kent

Saint John

Allagash

Grand Falls

ALLAGASH
WILDERNESS
WATERWAY

Presque Isle

N E W

B R U N S W I C K

Saint John

8

Moncton

M O U N T A I N S

BAXTER
STATE
PARK

Fredericton

95

Moosehead
Lake

APPALACHIAN
NATIONAL
SCENIC TRAIL

2

Penobscot

3

1

Saint John

M A I N E

MOOSEHORN
NWR

Bay of Fundy

Bangor

Grand
Manan
Island

101

N O V A

Augusta

Bar Harbor

ACADIA
NATIONAL
PARK

FERRY

S C O T I A

1

FERRY

Yarmouth

103

Gulf of Maine

A T L A N T I C

O C E A N

North Atlantic Coast
P. 14

0	miles	80
0	kilometers	120

Kayaking in Groton State Forest, Vermont

New England Waltz

MY FIRST DANCE WITH New England began in 1988, a slow, seven-month
waltz through the wilds, researching what would become the third in a
series of natural history guides I'd been writing for different regions of
the country. To this day, I remember my astonishment at the diversity
of this region. Within a relatively small stretch of land was an uncanny
mix of bogs and rivers, meadows and hardwoods and conifers, each a
powerful reminder of how even tiny variations in geology and soil, sunlight and moisture can lead to vastly different webs of life. On those few
days when I wasn't on the trail, I hung my hat in a small cottage on the
shore of Lake Willoughby, in Vermont's Northeast Kingdom. I recall the
sound of summer rain drumming on the roof, and at night, air that
smelled like grass and earth and deep water. As autumn began rolling
across the land, the scent of the place turned sharp, peppery, sweet with
the breath of dying leaves and earth, dampened by the November snows.

My second encounter came several years later. The experience this time
included hundreds of hours in libraries and museum collections in the
course of my work for a book called *Through the Woods: A Journey
Through America's Forests.* I began to understand the cultural significance
of natural New England; how it had not only produced wealth, but had
become a symbol of early America's fondest hopes and aspirations.

And now this book. Another seven months on the trail, rambling
through places that seem like old friends, as well as through a host of new
forests, coasts, and mountaintops. For all the thrill of being neck-deep
again in New England nature, what caught my attention most this time
were the residents. There are in these hills and forests, along these coasts,
so many who have a steadfast commitment to saving the beauty that
remains, who see landscape as a critical part of heritage. They taught me
a great deal about building a relationship to the land and about the vigor
that comes to a people wise enough to hold fast to place.

Gary Ferguson

The Worlds of New England

NOWHERE HAS AMERICA'S LOVE AFFAIR WITH NATURE been pursued with more passion than through the woods, mountains, and shorelines of New England. It was in 18th-century New England that pundits predicted artistic greatness for the nation—a boast rising from the idea that creativity would come first and best to those in constant relationship with the woods. It was here, during the early 1800s, that urban preachers routinely went on guided sojourns through the unexplored interior of Maine—fasting, climbing mountains, seeking inspiration to share with their congregations back in Boston and New York. It was in New England that the Hudson River school of landscape art unfolded, resulting in a rendering of mountains and woods so stirring that the painters came to be thought of as holy men. It was life on the land in early New England that led one of the nation's most prominent historians, Frederick Jackson Turner, to declare in 1892 that in America, freedom was a forest product.

Over the centuries, New England's wild places have suffered from periods of neglect and abuse, as have wild places throughout the country. But the way that New Englanders saw nature—a source of fear for the Pilgrims, a source of identity for their descendants fighting the Revolution—has added a unique cornerstone to our culture. Aided by the inspirational writings of men like William Cullen Bryant, John Greenleaf Whittier, Walt Whitman, and Ralph Waldo Emerson, the people of these fields and forests developed a powerful philosophy that nature, patriotism, and religion would be forever linked. New Englanders came to believe that who we are as a people would be understood best through our relationship with the land.

Happily, the New England of today remains rich almost beyond imagining. The mix of soil, climate, and topography is such that a half dozen miles of hiking or bicycling can offer up vastly different worlds, from meadows and bogs to fern gardens and oak groves, from rich tide pools to boreal forests, with all the diversity of bird- and animal life that such variety provides. That said, as you make your way along the roads and trails highlighted in this book, be aware that the New England of today is dramatically different from its past. The same Massachusetts and Connecticut lands that were mostly pasture in the 1880s are now more than 80 percent forest, the result of farmers abandoning their stony fields for more productive lands in the Midwest. The woods blanketing those former fields are far different too—both in the type of trees and in their stature—from the forests early European explorers found here in the 1600s.

The striking natural dynamics of wild New England, from wind and waves to fire and ice, combined with countless changes wrought by humans, make this a land in constant transition. One of the joys of hiking, canoeing, and biking here is encountering traces of nature's twisted tales: stumbling across a stone wall deep in the woods—silent witness to a time when this was open ground for sheep and cattle; long scars on the trunks of white oak—signatures of a major fire now a half century past; mixed hardwoods leveled by a recent ice storm—with the land being reclaimed by sun-loving birch.

When it comes to understanding how the natural world works, this is an especially exciting time in New England. In the course of the last ten years, conservation biologists have uncovered a great deal about the relationships among the plants and animals that make up the different ecosystems here, as well as about the specific needs of such life. This has led to a sophisticated effort to remap New England, trading state and township lines for boundaries drawn according to natural communities. Defined largely by the plants inhabiting them, these communities are referred to as "ecoregions."

The goal of the ecological analysis is to allow more effective management of our remaining natural resources. When it comes to saving threatened or endangered species, for example, past efforts have tended to focus on protecting all of the critical habitat of a single organism— a strategy often referred to as the "Noah's Ark approach." By contrast, management based on ecoregions allows scientists to spend limited funds more effectively by focusing on the most viable populations in the system. Furthermore, ecoregions promote biodiversity by shifting attention from single species toward so-called representative communities. Ultimately such models could allow decisions to be made about everything from tree harvests to housing developments based on the cumulative impacts such projects have on the larger system.

Clearly, this guide to New England is recreational, not scientific. Yet it has been designed with the spirit of this unprecedented conservation effort in mind. Of course, you'll find plenty of state lines and other recognizable boundaries to keep you on track as you make your way around the region. But the trails, rivers, parks, roads, and preserves highlighted in these pages are organized by New England's four major ecoregions: the North Atlantic Coast, the Northern Forest, Lower New England, and the Champlain Lowlands, which are limited to extreme northwestern Vermont.

Learning some of the basic plants and animals of these systems—and learning why they live where they do—can add greatly to your enjoyment of the outdoors, creating over time a stronger sense of connection to the land. Moving north out of Lake Winnipesaukee, New Hampshire, on N.H. 109 will suddenly mean more than the fact that the village of Center Sandwich is just a few miles up the road. The sugar maples, balsams, beeches, and birches drifting by the window are also sure signs that you've entered the southern edge of the boreal forest—an ecological community that will deepen and finally dominate the landscape all the way through northern Maine.

This book has been designed to help you forge that sense of place. For starters, each of New England's ecoregions is introduced with an essay explaining the natural dynamics of the area. In addition, the sites in the book were chosen according to a) the level of interpretation offered—guided walks, canoe trips, and other programs, or b) by how well they represent that particular region's environment.

As you can probably guess, moving beyond traditional land management models to see the world in terms of ecoregions has required a tremendous degree of cooperation. In that, New England is as fortunate as any place in America. One quickly loses count of the number of town forests, land trusts, conservation groups, museums, and private land owners now involved in grass-roots efforts to preserve what is left of this region's precious natural heritage. Besides traditional state and national parks, many of the preserves you'll find in this book—and often the very best examples of a specific kind of nature—are sites managed by local citizen members of groups such as the Maine Coast Heritage Trust, the New Hampshire Society for the Protection of Forests, the Green Mountain and Appalachian Mountain Clubs, as well as local chapters of the Nature Conservancy and Audubon Society.

And now it's time to grab your walking shoes, load up the bike, the kids, and the canoe, and head out for some of the most enticing nature adventures of your life. ■

Grasses on Block Island, Rhode Island

North Atlantic Coast

Sunset at Wells National Estuarine Research Reserve, Maine

TRUE TO ONE OF THE GREAT themes of outdoor New England, the coasts of Connecticut, Rhode Island, Massachusetts, New Hampshire, and Maine bring with them an extraordinary level of variety. To the south are the long, soothing tidal marshes of Long Island Sound, tossed with mats of cordgrass, spike grass, and black grass, the smooth, muddy bottoms pockmarked with the burrows of fiddler crabs. To the north are the sandy spits of Cape Cod, and at Martha's Vineyard, the brightly colored, chiseled cliffs

Camden Hills State Park overlooking Camden, Maine

of Gay Head. Southern Maine contains the quiet marshes and seaside forests of Wells National Estuarine Research Reserve, while a short distance to the north begins a maze of granite islands, in summer thick with the cries of a thousand seabirds.

To understand the varied look and feel of the New England coast, we must first turn to the comings and goings of glaciers. Ice has covered New England in separate periods of advance and retreat, the last one ending roughly 12,000 years ago. The retreat of these ice sheets in the face of a warming climate happened not in one smooth movement, but haltingly, in stages. During times of relative inactivity, the glaciers dumped the massive amounts of sediment they carried along their retreating edges, which in turn created sizable hills or deposits called moraines. The lower portions of Cape Cod, as well as the surrounding islands, were fashioned in exactly this way.

Later, as the glacial ice continued to melt, it produced enormous amounts of meltwater. (Keep in mind that these ice sheets were in some places more than a mile thick!) Much of the sediment contained in that meltwater traveled down to the sea and spread out over bare rock, creating vast outwash plains. Ocean currents and waves sculpted this material into the spits and beaches we see along the southern portions of the coast. Nor was this the only form of beach building. The southern portions of New England contain headlands made up of soft, sedimentary rock and glacial outwash (such as sandstone), which is easily eroded by ocean waves; even today the remaining headlands continue to peel away, sometimes at the rate of several feet per year. This eroded material doesn't just wash out to sea: It becomes the sand that is pushed around by currents and waves, maintaining, or even expanding, existing beaches. Geologists often refer to a relatively even shore such as those you'll find in

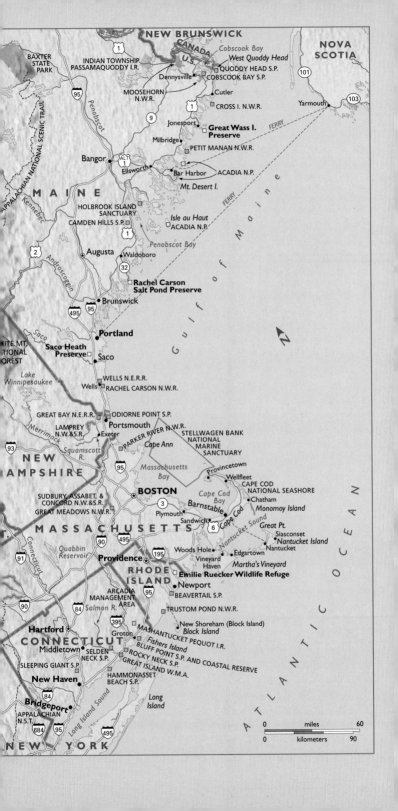

Rhode Island or Connecticut—a shore without headlands, deep bays, or other irregularities—as a "mature coast."

Farther to the north, by contrast, especially Down East in Maine, the coast is anything but mature. In fact, if you could manage to wind your way around each inlet and cove in some stretches of the north, you'd end up traveling roughly ten times the distance you would have covered if you'd moved in a straight line. This is because the coast here is made up of extremely hard, metamorphic and granitic rocks. Harder rock is slower to erode, so waves and weather have been unable to smooth out the Maine coastline, leaving it full of ragged bays and coves. These rocks also yield much less sand, so beaches are far harder to come by in Maine. Nor did the state benefit from all that glacial meltwater sediment. In southern New England it went into creating beaches, but in what is now Maine most of that material ended up south and east of the present coastline.

Although the look and feel of this portion of the North Atlantic coast may be a relatively simple matter of geology, the plants and animals that live here are subject to an enormously complex mix of weather, temperature, and salt levels, or salinity. It's one thing to eke out a living in harsh yet stable conditions. But some of the most fundamental aspects of life on this coast are not stable at all. They can change in profound ways—sometimes with the seasons, other times by the day. In a shallow salt marsh, for instance, plants may enjoy reduced levels of salinity when the tide is low, since at those times fresh water from inland streams and rivers flows through and flushes the system. At high tide, on the other hand, salinity may be much higher as seawater enters the marsh. Salinity also varies widely depending on the season; when snow is melting in interior lands during spring, for example, fresh water will be in great abundance, which will lower salinity levels again. Add to all this the fact that harsh winters freeze and thaw portions of coastal coves from Cape Cod northward, while gale-force winds drive waves with such fury that they rip poorly anchored plants from their moorings, and you begin to see why life on much of the New England coast is anything but easy.

As a rule of thumb, the number of different organisms in any given place is determined by the severity of the conditions; the tougher the environment, the fewer the plants and animals that can survive there. In the far northern reaches of New England, chunks of ice abrade the shoreline rocks, damaging everything in their path. As you move south, conditions on most of the New England coast become less intense. Thus it makes sense that a far greater number of creatures populate the more southerly reaches of the New England shore. Continuing on that theme, southern New England waters are a far cry from the fairly stable, relatively easy living conditions of the tropics, which have greater variety still.

And yet life in the tropics has another kind of problem: Many more organisms mean much higher levels of competition. You can see this basic ecological principle at work in what is surely the most intriguing and difficult of the New England coastal environments, the intertidal zone. For starters, this area between the high and low tides is covered by water only when the tide is in, leaving plants and animals exposed to desiccation—and, to a lesser extent, to predators as the tide moves out. The intertidal zone also feels the full fury of ocean waves (especially on steep coastlines), so plants and animals must find a way to anchor themselves—either with glue, like the barnacles, or with specially adapted feet, like the dog whelks. Many of the life-forms you'll see in the tide pools have taken up residence not because they have no other choice; many are quite capable of living beneath the low-tide line. But by living in this difficult place, they can survive with fewer organisms around to compete for resources.

The coast of New England, perhaps more than any other environment, exudes a feeling not just of power, but of timelessness, of the unbroken circle of life and of passing that rims the world. "The sea is all about us," as Rachel Carson wrote in her 1950 classic, *The Sea Around Us.* "In its mysterious past it encompasses all the dim origins of life and receives in the end, after, it may be, many transmutations, the dead husks of that same life. For all at last returns to the sea. . . ." ■

Racing the waves at Hammonasset Beach State Park, Connecticut

Wells National Estuarine Research Reserve

Wells National Estuarine Research Reserve

MAINE ■ 1,600 acres ■ Southwest Maine, just east of Wells ■ Best months May-Oct. ■ Hiking, guided walks, kayaking, bird-watching, wildlife viewing ■ Parking fee in season; reservations required for parties over 8 people ■ Contact the reserve, 342 Laudholm Farm Rd., Wells, ME 04090; phone 207-646-1555. www.wellsreserve.org

FORGET FOR A MOMENT the traffic and outlet malls, the fish shacks and miniature golf courses, the water parks and go-cart tracks screaming for your attention all summer long on US 1. The real treasure in this part of the world—and the reason tourism got started here in the first place—is the fragile, stirring beauty of the coast. Perhaps nowhere does that beauty show itself more profoundly than in the Wells National Estuarine Research Reserve. For all its remarkable open space and unforgettable scenery, Maine has a smaller percentage of land in public ownership than nearly any other state in the nation. Furthermore, less than half of these lands are located in the more populated and more heavily traveled southern third of the state. (Thankfully, recent land purchases by organizations such as the Nature Conservancy are helping to balance the equation.)

This beautiful land, once known as Laudholm Farm, was first settled by an English family named Boade in 1642. After surviving ice and fire and the ravages of angry Native Americans during the infamous King Philip's War, the farm reached its heyday from roughly 1910 to 1930 under a gentleman farmer named Charles Lord, and later under his son George. In those years there were chickens and guernseys in abundance here; whatever scientific breakthrough in agriculture happened to be brewing, it was likely to show up at Laudholm Farm.

George Lord started the preservation process in the 1960s by selling 200 acres, including Laudholm Beach, to the state. Twenty years later his family members found themselves facing the prospect of having to sell off the property to developers. Residents of the area banded together to save the remaining 250 acres of the farm even as plans were being drawn up to subdivide it. Learning from the state that the National Oceanic and Atmospheric Administration (NOAA) had a program to protect marine estuaries, and given that this property was ideally situated between two such habitats, the townspeople of Wells rallied to the cause. Beginning with such simple efforts as bottle returns and raffles, in only four years the town raised the funds needed to match NOAA grants and buy the land. The farm was combined with Laudholm Beach, the Rachel Carson National Wildlife Refuge, and 26 acres owned by the town of Wells to create what is today a fantastic 1,600-acre sanctuary, including critical habitat for endangered least terns and piping plover.

What to See and Do

Few places in Maine offer more thoughtful interpretive programming than you'll find here, especially in the months of April through November. If you have kids, be sure to stop by the visitor center on your way in to purchase a "Family Discovery" booklet. Along with the booklet, the center will loan you a backpack full of everything you'll need to make discoveries on your own, from identifying wildlife tracks to humming periwinkles out of their shells to taking soil samples. Adults, meanwhile, will find excellent bird walks led by members of the York County Audubon Society, as well as general nature and coastal geology walks, sky watches, half-day kayaking trips on the Little River, artist workshops focusing on field sketching, photography, and pastels, and an annual series of readings, lectures, and slide shows on a variety of natural history and conservation topics.

If you're more inclined to head out on your own, spend an hour or so getting your sea legs at the displays at the visitor center. Pick up a trail map and set off on the 7 miles of trails that crisscross the reserve. A particularly enjoyable 1-mile (one way) journey begins on the **Cart Path** directly behind the visitor center. Follow this to the **Farley Trail** and turn right to the **Little River Overlook,** which offers a striking view of the salt marshes cradling the Little River. If time is limited, retrace your steps on the Farley Trail to the **Laird Norton Trail,** which includes a wonderful boardwalk through a red maple swamp, as well as yet another fine overlook.

Continue on the Laird Norton Trail to Beach Road and turn left. Behind the dunes is a wash of wetlands where you'll catch glimpses of a number of wading birds, including the great blue heron, snowy egret, whimbrel, short-billed dowitcher, lesser yellowlegs, willet, green-backed heron, and greater yellowlegs. Shortly after this, the road breaks out onto the rocky shore of **Laudholm Beach**. If you feel like rubbing elbows with the Atlantic for a while, turn left and walk north for another 0.75 mile, coming out at the mouth of the Little River. ∎

Pitcher plants

Saco Heath Preserve

MAINE ■ 876 acres ■ Southwest Maine, northwest of Saco off Me. 112 North (Buxton Road) ■ Best months May-Oct. ■ Camping, hiking, wildflower viewing ■ Contact the Nature Conservancy, 160 Main St., Sanford, ME 04073; phone 207-490-4012

ALTHOUGH THERE ARE certainly easier places to find (you can almost count on blasting by the entrance on the first try), 876-acre Saco Heath Preserve, owned by the Nature Conservancy, can nonetheless be a welcome respite from the heavy summer traffic on I-95 or US 1. Besides being beautiful and blissfully quiet, Saco is a great place to see some unique examples of wetlands plants and animals.

For starters, this is the southernmost example in North America of the kind of peat land biologists refer to as a coalesced raised bog—a rather complicated way of saying that the surface of the bog has actually grown above the level of the local water table. There were once adjacent natural ponds here, which over time filled in with layer upon layer of decaying plant material. These organic layers, which can absorb many times their own weight in moisture, eventually swelled above the existing water table, forming two raised bogs. These domes later grew together, or coalesced, resulting in the land features you see today.

Saco is also home to one of the state's largest stands of Atlantic white cedar. This species usually grows farther south, but because of logging, the draining of wetlands, or, alternatively, flooding for cranberry production, white cedar occupies only a tiny fraction of its former range. (Settlers drained many a white cedar swamp in the hopes of making productive farmland, only to discover that the soil was far too acidic to grow commercial crops.) Because of its remarkable resistance to decay, the Atlantic white cedar was long used for piers, fence posts, roof shingles, water barrel staves, boats, and telephone poles, and it was also bored out for use as water lines in many early American cities. Burned slowly, the tree makes a fine black charcoal, which was critical to the production of gunpowder during the Revolutionary War. It is entirely thanks to the cedars of Saco that this area remains home to the very rare Hessel's hairstreak butterfly, whose caterpillar feeds only on this species of tree.

Once out on a boardwalk crossing the bog, you'll have the pleasure of seeing a number of fascinating plants. The Atlantic white cedar is found on the highest portions of the bog, joined by black spruce and tamarack. Elsewhere, closer to the trail, are the insect-eating sundew and pitcher plants, as well as blueberry, Labrador tea, leatherleaf, iris, and an abundance of sheep laurel. Sheep laurel spreads in colonies from underground stems. In early to mid-June, you'll be treated to a wash of saucer-shaped, magenta-colored blooms flying in clusters along the stems. The stamens of these flowers are bent backward. When an insect lands on a bloom, the stamens uncoil like springs, dusting the insect with pollen, which it takes, thus ensuring cross-pollination. Sheep laurel is not so-named because it is good food for sheep. In fact, just the opposite is true. Many locals know this plant by its other common name, lambkill. ∎

Lobsters

Overwhelmed by the sheer number of lobsters off the New England coast, early settlers considered them despicable creatures, good for little more than animal food. But in the mid-1800s, lobsters began to catch on as a meal for humans—and then they went fast. Populations in southern New England were nearly wiped out in less than a century. Today, with roughly two million lobster traps off the coast of New England, a mature lobster has about a one-in-ten chance of avoiding the dinner plate. Those who manage to survive can live for decades, growing several feet long and weighing up to 40 pounds.

Rachel Carson Salt Pond Preserve

MAINE ■ 78 acres ■ Southern Maine, east of Brunswick off Me. 32 ■ Best months May-Oct. ■ Hiking, bird-watching, wildlife viewing ■ Contact the Nature Conservancy, 14 Maine St., Suite 401, Brunswick, ME 04011; phone 207-729-5181

FEW PEOPLE HAVE DONE MORE to improve our relationship to the earth than marine biologist Rachel Carson. Her decision to speak out against the wholesale use of pesticides in her 1962 book *Silent Spring* brought her tremendous criticism. In the end, Carson's skills as a scientist and writer, reinforced by her tremendous courage, enabled her to be a catalyst for political changes that ultimately saved countless species of wildlife. The next time you thrill to the sight of a fishing osprey—a species that was very nearly destroyed by DDT—whisper a thanks to Rachel Carson.

While *Silent Spring* is her most well-known book, Carson was also a talented writer of natural history. One of her best such works, *The Edge of the Sea*, was researched in part here at the salt pond, which was donated to the Nature Conservancy by Helen Williams and her two sisters, Anne and Elizabeth. Although this is a small preserve, it packs an extraordinary amount of pleasure. If you've ever yearned to get more familiar with the fragile weave of life that makes up the intertidal zone—that mysterious world that bridges land and sea—this is a wonderful place to start.

After a short walk through a ribbon of seaside rose, strawberry, golden-rod, and meadowsweet, you'll find yourself at the upper edge of the tidal zone—a line marked by rough periwinkles, tortoiseshell limpets, and

Bird-watching at Rachel Carson Salt Pond Preserve

blue mussels. Look for Irish moss (the source of carrageenan, which is a stabilizer for everything from chocolate milk to salad dressings), as well as rockweed and knotted wrack. The bulges visible near the tops of these last two plants are actually air chambers that allow the leaves to float near the surface of the water, maximizing exposure to the sun.

Some scientists use the term "ecozone" to describe an ecological niche with conditions that favor specific life-forms. What makes the intertidal zone so exciting is that so many different niches are only a few feet apart. Some species here, for example, require constant submersion, while others are submerged only twice a day, during high tide; still others may be submerged only during twice monthly spring tides. Some can cross back and forth from one niche to another. Directly below the rockweed and wrack and Irish moss you're likely to see species such as sea stars, Jonah crabs, and hermit crabs. Below that you'll find kelp, so well anchored to these rocks that this seaweed can withstand wave forces of 800 pounds per square inch.

At the center of the preserve is the salt pond—a wonderful spot to drop to your knees and look for dogwinkles, green sea urchins, green crabs, and smooth periwinkles. One note of caution is in order here. Many tide pool residents are living in very precise locations, chosen for food and security; if you disturb one of the creatures here, or even move a rock, it's essential that you return it to its original location.

Those looking for more of a leg-stretcher can follow a series of trails and old logging roads on the upland section of the preserve, part of a farm now reverting to woods. Access is across Me. 32 from the pull-off; you can find brochures at the trailhead registration box. ∎

Acadia National Park

MAINE ■ 35,000 acres ■ Southeast Maine, south of Ellsworth ■ Best months May-Oct. ■ Camping, hiking, guided walks, boating, biking, mountain biking, bird-watching, wildflower viewing ■ Adm. fee ■ Contact the park, P.O. Box 177, Bar Harbor, ME 04609; phone 207-288-3338. www.nps.gov/acad/

IN ALL THE MILES of America's Atlantic coast, from the sultry warmth of southern Florida to the foggy chill of West Quoddy Head, in no place does nature seem more fresh or urgent than in the 35,000 acres of Acadia National Park on Maine's Mount Desert Island.

The geology of Mount Desert Island is a complex tale, beginning some 500 million years ago, when vast rivers carried sediments to the floor of an ancient sea. These layers of sand, silt, and mud accumulated at the rate of roughly an inch every century, until they were thousands of feet thick. Pressure and heat fused these sediments into bedrock, which was then uplifted into an enormous mountain range; these mountains, in turn, were worn down by the forces of erosion. Periods of intense volcanic activity and massive intrusions of magma created the beautiful fine- to coarse-grained granites visible throughout the park. This dramatic geologic history, combined with the powerful forces of glaciation, has left a number of open, rocky vistas from which to survey the beauty of the Maine coast, including the famous view from Cadillac Mountain. Down along the sea, it has led to what is arguably the best place in all of New England for extended exploration of the intertidal zone. The largest of the Atlantic rock islands, Mount Desert Island is also blessed with an astonishing 500 species of plants and more than 300 species of birds.

What to See and Do

Acadia has an impressive assortment of ranger-led programs from late May to mid-October, including hikes to the park's highest peak, **Cadillac Mountain.** The park offers shoreline discovery walks, peregrine falcon-watching, boat cruises off the coast of Mount Desert Island, and regular evening programs at Blackwoods and Seawall Campgrounds. You'll find complete program listings in the park newspaper, The *Beaver Log.* Also worth a visit is the **Sieur de Monts Spring Nature Center** (*mid-June–late Sept.*), as well as the nearby **Wild Gardens of Acadia,** managed by the Bar Harbor Garden Club (both on the Park Loop Road, southeast of the visitor center). The wild gardens, open all year and free to the public, include a variety of Mount Desert Island habitats with hundreds of native species labeled.

One of the most enjoyable ways to see Acadia is by walking or mountain biking on the web of broken-stone carriage roads established by John Rockefeller, Jr., between 1913 and 1940. Although broken-stone construction was

Lighthouse, Acadia National Park

common in the early years of the 20th century, Rockefeller's 57 miles in and around Acadia are the best remaining examples of this type of road anywhere in America.

Amphitheater Loop

Walkers and bikers alike can enjoy an easy 5.5-mile loop on the carriage roads, beginning from a point just south of Upper Hadlock Pond. A small footpath at the rear center of the parking lot leads you to a carriage road; turn left to begin the loop walk.

The trek begins in a beautiful forest of white pine, striped maple, birch, and spruce. Along the edges of the carriage road are carpets of club moss, meadowsweet, huckleberry, wintergreen, and sweet fern, a native plant that grows on drier sites from Nova Scotia all the way to North Carolina. Builders

routinely planted sweet fern along these roads in an effort to make them blend in with the natural landscape. In addition to making a tasty tea, the leaves of sweet fern were often used by Native Americans throughout the Northeast as a compress for poison ivy.

In just over a mile, off to the right and slightly behind you, is a fine view of the Atlantic Ocean, broken here and there by the green tufts of the **Cranberry Isles.** This is a good place to stop to consider the long, diverse relationship humans have had with this part of the world. Mount Desert Island was a food-rich haven for native people for at least 6,000 years. The Indian names for various parts of Mount Desert Island, for example, are filled with references to gathering and baking clams. In the 17th century, Frenchman Antoine Laumet attempted to turn the island into a feudal estate. Fishermen and farmers grew wheat, corn, and potatoes through much of the 1800s. Then, in the middle of that century, Mount Desert Island also became a playground for the rich (see p. 32).

At the intersection 0.2 mile from this viewpoint keep left, reaching **Amphitheater Bridge** in another half mile. This is the longest of 16 magnificent, hand-hewn stone bridges that were built by Rockefeller as part of his carriage road system. At the next two forks in the road (mileposts 21 and 22), bear to the right, and cross **Little Harbor Brook Bridge** at 3.3 miles. At the final intersection (milepost 20), turn left,

Nearby

Acadia is not the only seaside park in Maine worthy of your attention. Not far down the road from the national park is the small but beautiful **Holbrook Island Sanctuary** (S of Bucksport off Me. 176. 207-326-4012). Here you'll find mixed hardwoods and open hills rich with wildflowers. It's a great place to walk and to observe how nature goes about reclaiming an abandoned farm. The **Backshore Trail** is especially nice, leading in one-half mile to the rocky shore of Penobscot Bay.

Moored sailboats, Acadia National Park *Following pages:* Seaside spray in Acadia National Park

Beach visitors, Acadia National Park

Rusticators and Rockefeller

Few natural areas in America have had such strong links to the wealthy as Mount Desert Island, home of Acadia National Park. In summers stretching from roughly 1880 until the Depression, a stream of people with names like Rockefeller, Morgan, Vanderbilt, Kennedy, Ford, Carnegie, Pulitzer, and Astor flowed into the area. They transformed the island from a mix of modest farms, fishing huts, shipyards, and fish racks to the site of some of the most elegant vacation estates in the country.

To understand how Mount Desert Island became a playground for the wealthy, we need to go back to 1844, when the artist Thomas Cole returned from a summer on the island with a fabulous array of landscape paintings. Soon other artists arrived, among them Frederic Church and Fitz Hugh Lane, creating work that was not only beautiful but in tune with the back-to-nature sentiment of the times. Before long, friends of the artists and other social movers and shakers began flocking to the island. Most preferred to stay with area farmers

and fishermen, usually in spare rooms of the family house or in fish shacks—a habit that earned them the name rusticators.

By the late 1800s, the richest of the new arrivals were building magnificent estates, many of them showcases of local wood and stone. For some the decision to build a mansion was in part fueled by an outbreak of typhoid—a disease that sparked a fear of using commercial hotels and cottages. (Many years later, in 1947, massive wildfires destroyed 67 of the oceanfront estates between Bar Harbor and Salisbury Cove.)

Before long, Mount Desert rivaled Newport, Rhode Island, as the center of the summer social scene. To their credit, some members of the wealthy class, most notably George Dorr, worked to protect the natural areas of Mount Desert from rampant development. By establishing public preserves, Dorr and others ensured that much of the land now included in Acadia became protected as a national park—the first such preserve east of the Mississippi River.

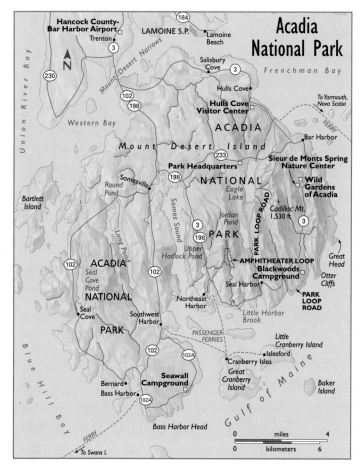

Acadia National Park

Hancock County-Bar Harbor Airport
Trenton
LAMOINE S.P.
Lamoine Beach
184
Mount Desert Narrows
Salisbury Cove
Hulls Cove
Hulls Cove Visitor Center
Frenchman Bay
To Yarmouth, Nova Scotia
FERRY
Bar Harbor
ACADIA
Mount Desert Island
Park Headquarters
233
Sieur de Monts Spring Nature Center
Wild Gardens of Acadia
NATIONAL
Somesville
Round Pond
Eagle Lake
PARK LOOP ROAD
Cadillac Mt. 1,530 ft
Bartlett Island
Somes Sound
Jordan Pond
Western Bay
Union River Bay
Great Head
PARK
Upper Hadlock Pond
AMPHITHEATER LOOP
Long Pond
ACADIA
Seal Cove Pond
Blackwoods Campground
Otter Cliffs
Seal Harbor
NATIONAL
Northeast Harbor
PARK LOOP ROAD
Seal Cove
Southwest Harbor
Little Harbor Brook
PARK
PASSENGER FERRIES
Little Cranberry Island
Islesford
Cranberry Isles
Seawall Campground
Bernard
Bass Harbor
Great Cranberry Island
Gulf of Maine
Baker Island
Blue Hill Bay
Bass Harbor Head
FERRY
To Swans I.
miles 0 — 4
kilometers 0 — 6
230
3
102
198
198
102
3
198
3
102
102A
102A

reaching the parking area again in just a little over a mile.

Biking

Biking the carriage roads is a fine way to see Acadia; keep in mind that they can get busy on summer days after 10 a.m. Ride on the right side of the road, watch your speed on descents, and be aware that the route has patches of loose stone.

If you'd like to expand your riding beyond the carriage roads, you can make a fine, moderately challenging 26-mile loop by following the **Park Loop Road** south from the Hulls Cove Visitor Center *(Me. 3 just NW of Bar Harbor)*. The loop will pass the Sieur de Monts Spring Nature Center and Wild Gardens of Acadia, as well as the fabulous **Otter Cliffs, Jordan Pond,** and **Eagle Lake.** The more gnarly among you should consider a side trip to Cadillac Mountain, the highest peak in the park. It will mean a thousand feet of climbing along the 3.5 miles of road, but your effort will be rewarded by outstanding views in every direction. ■

Puffin with catch

Petit Manan National Wildlife Refuge

MAINE ■ 6,918 acres ■ Southeast Maine, south of Milbridge ■ Best months May-Oct. ■ Hiking, boating, bird-watching, wildlife viewing ■ Contact the refuge, P.O. Box 279, Milbridge, ME 04658; phone 207-546-2124

THE COASTAL ISLANDS and peninsulas of Maine have long been the site of human enterprise. Algonquian tribes that hunted and fished there for centuries were followed by saltwater farmers who grew hay and grazed sheep. Miners, lumberjacks, and developers also moved in. As all such activity intensified, it had profound effects on the seabirds, songbirds, and raptors that used these windswept lands as stepping stones for seasonal migrations. Through the establishment of places such as Petit Manan National Wildlife Refuge, stitched together across the mainland and islands near Milbridge by the U.S. Coast Guard, the Nature Conservancy, local land trusts, and private individuals, populations of many such birds have stabilized or are on the comeback.

Places such as the Petit Manan National Wildlife Refuge are actively managed to preserve specific wildlife values. Blueberry fields, for example, may be maintained by mowing and burning to keep courting areas open for woodcock, as well as to provide food for small mammals, whimbrels, and songbirds (yes, humans can collect the berries as well). Refuge managers may raise or lower water levels in former cranberry bogs to create additional food sources. On **Petit Manan Island**—a critical area for a variety of nesting seabird colonies—managers began reducing populations of herring and black-backed gulls in 1984 to limit competition for nesting space with less common species. As a result, laughing gulls, guillemots, and three species of tern are doing well; even nesting puffins came back, after having been absent from the island since 1887. In addition, naturalists count birds through mist netting, part of an ongoing effort to improve understanding of how migrant and resident species use these lands.

There are two foot paths in Petit Manan. The **Birch Point Trail** begins at the parking lot and takes you 2 miles to the north end of the point, on **Dyer Bay.** Along the way it passes through a delightful weave of tamarack, northern white cedar, gray birch, speckled alder, balsam fir, aspen, white birch, and black and white spruce. The 1.5-mile **John Hollingsworth Trail** also begins from the parking lot. It is a self-guided loop trail with a variety of interpretive signs, leading through an upland forest and past a cedar swamp to a cobbly beach on the east side of the peninsula. Both paths offer fantastic opportunities for bird-watchers, who stand a chance of seeing oldsquaws, mergansers, and cormorants, as well as a variety of sea ducks, including common eiders, which at this point are near the southern edge of a breeding range that extends all the way to Greenland.

In spring, after laying her eggs on nearby offshore islands, the female eider will sit with them faithfully for nearly a month, taking no food the entire time. The young are ready for travel soon after hatching, at which point the mother will lead them from the islands to the sheltered waters of the mainland to dine on such shellfish as mussels, clams, and crabs. Unlike other birds, eiders don't have to worry about cracking open the tough shells to get at the delicious insides of the mollusks; instead, they gobble them down whole, relying on a powerful set of stomach muscles to crush the shells. If you happen to be here in the fall, you may well see male and female eiders together, often floating by the thousands in masses called rafts. ■

Great Wass Island Preserve

MAINE ■ 1,579 acres ■ Southeast Maine, off Me. 187 near Jonesport ■ Best months May-Oct. ■ Hiking, bird-watching ■ No pets ■ Contact the Nature Conservancy, 14 Maine St., Brunswick, ME 04011; phone 207-729-5181

THE GREAT WASS ARCHIPELAGO consists of 68 islands—each one beautiful, and on many days wrapped in far more fog and bluster than the mainland just a few miles away. These cool, moist conditions have created a fascinating oceanic microclimate, populating the archipelago with plants normally found much farther north in subarctic regions. Great Wass Island Preserve, for example, where our walk takes place, contains a medley of pink granite shorelines dotted with beach-head iris and bird's-eye primrose, and on the interior, sizable stands of jack pine, here reaching the southern limit of its Maine range. You'll also find open peat lands layered with sphagnum moss, cranberry, sundew, pitcher plant, and baked-apple berry. Bird-watchers will absolutely love Great Wass, as it's a wonderful place to spot spruce grouse, downy and hairy woodpeckers, eastern kingbirds, Swainson's and hermit thrushes, and cedar waxwings. You might also see a multitude of warblers—including Nashville, yellow, chestnut-sided, magnolia, palm, Blackburnian, black-and-white, and black-throated green—as well as black ducks; spotted sandpipers; black guillemot; and savannah, white-throated, and swamp sparrows.

Two trails, **Little Cape Point** and **Mud Hole,** begin at the parking area, each going to different parts of the eastern shore. If you have the time and energy (roots and rocks and wet spots can make for slow going), by all means consider a 5-mile loop walk. Head out to the shore on the Little Cape Point Trail, passing through stands of jack pines and stopping at fine viewpoints of the coastal plateau bogs. On reaching the shore turn left and walk north, following a series of rock cairns and markers. Be sure to take your time here, pausing along the way to explore the tidal pools. Eventually you'll reach the Mud Hole Trail, which will take you back to the parking lot through a blanket of spruce and fir.

Those with even more ambition can turn right instead of left at the shore end of the Cape Point trail, making for the southern tip of the island at **Red Head.** Be aware that this amounts to a 9-mile trek over rather grueling, rocky terrain, though in truth it would be hard to imagine a more satisfying way to wear yourself out.

Quoddy Head State Park

MAINE ■ 481 acres ■ Southeast Maine, off Me. 189 near South Lubec ■ Mid-May–mid-Oct. ■ Hiking, bird-watching ■ Adm. fee ■ Contact the Bureau of Parks and Lands, 106 Hogan Rd., Bangor, ME 04401; phone 207-733-0911 summer, 207-941-4014 winter

You'll find a magnificent slice of the Maine coast at Quoddy Head State Park. **West Quoddy Head** is famous for being the easternmost location in the contiguous United States. Try the walk to **Carrying Place Cove,** an inlet fringed with wildflowers. In autumn, it is the perfect place to watch migrating seabirds; in summer, look for Lincoln sparrows and palm warblers.

Also of interest nearby is a wonderful peat bog, the north side of which has been exposed to a height of more than a dozen feet by rain and the action of waves. So rare is it to have this kind of cross-sectional view of a bog that the site has been designated a National Natural Landmark.

As you explore this area, keep your eyes to the water, and you may well spot any number of harbor seals. They're especially visible during high tide, busy feeding on a variety of fish, including cod, flounder, herring, and rockfish. During low tide harbor seals settle onto rocks for a bit of shuteye, and therefore become more difficult to see. Should danger arise during these siestas, a sharp bark of alarm goes out, at which point they all bail off the rocks for the safety of the water. Watch Quoddy Head's waters for migrating whales as well; the park has a plaque explaining which species to look for. ■

Fog at Quoddy Head State Park

On the waterfront at Cobscook Bay State Park

Cobscook Bay State Park

MAINE ■ 888 acres ■ Southeast Maine, off US 1 in Dennysville ■ Best months mid-May–mid-Oct. ■ Camping, hiking, boating, kayaking, bird-watching, whale-watching ■ Adm. fee ■ Contact the park, R.R. 1, Box 127, Dennysville, ME 04628; phone 207-726-4412

IN DOWN EAST MAINE, you'll encounter a slice of the natural world that seems both sublime and overwhelming—one day restful, with the blue waters of the Atlantic calmly flashing in the sun, the day next wild and furious. Cobscook Bay State Park is a good example of this. The park is known for its wildlife, beautiful campsites, and some of the highest tides in the United States. Indeed, nearby are **Reversing Falls,** created by an incredible 25-foot tidal drop that causes the water flow in Cobscook Bay to change directions. Park rangers can give you exact directions to Reversing Falls; they will also have the necessary tide tables to help you plan your visit for the optimum time, roughly two hours before high tide.

Although there are no boat rentals in the park, the area in and around **Cobscook Bay** offers some of the best sea kayaking to be found on the Maine coast. Launch points are located near the middle of the park and in the northwest corner. Keep in mind that the powerful tidal surges in this part of Maine can be dangerous to uninformed boaters: By all means talk to a park ranger before you launch. Those wanting to get on the water, but not under their own power, may want to secure a spot with kayak outfitter Tidal Trails *(207-726-4799)*. You can try your hand at another kind of ocean adventure with Harris Whale Watching *(207-853-4303);* the Harrises not only help you find whales but may run you past a feature named **Old Sow,** one of the largest whirlpools in the world.

Other worthwhile pursuits include a predawn hike up the 0.2-mile trail to **Cunningham Mountain** to watch the sunrise, an afternoon ramble down **Anthony's Beach Trail** *(0.75 mile one way),* or a couple of hours spent clamming for dinner on **Whiting Bay.** ■

Great Bay National Estuarine Research Reserve

NEW HAMPSHIRE ■ 5,300 acres ■ Southeast New Hampshire, off N.H. 33 ■ Visitor center open May-Sept. Wed.-Sun., weekends Oct. ■ Hiking, guided walks, canoeing, bird-watching, wildlife viewing ■ Contact the reserve, 89 Depot Rd., Stratham, NH 03885; phone 603-778-0015. www.greatbay.org

NEARLY 400 YEARS AFTER a European explorer named Captain Pring reported seeing "sundry sorts of beasts, as stags, deere, bear, wolves, foxes, and dogges with sharp noses," there are still a great many riches to be found at the Great Bay National Estuarine Research Reserve. **Great Bay,** 15 miles from the Atlantic, is one of the most recessed estuaries in America. Consisting of roughly 4,500 acres of tidal marsh and wetlands, along with another 800 acres of coastal lands, the bay is a large and diverse reserve. No fewer than six habitats are found here. The upland forests are home to deer, ruffed grouse, and fox, while upland fields offer a haven for bluebirds, cottontails, and woodchucks. Salt marshes abound with glossy ibises and great blue herons, muskrat, and green crabs, and mudflats are home to soft-shell clams, mud snails, and birds such

Signpost, Sandy Point Discovery Center

as lesser yellowlegs. Leading off the bay, tidal creeks are filled with smelt and flounder and patrolled by the common tern, while the bay's rocky shores are alive with harbor seals and cormorants.

What to See and Do

There's no better place to discover at least a portion of these habitats than at the reserve's **Sandy Point Discovery Center.** The center offers excellent cultural history exhibits, and the interactive learning areas are as much fun for adults as they are for kids, especially the tank with the big floating magnifying glass, where you can spy on horseshoe crabs, lobsters, flounder, and soft-shell clams.

In July and August, the center offers a variety of interpretive activities. During most Saturday mornings, for instance, naturalists lead free waterfront explorations, offering visitors the chance to see firsthand the life of either the mudflats or the upper tidal zones.

On Saturday afternoons you can head out with a naturalist along the beautiful **Sandy Point Boardwalk.** On weekdays you'll find opportunities for children's programs on everything from how to attract wildlife to your yard to simulated archaeological digs. The center also offers longer explorations *(reservations required)*, such as canoe trips down the **Squamscott River** from Exeter to Chapman's Landing.

If you can't make any of the above programs, you can still have a wonderful time by walking the half-mile **Sandy Point Trail,** which departs from the Discovery Center. This trail will take you to the edge of the 19-square-mile estuary, as well as through a forested upland stitched with shagbark hickory, yellow birch, and ironwood.

As you walk the outer sections of the Sandy Point Trail, keep an eye to the open water for signs of large groups of feeding gulls; these birds often dine on the leftovers of creatures eaten by bluefish, including crabs, clams, shrimp, mackerel, and alewives. Those fond of fishing should note that Great Bay is known for its bluefish, which is perhaps the most popular of all the species sought by recreational anglers.

Bluefish are migrators, spending their winters in offshore waters on the outer continental shelf; they also travel south, between North Carolina and Florida. Prompted by rising water temperatures, bluefish begin arriving in Great Bay in June and stay on until September, when the water temperature drops to around 60°F, pushing them southward again. Spawning occurs in offshore waters, and an adult female will produce over a million eggs. The bluefish larvae are at the mercy of prevailing currents, which carry them toward shore, into suitable feeding grounds like this one. ∎

A Special Note for Bird-watchers

Great Bay is a fine place for birdwatching. In the summer months alone you are very likely to spot glossy ibises, green-backed herons, snowy egrets, wood ducks, greater and lesser yellowlegs, American woodcocks, great horned owls, kingfishers, and a full array of migratory songbirds.

An even better location for birding than the reserve's Sandy Point Discovery Center is **Adams Point,** located to the north, in Durham at the mouth of Great Bay. The **Evelyn Browne Trail** at Adams Point, named for the feisty 20th-century conservationist who led efforts to protect Great Bay, offers a 45-minute walk around the peninsula that separates Little Bay from Great Bay. A trail guide explaining the natural and cultural history of Adams Point is available at the trailhead.

Odiorne Point State Park

NEW HAMPSHIRE ■ 330 acres ■ Southeast New Hampshire, 50 miles north of Boston on N.H. 1A ■ Best months May-Oct. ■ Camping, hiking, guided walks, biking, wildlife viewing ■ Adm. fee; fee for naturalist-led tours ■ Contact New Hampshire Division of Parks and Recreation, P.O. Box 606, Rye Beach, NH 03871; phone 603-436-8043. www.seacentr.org

NEW HAMPSHIRE BEGAN, some might say, at Odiorne Point. Here the intrepid Scotsman David Thompson dropped anchor in the spring of 1623, to let off a group of settlers and their supplies in what was to become the first European settlement in this state. Purchased more than 300 years later by the federal government at the onset of World War II and turned into a coastal defense installation, today the point remains the last significant stretch of undeveloped shoreline in New Hampshire.

And what a beautiful shoreline it is. Odiorne is a wealth of natural splendor, from intertidal zones to salt marshes to forests—seven distinct coastal habitats in all. Here you'll find rocky bluffs fringed by sumac, alder, rose, tansy, and St. John's wort, as well as a tremendous variety of creatures in the tidal pools, from chitons to limpets, green crabs, periwinkles, spiral worms, dog whelks, rock crabs, and sea urchins. You'll also see plenty of barnacles—perhaps not the most exotic of residents, but remarkable creatures nonetheless. To stay put in the face of powerful wave action, barnacles anchor their shells—actually, a series of plates made up of calcium carbonate—with a cement that has tremendous holding power. Indeed, millions of dollars are spent each year removing barnacles from the hulls of ships, piers, and buoys. When covered with water during high tide, the barnacles in Odiorne's tidal pools project a set of fan-shaped appendages, using them to gather particles of plankton and other food. Barnacles in the intertidal zone can withstand an extraordinary range of conditions, surviving temperature fluctuations of more than 100°F. If you plan to explore the tidal pools on your own, remember that everything you touch should be returned exactly as you found it. Through nothing more than flipping over a rock and leaving it bottom up, you can expose tidal-pool residents to predators, as well as to the drying effects of the sun.

Adding in no small amount to the appeal of this place are the excellent exhibits, programs, and trails of the **Seacoast Science Center,** located at the state park. The center offers year-round activities, including naturalist-guided talks, and presentations on the social history of Odiorne Point and the Gulf of Maine. Indoor programs are free with admission to the Science Center, while a small fee is charged for tours led by a naturalist. Indoor activities include lighthouse tales, sea rescue presentations, and coastal wildlife walks, while guided walks offer visitors hands-on explorations of the intertidal zone, geology walks, and even outings around the park to examine World War II history. ■

Following pages: Evening on a wildlife refuge

Cape Cod

MASSACHUSETTS ■ Southeast Massachusetts, 45 miles southeast of Boston ■ Camping, hiking, walking, boating, kayaking, canoeing, swimming, biking, bird-watching, whale-watching, wildflower viewing ■ Contact the Chamber of Commerce, P.O. Box 790, Hyannis, MA 02601; phone 508-862-0700 or 877-332-2732. www.capecodchamber.org or www.capecodvisit.net

NOT TO SLIGHT THE EXTRAORDINARY mountains of northern New Hampshire, nor the dark, moose-filled woods of Maine, the fiery autumn colors of the Berkshires, or the fogbound granite lip of Acadia. But if there were one spot in all New England to visit—not just for the fine blend of nature still there today, but also for the lasting pull of the place on the minds of millions of people—it would have to be Cape Cod.

Compared with the Massachusetts mainland, which is about 300 to 500 million years old, Cape Cod is a newcomer. In fact, before the arrival of glaciers, the Cape simply did not exist. Some 15,000 years ago, when the glaciers stopped their southward advance, they dumped enormous

Sailing the waters off Cape Cod

piles of sediment—sometimes called moraines—along their leading edges. The lower portion of Cape Cod, along with the islands of Martha's Vineyard and Nantucket, began with these moraines. As the glaciers retreated, sediment fanned out in their wake, carried by the meltwater into vast outwash plains. These depositions provided much of the raw material that would then be fashioned by wind and water into today's Cape Cod. Nor is that shaping finished: The north-south arm of the Cape is losing about 3 feet of ground a year to erosion, while Cape Cod Bay is actually gaining land.

Besides extensive beaches and dune complexes, Cape Cod offers an intriguing mix of salt- and freshwater marshes, pockets of woodland, swamps, and kettlehole ponds. Such a diversity of habitat, combined with a climate moderated by the ocean and the fact that the Cape is a stopover for large numbers of migratory birds along the Atlantic flyway, makes this place a bird-watcher's dream. At this point, more than 300 species have been recorded along Cape Cod National Seashore alone.

To sample the full variety of the Cape Cod experience, a traveler should plan to visit not only the Cape's famous beaches, such as those on Sandy Neck (see p. 51), but also the marshes, swamps, and bogs found at

Cape Cod National Seashore (see p. 53). Worth visiting, as well, are two famous islands just to the south: Martha's Vineyard (see p. 57) and Nantucket Island (see p. 65).

   To say that the Cape is busy in the summer would be the height of understatement. And yet if it is nature you seek, you will find it with bells on. Those who walk a little farther down Nauset Beach or Sandy Neck, who take time to soak up the strange beauty of places like a red maple swamp, or who put out to sea to look for whales, will have a chance to revel in the splendor of this sand-laden gift from the north. The sites and activities featured below will begin to give you a taste of this edge country. "Edges," writes Robert Finch, "as every bird-watcher knows, are particularly rich habitats, producing more species than most. So this edge, where land meets sea, has proved to be a fruitful site for illuminating the human condition."

What to See and Do

As with any large area rich in nature, especially one so stitched through with colorful threads of history, it would take months, if not years, to get to know Cape Cod. For every place mentioned here, there are dozens of others worthy of your attention. Head to the bookstore or drop in on the Internet to get a better feel of what awaits you here. Carve out as many days as you possibly can to explore the area, especially if you plan to include Martha's Vineyard or Nantucket Island. Keep in mind that from early July through the end of August, lodging and camping can be tough to come by without reservations, and traffic —even on the islands—can be horrific. Your vacation will be infinitely more enjoyable if you use the bike trails or take a cab or bus. Finally, if you're an early morning person, so much the better, since the more popular trails and beaches often get crowded after 10 a.m.

Biking

In few places does travel by bike make more sense than on the Cape. There are a number of trails here, which for the most part traverse flat or only slightly hilly terrain; several rub elbows with marvelous slices of natural habitat, places that those stuck to their cars will never see. For information on this and other Massachusetts biking opportunities, a useful website is www.massbike.org/bikeways. The "Cape Cod & North Shore Bicycle and Road Map" (which includes the islands), by Rubel BikeMaps in Cambridge (www.bikemaps.com), is a helpful map that includes the location of bike shops and rentals throughout the area. Bike rental locations are also listed in Cape Cod Currents, which is available at visitor centers and ranger stations throughout the national seashore.

The **Cape Cod Rail Trail** is currently a 25-mile-long trail,

mostly off-road, running up the center of the Cape from South Dennis to South Wellfleet, where it connects with the Cape Cod National Seashore bike trails. This trail doesn't feature the ocean, but it does pass an excellent variety of wetland habitats rich in birdlife. Furthermore, this is a good trail for getting to various towns along the outer reaches of the Cape without having to ride the entire distance on vehicular roadways. Convenient parking areas for the Cape Cod trail include: south of US 6 (Mid-Cape Highway), at the South Dennis exit; the Harwich exit on the Mid-Cape Highway; Nickerson State Park in Brewster; National Seashore Salt Pond Visitor Center in Eastham; and National Seashore Headquarters in

Whale-watching

The waters off Cape Cod are a wonderful place to catch sight of cetaceans such as humpbacks and fin whales. A number of commercial outfitters offer trips, including the following:

Captain John Boats (Provincetown and Plymouth. 508-747-2400 or 800-225-4000 in Mass.).

Dolphin Fleet Whale Watch (Provincetown. 508-349-1900 or 800-826-9300).

Hyannis Whale Watcher Cruises (Barnstable Harbor. 508-362-6088 or 888-942-5392).

Provincetown Whale Watch (Provincetown. 508-487-3322 or 800-992-9333).

Exploring tide pools, Cape Cod National Seashore

Wellfleet. Good resources include the "Cape Cod Rail Trail Bicycle Map," published by the Butterworth Company of Yarmouth, Massachusetts.

Cape Cod Canal bike paths run on both sides of the Cape Cod Canal, offering more than 14 miles of flat, enjoyable riding, elbow to elbow with ship traffic going through the canal. The paths are maintained by the Army Corps of Engineers.

The **Cape Cod National Seashore Bike Trails** include three paved trails. The 1.6-mile **Nauset Trail** in Eastham runs from the Salt Pond Visitor Center on Mass. 6 to Coast Guard Beach (see p. 53). The 2-mile **Head of the Meadow Trail** travels through an intriguing mixture of dune habitats between Head of the Meadow Road and the High Head Road. The 5.25-mile **Province Lands Trail** can be reached through sites along the tip of the Cape, including the Beech Forest parking area, the Herring Cove and Race Point Beach parking areas, and the

Province Lands Visitor Center.

You'll find miles of fine bike trails on both **Martha's Vineyard** (*www.mvol.com/bikeinfo.html*) and **Nantucket Island** (*www.state.ma.us/ mhd/bikepath/webnant.htm*). Most parallel roadways and can be heavy with moped traffic in summer. Even so, bicycling can be a great way to see the scenery, especially in late spring and early fall.

Canoeing and Kayaking

With more than 300 ponds and an engaging coastline, Cape Cod can be a paddler's dream. Popular canoeing and kayaking areas include **Waquoit Bay** and **Washburn Island, Nauset Marsh** in Eastham, and **Pleasant Bay** in Orleans. **Nickerson State Park** i n Brewster also offers limited canoeing. You can rent canoes at Nickerson State Park through Jack's Boat Rental (*508-349-9808*). Tours are available through outfitters such as Cape Cod Coastal Canoe and Kayak (*508-564-4051. www.capecodcanoekayak.com*), Waquoit Kayak Company (*508-548-9722. www.waquoitkayak .com*), and Explore Cape Cod (*508-240-1211. www.explorecape cod.com*).

More Activities

As mentioned throughout this guide, what you see in New England today is far different from the forest that greeted the first Europeans. Cape Cod is no exception. Diaries of early explorers are filled with lengthy descriptions of rich woodlands made up of sizable trees spread across the Cape. As those trees were cut down, the topsoil that made such forests possible in the first place blew away. Today the Cape is mostly sand with scattered pockets of fertile soil and young forest.

Although much of the Cape is now highly developed, complete with fast-food restaurants and chain stores, at least some of the businesses along Mass. 6A—the northern route across the Cape, also known as the Old King's Highway—are fighting to keep the charm of Old America. Your impressions of the Cape will almost certainly depend on where you happen to be, and for those seeking the glories of nature, the strip malls, water slides and miniature golf courses that have spread through some shore communities don't necessarily cut it.

One fine place to begin your exploration of the Cape, while avoiding encounters with manufactured entertainment, is the **Cape Cod Museum of Natural History** (*Mass. 6A, Brewster. 508-896-3867. Adm. fee*). This is a small museum, not long on whistles and bells, but its exhibits are well thought out and presented in a way that doesn't leave you with a headache from information overload. The geology story is especially good. Docents offer regular walks on the trails leading from the museum to the salt marsh. You'll also find lectures and live animal shows, a marine room and tidal tank with live sea creatures, family field walks, a working beehive, and even some fairly good bird-watching from the Marshview Room. If you know ahead of time that you're coming to the Cape, be sure to give the museum a call and find out what touring events are scheduled. It typically features a great lineup, from summer nature camps to whale-watching adventures to an overnight stay in the lightkeepers' house on **Monomoy Island.**

The island is famous not only for its gray seals but for being one of the great bird-watching spots in all of eastern North America. Its birds include more than a dozen species of sandpipers, Hudsonian godwits, roseate terns, American avocets, American oystercatchers, black-bellied plovers, snowy and great egrets, northern harriers, and peregrine falcons.

If you can take the walk from the museum to **Cape Cod Bay** with a docent, so much the better, but if not, by all means make the trek on your own. This is new land, just 3,000 to 5,000 years old. The path begins in an upland forest of black and white oak, pitch pine, even tupelo and cherry, under which you'll find a tangled web of poison ivy, arrowwood, honeysuckle, bayberry, catbriar, and fox grape.

Soon the path drops out of the woods into a wonderful world of dunes and salt marsh, the former sprouting beach grass, beach plum, beach pea, dusty miller, beach heather, and seaside rose; the latter is rich with pickle weed, seaside goldenrod, and long waves of spartina grass. (If you look closely at the seaside goldenrod, you'll see that many of the lower leaves are dead. This isn't the result of sickness or disease; rather, the plant deals with the high salinity here by letting the lower leaves absorb most of the salt, which ultimately kills them.)

Moving toward the tide line, slow down and keep your eyes to the ground, where you'll find a wonderful array of creatures —or the remains of creatures— including decorator worms, hermit crabs, green crabs, periwinkles, razor clams, quahog shells, and sea cucumbers. Scattered about the beach you'll see blackened, dried pods with spines that look like antennae. These are skate cases, from which young skates have hatched.

This shoreline is also a place to look for the brown, armored shells of the horseshoe crab. If this creature appears downright prehistoric, it's with good reason. Horseshoe crabs—whose fossils date from the Ordovician period—have been around for 500 million years.

In May and June, horseshoe crabs move ashore in pairs, the female in the lead, the male clinging to her shell. Eggs are laid in a shallow nest in the sand and are then fertilized by the male; afterward, the two adults crawl back into the ocean. Curiously, on land horseshoe crabs always seem to know the direction of the sea, even if they can't see it. Researchers believe they take bearings from the sun, much as birds do. Horseshoe crabs have had a rough go of it at the hands of humans. For decades people considered them a "trash fish" and trapped them in great quantities to be used as fertilizer. ∎

Anglers at Cape Cod

Sandy Neck

MASSACHUSETTS ■ 8,000 acres ■ Cape Cod, off Mass. 6A near Barnstable
■ Best months May-Oct. ■ Hiking, swimming, bird-watching, wildflower viewing
■ Adm. fee (summer) ■ All cottages on Sandy Neck are owned or leased: Please
respect private property ■ Contact the Department. of Natural Resources,
Sandy Neck Rd., West Barnstable, MA 02668; phone 508-790-6272

SANDY NECK, which has long been a favorite of local beach lovers, was
first acquired from Native Americans more than 300 years ago in a land
deal that was typical for the time, but by today's standards seems utterly
unconscionable. Settlers purchased the western portion of Sandy Neck
from Sachem Serunk in 1644 for the grand sum of four coats and three
axes; they bought the eastern portion from Sachem Nepoyetum for two
coats and one day's worth of plowing. During the Revolutionary War, this
area held a large saltworks and, later, a vigorous whaling station.

There are five trails on Sandy Neck, each of which is described in an
interpretive brochure available at the entrance station. If time is limited,
try **Trail No. 1,** which will carry you through a fine coastal barrier beach,
laced with beach grass, beach plum, cranberry vines, rugosa rose, and
poverty grass, as well as the rare Plymouth gentian. Some of these dunes
are nesting areas for the endangered diamondback terrapin, which moves
each spring from the nearby marsh onto these sandy areas to nest.

If you happen to be here in fall or winter, you'll see that the waters off
Beach Point (the eastern section of Sandy Neck) support large rafts of
scoters and eiders. Other migratory waterfowl include grebes, mallard,
black ducks, brant, and mergansers. Be aware that permits are available
for driving on this beach, which is a matter of concern to many people.
Recently a group of scientists from all over the North Atlantic region
were asked to identify the biggest threats to endangered plants and animals.
Their responses were, in order of priority: a) development, b) off-road
vehicles, and c) water drawdowns. ■

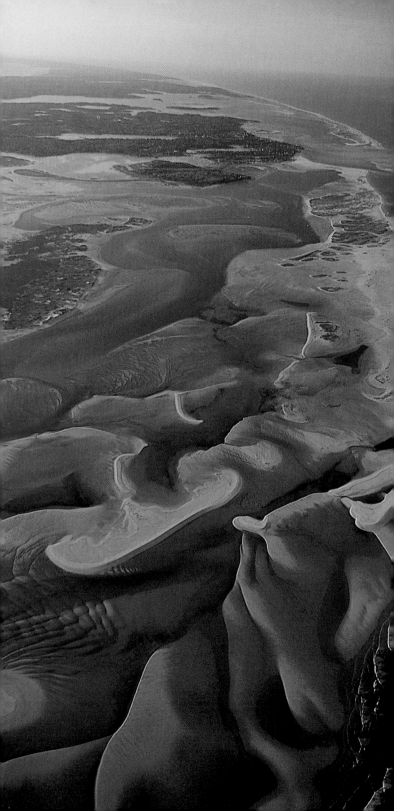

Cape Cod National Seashore

MASSACHUSETTS ■ 27,700 acres ■ Cape Cod, off US 6 ■ Year-round
■ Camping, hiking, walking, canoeing, bird-watching, wildlife viewing ■ Adm. fee
■ Contact the seashore, 99 Marconi Rd., Wellfleet, MA 02667; phone 508-255-3421. www.nps.gov/caco

CAPE COD NATIONAL SEASHORE, truly one of the great jewels of New England, was established in 1961 to protect the coastal environment along a 40-mile stretch of land between Chatham and Provincetown. Although many visitors think of Cape Cod as a land of surf and sand, the national seashore's many habitats—from woods to swamps to bogs—prove that there's more to the Cape than beaches.

What to See and Do

You'll find excellent interpretive offerings at either of two Park Service visitor centers *(hours vary according to season)*: **Salt Pond Visitor Center** *(US 6, Eastham. 508-255-3421)* and the **Province Lands Visitor Center** *(Race Point Rd., Provincetown. 508-487-1256)*. Salt Pond, for example, provides naturalist-led canoe trips into Nauset Marsh, as well as the more typical walks, talks, and presentations. In addition, the national seashore contains 11 engaging self-guided nature trails. Especially noteworthy are the Red Maple Swamp Trail and Nauset Trail in Eastham, the **Atlantic White Cedar Swamp** and **Great Island Trails** in Wellfleet, the **Pamet Cranberry Bog Trail** in Truro, and the **Beech Forest Trail** in Provincetown.

Either before or after stopping at the Salt Pond Visitor Center, you can enjoy an excellent walk by following foot trails to **Doane Memorial** (or if you're on a bike, take the bike path leaving from the visitor center). Continue on to **Coast Guard Beach,** where you can head south for nearly 2 miles along the lovely, fine-grained sand of **Nauset Spit.** This striking edge of the world, framed to the west by **Nauset Marsh,** has been the scene of a variety of intriguing events, from dramatic rescues of grounded ships by U.S. Coast Guard surfmen to the presence of Henry Beston, author of *The Outermost House,* a masterly work based on time he spent in a simple cottage here in the 1920s.

Fort Hill to Red Maple Swamp Trails

Less than a mile south of the Salt Pond Visitor Center off Governor Prence Road is the trailhead for the **Fort Hill Trail** leading to Fort Hill, offering one of the finest views for miles around, and ultimately leading to the **Red Maple Swamp Trail.** This may not be the environment you most came to see, but it's certainly not one you'll soon forget. Behind the stately home of whaling captain Edward Penniman, the trail enters what

Aerial view of Cape Cod National Seashore

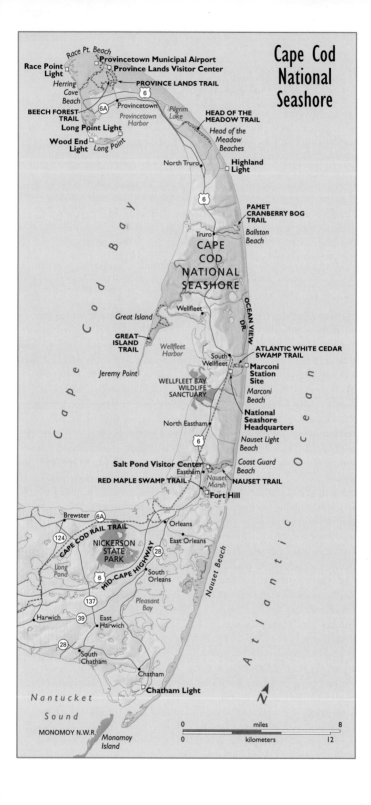

Cape Cod
National
Seashore

Race Pt. Beach

Race Point
Light

Herring
Cove
Beach

Provincetown Municipal Airport
Province Lands Visitor Center

PROVINCE LANDS TRAIL

6

BEECH FOREST
TRAIL

6A   Provincetown

Long Point Light

Wood End
Light   Long Point

Pilgrim
Lake

Provincetown
Harbor

HEAD OF THE
MEADOW TRAIL

Head of the
Meadow
Beaches

North Truro   Highland
Light

6

PAMET
CRANBERRY BOG
TRAIL

Truro   Ballston
Beach

CAPE
COD
NATIONAL
SEASHORE

Cape Cod Bay

Wellfleet

Great Island

GREAT
ISLAND
TRAIL

Wellfleet
Harbor

Jeremy Point

OCEAN VIEW DR.

South
Wellfleet

ATLANTIC WHITE CEDAR
SWAMP TRAIL

Marconi
Station
Site

WELLFLEET BAY
WILDLIFE
SANCTUARY

Marconi
Beach

National
Seashore
Headquarters

North Eastham

Nauset Light
Beach

6

Coast Guard
Beach

Salt Pond Visitor Center
Eastham

RED MAPLE SWAMP TRAIL

Nauset
Marsh

NAUSET TRAIL

Fort Hill

Brewster   6A

Orleans

CAPE COD RAIL TRAIL

124   East Orleans

NICKERSON
STATE
PARK

28

Long
Pond

6   South
Orleans

MID-CAPE HIGHWAY

137

Pleasant
Bay

Harwich   39   East
Harwich

28

South
Chatham

Chatham

Chatham Light

Nantucket

Sound

MONOMOY N.W.R.   Monomoy
Island

Atlantic Ocean

Nauset Beach

N

miles   8
0

kilometers   12
0

was once an old orchard but is fast becoming an enchanted tangle of black cherry, red cedar, black locust, and, yes, poison ivy, this yielding to sun-drenched meadows sprinkled with chicory and milkweed. (Because this trail is so close to the ocean, it seems appropriate to mention that milkweed once came to the rescue of sailors in peril. During World War II, America lost access to the silk cotton trees that provided flotation material in Navy life jackets; the silky seed hairs of the milkweed plant were the perfect alternative.)

From Fort Hill you'll drop past pokeweed and honeysuckle and salt spray rose, keeping left to pass Indian Rock, then taking the next left, following signs to the **Red Maple Swamp.** This second-growth forest, full of gnarled trunks and tangled branches covered in greenbrier vine, is eerie to some, hauntingly beautiful to others. It is a place thick with shadow, perfect for exploring on those days when the Cape is wrapped in blankets of fog. Also here are bayberry, sweet pepper-

Nearby
If you have more time to explore the area, you might want to pay a visit to some other interesting spots:
Wellfleet Bay Wildlife Sanctuary (South Wellfleet. 508-349-2615. Adm. fee) Salt marsh boardwalk; natural history programs for families.
National Marine Fisheries Aquarium (Woods Hole. 508-495-2000 or 508-548-5123) Woods Hole is world famous for its oceanographic research.
Ashumet Holly Wildlife Sanctuary (East Falmouth. 508-563-6390. Adm. fee) Featuring 65 varieties of holly trees and rare wildflowers.

bush, arrowwood, and the beautiful swamp azalea. Stay left at the next two forks, and at the next junction, nearly 2 miles from your starting point, take a right turn, then quickly take another right to end up back at the parking lot. ■

Magnolia fruit

Ornamental grass

Martha's Vineyard

MASSACHUSETTS ■ Island south of Cape Cod ■ Best seasons spring, summer, and fall. Access via ferry (see information p. 281). If you plan to take your car in summer (not recommended), ferry reservations are strongly recommended ■ Camping, hiking, walking, boating, kayaking, swimming, biking, bird-watching, wildflower viewing ■ Contact the Chamber of Commerce, P.O. Box 1698, Beach Rd., Vineyard Haven, MA 02568; phone 508-693-0085. www.mvy.com

DESPITE THE CRUSH OF SUMMER CROWDS, as well as a significant increase in development over the past 20 years, there is still something of the old days floating on the salt air that drifts across the island of Martha's Vineyard. The Wampanoag Tribe tells stories of the giant Moshup's visits to these cliffs and his decision to bring his people there. As they traveled, Moshup dragged his big toe, creating the beautiful island. That beauty also attracted the English explorer Bartholomew Gosnold, who named the island for his daughter Martha.

Helping enormously in maintaining the timeless feeling of the Vineyard is a fascinating collection of wildlife preserves and natural areas. Many of these are managed by the Massachusetts Audubon Society, the Wampanoag Tribe, and the Martha's Vineyard Land Bank Commission. The commission has used a 2 percent surcharge on most real-estate transactions to fund purchases of more than 1,100 acres of critical habitat and open space.

What to See and Do

One of the best ways to orient yourself to the nature of the Vineyard is to spend several hours at the **Felix Neck Wildlife Sanctuary** *(Felix Neck Dr., Edgartown. 508-627-4850. Visitor center closed Mon. Sept.-May; adm. fee).* Located at the edge of **Sengekontacket Pond,** the sanctuary is managed and operated by the Massachusetts Audubon Society. (Felix, by the way, lived in the 1600s, and was the last Native American to reside along the west shore of Sengekontacket Pond.) Like many of the best sanctuaries, Felix Neck has been less concerned about creating expensive virtual experiences inside a multimillion-dollar

museum than about putting its energy into helping the public experience the fantastic mix of bird, plant, and animal life to be found here. There are good exhibits, to be sure, and field guides and books are available for sale, but most of the magic will be found along the relatively short, flat trails through a variety of habitats, all of them perfect for families. Interpretive brochures do a good job of keying you into the life all around; birders will find a fine observation blind along the **Orange Trail** at the edge of **Waterfowl Pond.**

Note that Felix Neck offers a number of special events

Riding the roads, Martha's Vineyard

throughout the year. Among them are an Osprey Festival in March and a Fall Festival on the Friday after Thanksgiving.

Polly Hill Arboretum

There's something of Polly Hill smiling back in every tree and wildflower, every witch hazel and dogwood and azalea in the Polly Hill Arboretum *(State Rd., West Tisbury. 508-693-9426. Columbus Day–Mem. Day Thurs.-Tues.)*, and that's worth going out of your way for. Established in 1957, this collection of cultivated and wild plants is the expression of one woman's 40-year passion, to bring the beauty of new varieties to her home ground, as well as to provide sanctuary for those plants threatened in their native habitats.

In the early years, Polly Hill was mostly interested in finding coniferous trees that could thrive on the Vineyard as ornamentals and as shelter belts. Later she turned her attention to rhododendrons, which would become her signature species, as well as to Japanese azaleas, starting with seeds obtained from a colleague in Japan. Catering to the island's summer visitors, Polly Hill focused on securing low-growing varieties that would bloom during June and July, instead of later in the year.

During your visit you can walk through 20 acres of cultivated gardens, reach another 40 acres that remain in native woodland, and weave between the two through meadows thick with those wildflowers most common to the up-island stretches of the Vineyard. When you're stressed out with Vineyard traffic, crazed

moped riders, and long waiting lines for lunch, there are few places better than Polly Hill Arboretum to restore your sense of calm and contentment.

A new, beautifully designed visitor center will help you get oriented to the arboretum, and the staff there can answer any questions you might have about the grounds. Notable areas for strolling include **Polly's Play Pen** on the southwestern edge of the property, which contains a number of rare plants as well as some of Polly Hill's introductions, including the group for which she is perhaps most famous—the North Tisbury azaleas. If you're here from the middle of June to July, take a stroll down the 284-foot **Dogwood Allée,** which contains two rows of Kousa dogwood—some of which, once again, are introductions. From early June through the middle of September the arboretum sponsors an excellent Wednesday evening lecture series, featuring noted horticulturists and botanists from around the world.

Land Bank Properties

Besides the three Land Bank properties described on the following pages, nearly three dozen more await your exploration on Martha's Vineyard. The Land Bank office *(508-627-7141. www.mvlandbank.com)* has a complete listing of properties that have trails open to the public.

Waskosim's Rock Reservation

The 185 acres of field, forest, and lilting uplands in Waskosim's Rock Reservation *(North Rd.,*

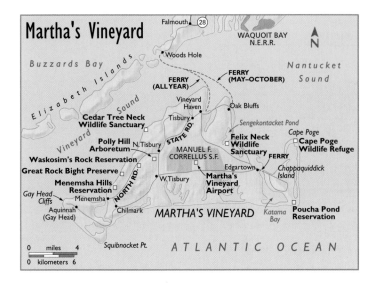

Martha's Vineyard

Falmouth ⊙ 28
Woods Hole
WAQUOIT BAY
N.E.R.R.
N

Buzzards Bay
FERRY
(MAY–OCTOBER)
FERRY
(ALL YEAR)
Nantucket Sound

Elizabeth Islands

Vineyard Sound

Vineyard Haven
Oak Bluffs
Tisbury
Sengekontacket Pond
Cape Poge

Cedar Tree Neck
Wildlife Sanctuary

Polly Hill
Arboretum
N. Tisbury
STATE RD.
MANUEL F.
CORRELLUS S.F.
Felix Neck
Wildlife
Sanctuary
Cape Poge
Wildlife Refuge

Waskosim's Rock Reservation
Great Rock Bight Preserve
NORTH RD.
Edgartown
FERRY
Chappaquiddick
Island

Menemsha Hills
Reservation
W. Tisbury
Martha's
Vineyard
Airport

Gay Head
Cliffs
Menemsha
Aquinnah
(Gay Head)
Chilmark
MARTHA'S VINEYARD
Katama
Bay
Poucha Pond
Reservation

0 miles 4
0 kilometers 6
Squibnocket Pt.
A T L A N T I C   O C E A N

Chilmark) will introduce you to a world far different from that of the salt ponds and wave-brushed beaches most people usually associate with the Vineyard. As massive ice sheets from the last three glacial epochs pushed to the southeast and then finally retreated, they left in their wake a series of steeply rising ridges, cut by low, linear stream valleys. As a result, this "up island" or morainal section of Martha's Vineyard contains a wide variety of dry to wet areas, all of it utterly unlike the fairly flat, sandy outwash plains lying to the east. (You can always tell when you're up island, locals say, because this part of the Vineyard is characterized by stone walls, whereas down island is characterized by outwash, and building walls out of stone there was not a good option.) As on many small preserves, you may or may not find descriptive trail brochures waiting for you at the trail. Come

prepared to make a quick sketch of the possible routes using the map posted at the trailhead.

On this reservation you'll find red maple and shrub swamps along **Mill Brook;** a moderately wet hardwood forest on the north-facing slopes above Mill Brook; a mixed oak and pine woods on the uplands to the south; grasslands; and finally, wind-tossed heath, which is located directly above **Waskosim's Rock.** This massive rock (whose name is said to mean "whale turned to stone") was carried in the belly of glacial ice some 15,000 years ago to its present-day resting place along the **Red Trail.** In the 1600s the rock was used as a property marker to divide settlers' lands from those of the Native American people.

The upper stretches of the **Green Trail** offer great views of vast, timbered-covered hills, while the **Blue Trail** will take you past some excellent edge habitat that is perfect for bird-watching.

Sandpiper

This reservation is home to a surprising array of flora and fauna, some of it quite rare, from brook lampreys in Mill Brook to southern lady ferns, bushy rock-roses, green wood orchids, and the rare LeConte's violet and cranefly orchids. The Vineyard in general is also noted for its exceptional diversity of butterflies and moths.

Great Rock Bight Preserve

You'll find one of the newest Land Bank properties, acquired in the fall of 1996, at **Great Rock Bight** (*off North Rd., Chilmark*). Though not nearly as popular as the trail to the base of the clay cliffs at **Gay Head** (that trail, after all, leads to one of the all-time great swimming beaches), Great Rock Bight provides a thoroughly delightful half-mile stroll, ending at a narrow, sickle-shaped sand beach on a coastline dappled with rocks. It begins in a forest of black oak— a gnarled, rough-looking species that was seldom sought out by lumbermen, but whose yellow inner bark produces a beautiful, and once highly sought-after dye, still used by some native weavers. The black oak also served the arts by fueling many a potter's kiln.

Soon the trail makes a short detour past the haunting, tea-colored waters of **Marl Pond,** then resumes its march to a bluff high above the beach. Whereas the coast of Gay Head is dramatic, Great Rock Bight is restful, calming —the kind of place that makes you want to linger through sun-down. To the west are views of the Elizabeth Islands (named, as was the Vineyard itself, by Bartholomew Gosnold, but for a queen this time), littered with glacial rocks and boulders, cut and scoured by numerous floods.

Poucha Pond Reservation

Poucha Pond Reservation (*Chappaquiddick Rd., Chappaquiddick Island via ferry from Edgartown*) is a salt-marsh lover's dream, with more waterfowl than you can shake a camera at. The Blue Trail is the most direct route, with the Yellow Trail and Red Trail forming side paths that rejoin the Blue a short distance from the trailhead. On the early stretches of the Blue Trail, oak and pitch pine forest predominate, with chickadees, towhees, mourning doves, and goldfinches to keep you company. At 0.75 mile you cross a ribbon of the salt marsh. Following this is another pocket of oak woods, then another crossing of an open area with a view of **Poucha Pond,** rimmed on the far side by an impressive barrier beach. Now it's into the woods one last time, with the end of the trail coming at roughly a mile, a mere 60 yards from the pond. A chest-high curtain of shrubs here, which serves as a great bird blind.

One of the many birds you're likely to see here is the green-backed heron—smaller and less regal-looking than other herons, but nonetheless distinctive with its green wings, black crown, and red-brown neck. You'll probably spy this bird along the shore, bent over with head near the water, stalking its prey. When startled the green-backed heron will rise sharply, with rapid wing beats, and take refuge in the nearest tree. This is also a good place to see that consummate fishing bird, the osprey, which has made a fabulous recovery from the 1960s, when the entire species was threatened by poisoning from pesticides. Finally, Poucha is also home to mute swans. These are large, extremely aggressive birds, perfectly willing to use their beaks and wings to defend their nests against all intruders, including humans.

Though many of us tend to be drawn to the drama of pounding surf, the salt marsh, protected from the trauma of waves and rushing currents by barriers of sand and rock, quietly goes about its miraculous business. As tides rise and move through the marsh, spartina grasses slow the flows, causing the water to drop its enriching load of silt. Microbes eat the dead leaves of the grass, causing it to decay into detritus, which then feeds mussels, clams, plankton, and even some fish, which in turn feed larger animals. No acre of farmland in the world can support as much life as an acre of the salt marsh you see before you. ■

Nearby

If you have the time, check out the hiking, bird-watching, and wildlife observation in these two areas on Martha's Vineyard:

Cedar Tree Neck Wildlife Sanctuary (Obed Daggett Rd., North Tisbury. Call for directions, 508-693-5207) Note that, in order to allow better wildlife viewing, this 315-acre sanctuary does not allow swimming, picnicking, sunbathing, or fishing. All dogs must be on a leash.

Menemsha Hills Reservation (North Rd., Chilmark. 508-693-7662) This 211-acre reservation features hiking and bird-watching.

Following pages: Birders on Sengekontacket Pond, Martha's Vineyard

Nantucket Island

MASSACHUSETTS ■ Island south of Cape Cod ■ Best seasons spring, summer, and fall. Access via ferry (see information p. 281) ■ Camping, hiking, walking, biking, bird-watching, wildlife viewing ■ Contact the Chamber of Commerce, 48 Main St., Nantucket, MA 02554; phone 508-228-1700. www.nantucketchamber.org.

WITH ALL DUE RESPECT to Herman Melville and Captain Ahab, the fame Nantucket once earned as a whaling center may in the end not be nearly as enduring as the reputation it has established as a repository for some irreplaceable natural treasures. This tiny island, just 14 miles long and 3.5 miles wide, contains a greater variety of vegetation than nearly any place of equal size on the continent. Eighty percent of the Western Hemisphere's remaining sand-plain grasslands are on Nantucket. Birds live here in abundance, as well as more than a few rare and endangered species of plants. Happily, Nantucket also has a consortium of organizations dedicated to preserving the best of this precious island against the pressures of development. Thus far more than 12,500 acres (roughly 40 percent of the island) has been protected by various private, nonprofit conservation groups and governmental agencies. In the interest of preserving Nantucket's environment, these groups have set up strict guidelines (which are stringently enforced) for those who would recreate here: no camping on the sand, no digging or picking of plants, no harassing of wildlife.

One of the best first stops for any outdoor lover coming to Nantucket is the **Maria Mitchell Association** (*2 Vestal St. 508-228-9198. Adm. fee*). This extraordinary organization, named for the Nantucket native who became America's first female astronomer, not only features two observatories and a fine aquarium but also offers a full slate of nature walks every other day throughout the summer.

If you'd like to get out and walk, one of the most enchanting places to do so is at a place called **Middle Moors,** a collection of lands totaling 4,000 acres, used during the 1800s as a commons for grazing. These lands are protected by various organizations and local governments, but most significantly, by the Nantucket Conservation Foundation (*508-228-2884. www.nantucketconservation.com*), which controls 3,200 acres of the property. This membership-supported organization was incorporated in 1963 on the eminently practical and thoroughly American notion that the best way to protect land is to own it—an idea given life with the first donation of less than an acre. The NCF's lands have since grown to well over 8,000 acres, making the organization the largest single landowner on Nantucket Island. In the eastern part of the Middle Moors is **Heath House,** a contact station with a seasonal ranger who can answer your questions and help you plan your outings throughout this vast area.

Waterfront house, Nantucket

What's in a Name?

Some have suggested that the name Nantucket is linked to the notion of a faraway place, but it's more likely to have come from an Algonquian phrase, best translated as "at the point of land on a tidal river" (perhaps the flow between Tuckernuck and Nantucket Islands). The town we know today as Nantucket was once called Wesco—from the Algonquian word "woskech-quett," meaning "top of the rocks." It was from Nantucket that Captain Ahab set out to find the infamous *Moby-Dick*, a story Melville based on an actual event in 1820, when the *Essex* was rammed and sunk by an aggressive whale.

Also nearby is the **Milestone Cranberry Bog,** which was the largest cranberry bog in the world until the 1960s, when it was subdivided into more water-efficient parcels. (A portion of the profits from each year's cranberry harvest is paid out as rent to the NCF, which uses it to buy additional conservation land.) During your outings, plan to visit a hilltop called **Altar Rock,** which offers great views of the surrounding moors, as well as of Great Point and Sankaty Head lighthouses, Pocomo Head, and Siasconset Village. In the western portion of the Middle Moors are the beautiful **Shawkemo Hills,** which contain a number of wetlands known as kettlehole ponds, so named because they have no in-flowing or out-flowing streams. While geologists say that these formations were the result of slow-melting glaciers, more beguiling, perhaps, is the Native American legend that tells of the ponds being the footsteps of a giant, later filled in with water. The lush vegetation around the edges of these ponds—highbush blueberry, swamp azalea, and sweet pepperbush—provides good cover for a number of birds, including wood ducks, green-winged teal, mallard, black ducks, and hooded mergansers.

The Middle Moors are also home to a number of rare and endangered animals and plants, from the northern harrier and short-eared owl to Nantucket shadbush, St. Andrew's cross, bushy rockrose, sandplain blue-eyed grass, and sandplain flax.

If time allows, explore other NCF properties, including the beautiful 123-acre **Eel Point** on the northwest part of the island. This medley of sand dune, barrier beach, cranberry bog, tidal flat, and salt marsh contains an abundance of birdlife, from endangered piping plovers to American oystercatchers, as well as dowitchers, sandpipers, herons, egrets, and terns. Detailed maps of these and other Nantucket Conservation Foundation properties are available by contacting the organization.

Other key organizations involved with Nantucket conservation efforts include the Massachusetts Audubon Society *(781-259-9500),* which manages properties on Hummock Pond and Sesachacha Pond; Nantucket Island Land Bank Commission *(508-228-7240);* and the Trustees of Reservations *(508-693-7717),* which manages properties at Great Point, Coskata, and Coatue, Massachusetts. ∎

Emilie Ruecker Wildlife Refuge

RHODE ISLAND ■ 50 acres ■ Southeast Rhode Island, 3 miles south of
Tiverton on R.I. 77 ■ Best months May-Oct. ■ Hiking, bird-watching, wildlife
viewing ■ Contact Audubon Society of Rhode Island, 12 Sanderson Rd.,
Smithfield, RI 02917; phone 401-949-5454

THOUGH JUST 50 ACRES in size, this former farm, donated to the Audubon
Society by Emilie Ruecker in 1965, is absolutely awash with life. In the
course of a year, more than 150 species of birds will visit this refuge. Early
morning and late evening visitors to a pond located just off the Yellow
Trail will find an excellent opportunity to view a variety of species.

A fine web of trails here leads past a number of different habitats,
from bayberry and shadbush to cordgrass and seaside goldenrod, along
with limited stands of alder, maple, oak, and hickory. One favorite walk
is a 1.4-mile ramble along the Yellow Trail, breaking off on the Blue
Trail long enough to wander around a small peninsula jutting into the
Sakonnet River, and finally returning southward to the parking area
via the Red Trail. The edges of the peninsula reached on the Blue Trail,
and along the northernmost section of the Yellow Trail, are great places
to spot the occasional glossy ibis, snowy egret, and black-crowned night-
heron, and to see fiddler crabs dashing back and forth across the flats.

Fiddlers are amazing creatures, perfectly able to breathe in the water
like other crabs, but also able to store oxygen in their gill chambers and
take to the land for days at a time. When you see fiddlers crossing flats
like this, it's because they're scouring the area to munch on tiny plants
washed up on the mud, all the while trying to avoid ending up as dinner
for a hungry gull. Although fiddlers can't hear, they can pick up the
vibrations of your footsteps from many yards away, and will scurry en
masse ahead of you as you walk. ■

Arcadia Management Area

At 13,817 acres, the Arcadia
Management Area *(401-539-2356.
newportvisions.com/home/arcadia
3.html)* is the largest of the state
management areas, with broadleaf
and coniferous forest mixed with
wetlands. The **Wood River** is
among the finest waterways in the
state and a great place for both
fly-fishing and canoeing *(access
near parking area on R.I. 165).* Twelve
parking areas allow access to
roughly 100 miles of hiking trails of
varying difficulty, maintained by user
groups and the state Department
of Environmental Management.
The 3-mile **Mount Tom Trail,** the
4.5-mile **Narragansett Trail,**
and the 5-mile **Breakheart Trail**
are especially satisfying.

Because of hunting in the area,
winter visitors must wear at least
200 square inches of blaze orange
from the third week in October to
the last day of February.

Trustom Pond National Wildlife Refuge

RHODE ISLAND ■ 160 acres ■ Southern Rhode Island, south of US 1 near Charlestown ■ Hiking, bird-watching, wildlife viewing ■ Contact the Rhode Island National Wildlife Refuge Complex, Shoreline Plaza, R.I. 1A, P.O. Box 307, Charlestown, RI 02813; phone 401-364-9124

A SMALL REFUGE NEAR THE OCEAN, Trustom Pond has a diversity of vegetative habitats, and that makes it a splendid hiking place for those with an eye for birds. Just a few steps from the trailhead, for example, the path crosses a restored field of native grasses—a good place to spot meadowlarks—then moves into a patch of shrub land flush with thickets of viburnum, blueberry, raspberry, honeysuckle, and shadbush. The

Native grasses at Trustom Pond National Wildlife Refuge

shadbush, incidentally, takes its name from the fact that its beautiful white flowers appear in spring, about the time shad are making their way upstream to spawn. Finally, the path enters solid growths of red maple, apple, cherry, and scrub oak. In these last stretches you may see eastern towhees, brown thrashers, and orioles.

Perhaps the best part of the refuge is **Osprey Point,** reached by taking a left turn at a T-intersection roughly 0.75 mile into the walk. Here you'll find a lovely peninsula jutting into the brackish waters of **Trustom Pond,** with a small observation tower positioned above spartina grass, allowing you good glimpses of cormorants, terns, great blue herons, pintail, wood ducks, and ospreys. On the return walk, bear left at the first intersection, returning to your car by way of another gentle path, winding its way through shadbush, red pine, scrub oak, and fox grape. ■

Block Island

RHODE ISLAND ■ Island 10 miles south of Rhode Island in Block Island Sound
■ Best months mid-June–mid-Oct. Access via ferry (see information p. 282)
■ Hiking, guided walks, boating, kayaking, biking, bird-watching, wildlife viewing
■ Contact the Chamber of Commerce, P.O. Box D, Block Island, RI 02807;
phone 401-466-2982. www.ultranet.com/block-island

WHEN THE NATURE CONSERVANCY, one of America's most respected
conservation groups, came up with a list of significant lands throughout
the Western Hemisphere—the so-called Last Great Places—Block Island
was on the list. Built largely of clay and sand, Block Island is marked by
rolling, treeless moors and delicate saltwater habitats. Thanks to some
hard work by local citizens, fighting to preserve both their natural and
their cultural heritage, more than 30 percent of the land is protected,
including many areas that are critical for wildlife. Thousands of migratory raptors, songbirds, and waterfowl use the island as a resting and
feeding ground on their journeys
along the Atlantic flyway; more
than 40 species of rare or endangered animals can be found here.

The Nature Conservancy *(401-
466-2129)* offers an excellent
collection of guided nature walks
at selected preserves from mid-June
through Columbus Day. Because
the times and locations of these
outings vary, the best way to find
out about them is to pick up a
copy of the *Block Island Times*. The
Nature Conservancy also sponsors
summer children's programs and
offers custom group tours of Block
Island natural areas for groups of
six or more.

You might want to consider
an exploration of the beautiful
Great Salt Pond. You can do this
with the help of the Committee for
the Great Salt Pond *(401-466-5061.
www.blockisland.com/saltpond)*,
which offers a Water Nature Series
of guided explorations throughout
the summer. Alternatively, you can
explore the Great Salt Pond on your
own by kayak. Rentals are available

An Essential Rest Stop

In late September and early
October, when a series of
cold fronts descend sharply
across the region, bringing
strong winds from the northwest, Block Island can be one
of the finest places for bird-
watching of any location on
the Atlantic coast. These
winds routinely push migrating birds off their intended
route along the Atlantic flyway; as a result, thousands of
these fliers—unable to make
it to the mainland—alight at
the north end of Block Island
to rest and feed. In some
years you may spot more than
150 species on the island,
including virtually every bird
common to New England. The
bird-watching is enhanced by
the fact that the low vegetation marking much of the area
makes spotting relatively easy.

Mitchell Farm, Block Island

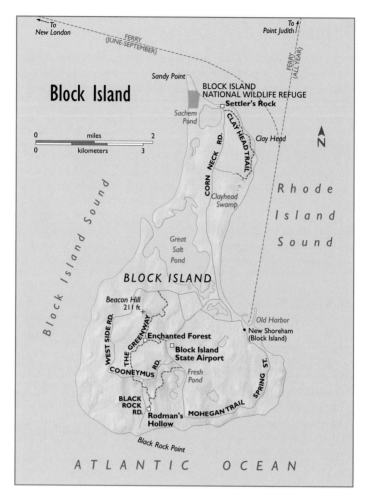

from the following sources: the Barrington Inn *(401-466-5510)*; Champlin's Kayak and Paddle Boat Rentals *(401-466-7777)*; Oceans and Ponds, The Orvis Store *(401-466-5131 or 800-678-4701)*; or New Harbor Kayak Rentals *(401-466-2890)*.

Rodman's Hollow

If you want to stretch your legs, be sure to visit Rodman's Hollow *(south end of island, off Cooneymus Rd. 401-466-2129)*, a glacial outwash basin with a grass scrubland community of arrowwood, bayberry, and shadbush. A small knoll provides fine views of the southern coastline. In mid-May, when the shadbush is in bloom, this is a lovely place to walk. The paths through the basin are part of **The Greenway,** an enticing network of trails stretching for more than 12 miles through the southern portion of the island, connecting Great Salt Pond with Black Rock Point.

Clay Head Trail

You'll find another fine hike on Clay Head Trail *(N end of Block Island, at the end of a small dirt road off Corn Neck Rd. 401-466-2129)*. Bicycle racks are located at the trailhead—bikes are not allowed on any preserve trail. This trail, my favorite walk on the island, begins in a dense blanket of vegetation, then skirts the beautiful **Clay Head Swamp,** which on most mornings is dizzy with birds. In 0.3 mile the trail reaches the coast, coming out at a cobbly beach, then climbs north to the top of a magnificent line of clay headlands. You can continue north for nearly 2 miles, weaving back and forth across these rose-bedecked bluffs, coming out again at Corn Neck Road just south of Settler's Rock. This area plays host to a fine variety of birds, including the song sparrow, yellow warbler, and red-winged blackbird; also here are probably the only nesting pairs of barn owls in all of Rhode Island. The bird you may see more often than any other, however, is the bank swallow, which builds its nests by excavating narrow chambers into the clay soils of the ocean bluffs. These tunnels, 2 to 4 inches wide, are bored into the cliffs for several feet, ending in a grass-lined chamber. ■

Bicycling on Block Island

Waterfront at Beavertail State Park

Beavertail State Park

RHODE ISLAND ■ 153 acres ■ Southeast Rhode Island on Conanicut Island just west of Newport off R.I. 138 ■ Best season summer ■ Hiking, guided walks, bird-watching, wildlife viewing ■ Contact the park, c/o Goddard State Park, Ives Rd., Warwick, RI 02818; phone 401-884-2010

BEAVERTAIL, LOCATED ON CONANICUT ISLAND near Newport, is a truly magnificent park—a generous helping of surf and seabirds and foghorns. This state park is as beautiful a piece of the southern New England coast as you'll find anywhere, and on any given day it can seem a thousand miles away from the urban bustle of south Rhode Island. On a windswept rocky stretch of beach you'll find the **Beavertail Light,** originally built in 1749 as only the third lighthouse in New England. The lighthouse is also the location of some fine seasonal naturalist-led activities, including tide pool explorations, geology, and special programs designed around an exhibit known as the Beavertail Aquarium.

Though the road system in Beavertail will take you close to most of the hot spots, this is also a wonderful park to explore on foot. Beginning at parking lot no. 3, for example, you can head along the beach toward Beavertail Light, then work your way around the peninsula past mats of pasture rose and plantain, horsetail and buttercups, and red cedar. There are tide pools as well, filled with a variety of shellfish and other creatures of the sea, ringed around the edges with bladder rockweed and Irish moss. ■

Project Oceanology

CONNECTICUT   ■ Southeast Connecticut, on Avery Point campus of University of Connecticut in Groton ■ Wildlife viewing, science experiments ■ Adm. fee ■ Contact the project, 184 Shennecossett Rd., Groton, CT 06340; phone 860-445-9007 or 800-364-8472. www.oceanology.org

IF YOU AND YOUR FAMILY are among those intrigued by the mysteries of the ocean, one of the best ways to answer the call is by spending half a day with Project Oceanology (Project O) in Groton. This is a hands-on educational experience involving a specially equipped research boat; in the course of your time at sea you can expect to participate in everything from retrieving mud-core samples to testing the clarity and dissolved oxygen content of the water. You'll also learn to use charts and other navigational aids. And then there's the best part of all: netting a host of sea creatures and recording information about them. On the day of my visit, our nets yielded a wealth of plants and critters, including kelp, dulce, sea lettuce, bread sponges, red jellyfish, clams, channeled whelks and knob whelks, squids, spider crabs and rock crabs, lobsters, summer flukes, window pane flounders, winter flounders, small-mouth flounders, sea robins, spotted hakes, porgies, and skates.

Spider crab

As good as the catch itself is the fact that alongside you at all times is a staff of research guides dedicated to helping you understand it all —and managing in the process to make the sea seem more strange and wonderful than ever. You may learn, for example, how lobsters have the ability to release an appendage to an attacking predator, then generate a new one; or how in times of danger the squid protects itself with a sack of ink. Then there's the intriguing story of the spider crab, which, being slow and easy prey, will sometimes camouflage itself with pieces of seaweed wrapped around the spines of its back. And tales of red jellyfish, with their long, dangling curtains of stinging tentacles—poisonous, to be sure, but also a shroud where young haddock and cod will swim to protect themselves from predators. ■

Autumn in Rocky Neck State Park

Rocky Neck State Park

CONNECTICUT ■ 710 acres ■ Southeast Connecticut, off I-95 near Old Lyme ■ Best months May-Oct. ■ Camping, hiking, swimming, fishing, biking, bird-watching ■ Adm. fee ■ Contact the park, P.O. Box 676, 244 W. Main St., Niantic, CT 06357; phone 860-739-5471

LIKE HAMMONASSET BEACH STATE PARK (see p. 86) to the west, Rocky Neck State Park attracts most people with one feature: the beach. On any hot summer day, you can count on the shore being nearly elbow to elbow with sun-seekers, the air thick with the smell of coconut-scented lotions. However, as you can easily see by walking the **Bride Brook Trail,** this park has much more to offer than just soaking up rays.

The Bride Brook Trail takes off from the northeast corner of a parking area near the bridge crossing **Bride Brook.** Marked at its beginning by red blazes, the trail will take you through an array of habitats, offering glimpses of tidal flowage, as well as fine stands of red maple, black oak, highbush blueberry, and thick clusters of Connecticut's state flower, the mountain laurel.

At 0.25 mile is a fork. Follow the white-blazed trail to the east (right), which leads in short order to the edge of the Bride Brook tidal wetland.

As you make your way along this wetland, keep your eyes peeled for breaks in the vegetation, the best of which comes roughly 0.25 mile beyond the last trail junction. Here you'll find a stage that on most days is busy with birdlife, including snowy egrets, great blue herons, belted kingfishers, bitterns, cormorants, red-tailed hawks, and ospreys. If time or energy is in short supply, this is a fine turnaround spot, which would make for a 1-mile round-trip. But if you pick your way along the path for another 0.3 mile, you'll find yourself in a virtual feast of ferns—Christmas, hay-scented, and cinnamon—all of which are cradled by rose, bittersweet, witch hazel, dogwood, winterberry, and hickory. You'll encounter many of these plants in your forays through southern New England lowlands. ■

Bluff Point State Park and Coastal Reserve

CONNECTICUT ■ 806 acres ■ Southeast Connecticut, off US 1 near Groton ■ Best months May-Oct. ■ Camping, hiking, fishing, biking, bird-watching ■ Adm. fee ■ Contact the park, c/o Fort Griswold Battlefield State Park, 57 Fort St., Groton, CT 06340; phone 860-445-1729

OF THE VERY FEW UNTRAMMELED slices of coast left in Connecticut, at more than 800 acres Bluff Point is not only the largest, but is well above average when it comes to catching the dramatic feel of Long Island Sound. For starters, there's a fine variety of birdlife, waxing and waning with the shifting seasons. In winter, for example, this is a good place to observe scaup by the hundreds, floating in great rafts and making dive after dive for crabs and barnacles. At other times look for mallard, buffleheads, mute swans, snowy egrets, and great blue herons. You'll also find that the great variety of vegetation at Bluff Point means a plenitude of songbirds. Don't forget your field guides!

Begin your walk by heading past the gate that marks the line between the state park and the reserve. In just a few hundred yards is a fork in the road; stay right, strolling by a gentle weave of oaks as well as rather typical thickets of greenbrier, black raspberry, rose, grape, and honeysuckle—the perfect place, incidentally, for catching sight of both bluebirds and mockingbirds.

In roughly a half mile, you'll see a grassy path taking off from the main road, leading down to the banks of the **Poquonnock River,** passing a loose toss of cherry, oak, and redcedar, finally arriving at the edge of an estuary. This low-lying area is yet another good place to watch birdlife, most notably wood ducks, blue herons, ospreys, and mute swans. During a devastating hurricane in 1938, flood waters here reached more than 11 feet above mean low-tide levels; surges up the Poquonnock were high enough to flood Trumbull Airport to the west.

In less than a half mile is another path on the left, leading back to the main road. Once there, take a right; a little farther, just past a boardwalk heading out to the beach, take the right branch of a fork in the road. This will let you climb onto the **Bluff Point Headland,** stitched through with beach plum, salt spray rose, beach pea, and bayberry. (The area accessed by the boardwalk is a good spot for beachcombing; look for the shells of crabs, blue mussels, scallops, and razor clams.)

This headland, the core of which is made of erosion-resistant volcanic rock, serves as an important protector of both Bluff Point and Bushy Point beaches, lying to the west. By the same token, the granite-like rock along the seaward face of the point is being steadily eroded by waves, then carried westward by currents to end up as sand for these same beaches. The island visible ahead of you and slightly to the east is **Fishers Island;** farther to the east, and part of the main coastline, is

Watch Hill in Rhode Island, so named because it served as an observation point for soldiers during the Civil War.

From here you can retrace your steps to the parking area, creating a walk of slightly over 3 miles. Or you can continue on, taking a right fork in the road onto a rocky beach, which in less than a half mile joins an obvious, grassy roadway. At the next intersection turn right, and then bear left, winding through a small forest back to the main road, where you'll make one last right, reaching the parking area at just over 4 miles.

Nearby Activities

This corner of Connecticut holds a number of interesting side trips. For instance, you'll enjoy a visit to the **Mashantucket Pequot Museum and Research Center** (*Mashantucket Pequot Reservation, 7 miles N of Mystic off Conn. 2. 800-411-9671. www.mashantucket.com. Closed Tues. in winter; adm. fee*). The museum offers excellent cultural and natural history exhibits tied to the native people of southeastern Connecticut. Here you can see multisensory dioramas, including a walk-through 16th-century Pequot village, as well as historical artifacts, films and videos, and 3-D interactive computer programs.

Denison Pequotsepos Nature Center

More than 7 miles of trails wind through the 125-acre Denison Pequotsepos Nature Center (*Off Conn. 27 in Mystic. 806-536-1216. Adm. fee*). This is a good place to see birds in a variety of natural habitats, or to visit abandoned or injured birds of prey.

Mystic Aquarium

Mystic Aquarium (*Mystic, via the Aquarium exit off I-95. 860-572-5955. www.mysticaquarium.org. Adm. fee*) is one of the finest facilities of its kind on the East Coast, containing over 3,500 sea creatures in 40 exhibits. Daily demonstrations feature beluga whales and Atlantic bottlenose dolphins. The aquarium is firmly tied to cutting-edge research (most notably through the Institute for Exploration, directed by Robert Ballard, finder of the RMS *Titanic*), making the learning opportunities here among the best in the nation. In the past, the aquarium's outings have included such adventures as underwater photography, gathering sea creatures with seine nets, boat-based whale-watching, and various studies aboard the EPA ocean survey vessel the *Peter W. Anderson*. The aquarium also conducts fine multiple-day programs for kids during the summer, including everything from exploring the world of ocean fishing to beach walks to whale-watching for teens.

Connecticut College Arboretum

Established in 1931, the arboretum (*Off I-95 on Conn. 32 in New London. 860-439-5020*) contains over 700 acres of native plant collections and gardens, as well as hiking trails. On Sundays from May through late October, it offers free public guided tours. ■

Canoeing the Lieutenant River, Old Lyme

Lower Connecticut River

CONNECTICUT ■ 30 miles long ■ South-central Connecticut ■ Best seasons spring, summer, and fall ■ Camping, hiking, kayaking, canoeing, bird-watching, wildlife viewing

THAT THE LOWER CONNECTICUT RIVER, which in the 1960s and '70s was described by some locals as little more than a toxic sewer, should today be teeming with life is one of the most heartening turns of events in modern American conservation history. Get into a canoe or a sea kayak in Middletown and head downstream, and you'll soon lose count of the ospreys and kingfishers and herons, of the flash of eagles in winter, shad in the spring. Some 30 miles later, on finally reaching the river's mouth at Long Island Sound, you will not see the typical industrial corridor that marks the vast majority of port cities around the country, but the wide, sweet drift of spartina grass cradling **Great Island,** and recreational fishermen at **Ferry Landing,** lowering traps for crabs and casting for mackerel and striped bass. The way the Connecticut River has risen from its deathbed has been a source of pride not just for the people who live here, but for the country as a whole. In 1994 the lower Connecticut was identified in a multinational convention as containing Wetlands of International Importance; in 1998 it was one of the first watercourses in the country to be designated as an American Heritage River. Give it a couple of days of your time, and you'll know why.

What to See and Do

Perhaps more than any other location in this book, the Connecticut River is best experienced by canoe or kayak. That said, keep in mind that summer weekends find this portion of the river filled with powerboats and personal watercraft (such as Jet Skis); if you can get out only on a Saturday or Sunday, begin paddling early in the morning, hug the shore on the way back, and spend the time in between at one or more of several wetlands, coves, or feeder rivers that lie to the side of the main channel. Bring a lunch, and bring your bird books.

If you have time constraints, be sure to plan a stop at the interpretive boardwalk taking off from the **Marine Fisheries Building** in Old Lyme (*northbound on I-95, take exit 70 and head south off the ramp onto Conn. 156. Take next right onto Ferry Rd. Boardwalk is at end*), where you can get out on Long Island Sound and experience some of the birdlife.

Chapman Pond

To reach Chapman Pond, put in a canoe or kayak at the the Salmon River boat launch, 1.5 miles north of East Haddam on Conn. 149 (*boat launch will be on the left*). As you head downstream, paddle on the east (left) side of the river for 2 miles, then look for an inlet at the south end of a small island on your right in the main channel. This inlet leads to the quiet waters of the pond itself. An outlet stream on the south side of the pond will take you back to the Connecticut, where you can head back upstream to the Salmon River ramp.

There is magic to this place, and it begins after no more than a couple of paddle strokes toward Chapman Pond. Alder and marsh grass cradle the inlet stream, while the occasional muskrat crosses in front of your boat. Mute swans, ever present in this part of New England, drift on without a whisper. Once on the pond itself, you're likely to catch sight of a heron in flight or an osprey fishing, or hear the shrill chatter of kingfishers. To the east of the pond rises a height of land now owned and managed by the Nature Conservancy (*860-344-0716 for directions and a trail map*), blanketed by a fine, open forest of white ash, sugar maple, beech, white oak, black oak, red oak, and sassafras. Those with a hankering to hike may want to pull up their boats on the east side of the pond, near the remains of an old stone foundation, where a 3.2-mile loop trail follows the edge of the pond. The trail also has an upland entrance off River Road in East Haddam. Unless you plan to hike the entire loop, however, a short detour from your paddling excursion may be the better option.

The color and texture of this forest includes stands of eastern hemlock, a tree species currently threatened by an invasion of a nonnative parasitic insect, the woolly adelgid. In feeding on the tree's sap, this insect injects a toxic substance that causes defoliation and often kills the tree. You may

Cleaning Up the Connecticut

It would be hard to name a river with a more dynamic blend of natural and historical significance than the Connecticut. It has been an inspiration and pleasuring ground for a remarkable array of people, including Harriet Beecher Stowe, Mark Twain, Emily Dickinson, Henry James, and even Albert Einstein, who on a vacation here in 1935 had a devil of a time trying to sail the lower Connecticut in a Cape Cod knockabout.

Yet the fact that today you have the chance to smile yourself silly over the wash of life to be found along the lower Connecticut—ospreys to herons, mink to muskrat—is tantamount to a miracle. Although the mouth of the river may never have suffered the pressures of industrial development seen on other waterways, the Connecticut nevertheless had its share of neglect and abuse. By the 1920s, bird populations along the river were greatly diminished. Shad fishing dwindled to the point that fishermen over an entire season were able to take less than half of what they'd formerly taken in a single day. As the century wore on, the riverbanks were strewn with the rusting flotsam of old factories, and a dramatic increase in pollutants rendered the lower river unsuitable for swimming or fishing. For a time the Connecticut was referred to by concerned observers as the best landscaped sewer in the nation.

Beginning in the 1950s, however, residents along much of the Connecticut's 410-mile length began a herculean effort to reclaim it, pushing for stringent laws against pollution as well as for the preservation of critical wildlife habitat. Within three decades, the river was nearly twice as clean as it had been, thanks in no small part to new municipal sewage treatment plants, many of them made possible by 1965's Clean Water Act. By 1980, most of the river was again open to swimming. Thanks both to improved water quality as well as to the installation of fish ladders, shad runs have rebounded, some years exceeding a million fish, while the reduction of pesticides and chlorinated hydrocarbons has allowed a phenomenal rebound in bald eagles, northern harriers, and ospreys. In 1993 the Nature Conservancy declared the Connecticut River tidelands one of the 40 "Last Great Places" in the hemisphere. Indeed, today there are few areas in the Northeast with such a high concentration of rare or protected species.

Egret, Rocky Neck State Park

note some hemlocks low down, in hollows near the water, that seem to be less affected than trees on sunny, dry, south-facing slopes. Research has shown that cooler and damper conditions give the trees a better chance to withstand the effects of the insect. The woolly adelgid has damaged vast stands of hemlock over hundreds of square miles, roughly from West Virginia to northeast Massachusetts. Foresters throughout the unaffected parts of New England are holding their collective breath, wondering whether this invasion might be heading their way. Given the hemlock's shallow root system, once a tree has died off it takes only a good nudge from the wind to knock it over. A downed tree opens up the forest floor to a wash of sunlight, which sets in motion the growth of other, more light-dependent species, each caught up in the great race for the sky.

Forest researchers have documented another widespread die-off of hemlocks across much of the tree's range some 5,000 years ago. The effect on the forest was pronounced then, too, as oak, elm, red maple, and pine moved in to claim the territory. By all indications, in some locations in the Northeast, hemlock rebounded after 1,000 to 2,000 years; in other locations it never reclaimed its former turf.

If you elect to leave your boat for the trails that wind through the preserve, two things may catch your attention. The first are the large patches of hay-scented ferns. In places these grow to the exclusion of nearly everything else, a condition that is often an indicator of an area being over-grazed by deer.

The second thing you may notice, if you are visiting during March through May or June, is the number of temporary water pockets, which ecologists call vernal pools (for the season in which they appear). These are wet areas—typically 20 to 50 feet across and 1 or 2 feet deep—with no inlet or outlet, fed by the winter snow or rain and usually drying up as summer unfolds.

At first they may seem utterly unremarkable; most of us have walked past such places hundreds of times without giving them more than a passing glance. But vernal pools are truly fascinating places, abounding with life. Mayflies, caddisflies, and

The Osprey

Relatively quiet waters, such as those on the lower Connecticut River, are great places to watch ospreys swing down to nab their dinners. The return of the these birds to New England and other parts of the country is one of the great conservation success stories of the 20th century. Even though the osprey has been protected in Connecticut since 1903, its numbers declined throughout the century, largely due to ingesting DDT from its prey. With the elimination of DDT from the environment, the osprey has made a remarkable comeback.

Kayaking near Great Island

damselflies—not to mention mosquito larvae—are plentiful here. Also found in ample quantities are such fascinating species as fingernail clams and fairy shrimp. In one of the great but seldom witnessed rites of spring, dozens of salamanders in the black of a rainy night will crawl from their underground chambers or from under logs and head for a particular vernal pool—the very same one used for generations before them—breeding there and laying eggs. As the pool dries, some species will enter a dormant phase as larvae or eggs, while others, such as adult insects and salamanders, will move on to take up residence elsewhere.

Lieutenant River to Great Island Wildlife Management Area

Another way to enjoy canoeing or kayaking in the lower Connecticut River is to paddle to **Great Island** beginning on the Lieutenant River, which empties into the Connecticut near the larger river's mouth. Begin at a state launch where Conn. 156 crosses the Lieutenant River just west of Old Lyme, a half mile east of I-95. If you've got the time, you may want to begin this trip by first going upstream on the Lieutenant for a couple of miles. You'll lose count of all the ospreys, swans, kingfishers, and ducks flying and floating past your boat. (If you get sidetracked on the Lieutenant, spending more time there than you planned, you can always launch later in the day closer to Great Island. Use the state ramp located on the Back River, reached by heading south on Conn. 156 from its intersection with I-95 for 1.7 miles; turn right on Smith Neck Road, and follow it to the end.)

As you paddle around in this area, one thing you're sure to notice is the tall, reedlike grass with plume-shaped flowers crowding much of the riverbank. Called phragmites, or common reed grass, this particular kind is thought to be a nonnative species carried here on ships as seeds mixed in with ballast stones. The grass was first documented on the lower Connecticut River in the 1960s and today is spreading along the riverbank at the rate of 2 percent a year, crowding out the native spartina grass. (Because phragmites favors brackish water, the placement of gates across estuaries throughout New England to restrict tidal flows may have helped create exactly the right conditions to support it.) Phragmites only rarely produces seed, but it spreads furiously by either underground or on-the-ground stems, some of which reach 35 feet; over time it crowds out nearly all other plants, including many that are important sources of food and shelter for wildlife. Some biologists consider phragmites one of the most serious problems facing tidal wetlands today.

When you're ready, head downstream on the Lieutenant for about a mile from the put-in point on Conn. 156 and you'll reach the mighty Connecticut. Turn left, paddling downstream for the final run before reaching Long Island Sound. Be aware that this is big water, made more so on some days by heavy boat traffic and blustery winds. Judge the conditions when you reach the mouth of the Lieutenant and use appropriate caution. Once in the Connecticut, keep to the east bank. The next water you come to will be the **Back River,** on your left, which serves as the perfect back door to the **Great Island Wildlife Management Area** *(contact state Dept. of Environmental Protection/Wildlife Division. 869-424-3011)* and the fabulous estuaries lying at the mouth of the Connecticut. This is a place of pure enchantment —islands crowned with loose blends of oak and other hardwoods, as well as accessible rock-slab shores, all surrounded by a tidal flowage rich with birdlife.

Continuing to paddle south past the state boat ramp on Smith Neck Road, you'll soon reach a large sand spit on your left, near the mouth of the **Black Hall River.** This is **Griswold Point,** a wildlife preserve managed by the Nature Conservancy, and probably the most pristine piece of shoreline anywhere in Connecticut. Nearly twice as big as it was 150 years ago, Griswold Point receives much of its sand supply from the erosion of glacial deposits lying to the east. (This may change with the recent stabilization of the glacial bluffs that for so long have provided the raw material.) Besides the visible neck of sand, there's also a large sandbar just under the surface of the water, extending from the western end of the point; at low tide it's possible to walk along this bar for nearly a third of a mile into the sound. ∎

Selden Neck State Park

CONNECTICUT ■ 550 acres ■ Southeast Connecticut; put in at the Salmon River boat launch off Conn. 149, 1.5 miles north of Conn. 82 junction ■ May-Sept. Accessible only by canoe or kayak; access may be flooded in spring ■ Camping, hiking, boating, kayaking, canoeing, bird-watching ■ Campsites one night only, mail-in reservations required ■ Contact the park, c/o Gillette Castle State Park, 67 River Rd., East Haddam, CT 06423; phone 860-526-2336

IN A SECTION OF THE Connecticut River that on weekends can be rife with powerboats, Selden Neck State Park—located on **Selden Island,** the largest island in the state—is a sweet breath of calm. Here you'll find a handful of primitive campsites along with a lazy string of trails coursing through the woodlands. It's a world away from churning wakes and the smell of marine gas. The tidal flow on the east side of the island is **Selden Creek,** which contains a myriad of watery nooks and crannies perfect for poking about by canoe. Expect to see a fine array of birdlife, including ospreys, swans, ducks, and northern harriers, as well as wild gardens of irises, cardinal flowers, and in some places on the island, enough poison ivy to set the whole state of Connecticut to itching.

On your way downriver, roughly 5 miles from the Salmon River state boat launch, you may want to consider pulling off at a sandy beach just north of the Chester-Hadlyme ferry dock for a climb up the hill to the amazing **Gillette Castle State Park** (*House under renovation and on restricted schedule. Adm. fee for house*). Here William Gillette, a turn-of-the-20th-century actor made famous by his role as Sherlock Holmes, spent five years and more than a million dollars designing his fantasy home—a 24-room castle with 4-foot-thick walls—including most of the furniture. Gillette was uncommonly fond of trains, so much so that he eventually built a miniature 3-mile-long railroad, complete with a tunnel and finely crafted bridges, to carry his friends and visitors through the castle grounds and down to the Connecticut River. ■

Leaves of Three

With the abundance of poison ivy in southeast New England, outdoor enthusiasts would do well to learn to recognize it. The 2- to 4-inch-long shiny leaflets of this woody-stemmed plant (which may grow as shrub, ground cover, or vine) come in threes, with the end leaflet slightly stalked. Older plants have greenish-white berries, growing in grapelike clusters, which appear in summer and fall. Even if you don't touch the plant directly, you can carry the oily poison on your shoes or clothes, and later transmit it to your hands. If you've touched it, wash promptly with strong soap or rubbing alcohol. Native peoples treated the itch with both sweet fern and jewelweed.

Hammonasset Beach

Hammonasset Beach State Park

CONNECTICUT ■ 1,100 acres ■ South-central Connecticut, off I-95 near Madison ■ May-Oct. ■ Camping, walking, canoeing, swimming, fishing, bird-watching ■ Adm. fee ■ Contact the park, P.O. Box 271, Madison, CT 06443; phone 203-245-2785

MAKE NO MISTAKE about it. Most people (and that means an awful lot of people) come to Hammonasset Beach State Park to swim, lie in the sand, and read books—pretending for a few hours that summer will go on forever. What most of them don't realize is that this is also a phenomenal place to wrap yourself in one of the state's great coastal ecosystems. Besides the **Meig's Point Nature Center,** filled with such creatures as live frogs, lobsters, fish, and many other residents of the intertidal zone, in summer there are six full-time naturalists on board, doing everything from giving talks about snakes to taking visitors on free canoe trips through the tidal marsh (minimum age, 12).

What to See and Do

You could begin your visit with a thoroughly enjoyable self-guided walk on the **Willard Island Nature Trail,** located near the eastern end of the park, just north of the Meig's Point Nature Center. Farmed until 1920, **Willard Island** was used as a field campground until 1972; since then it has been allowed to go wild, and thus serves as a wonderful example of plant succession. While you can still find apple, pear, and crabapple trees, all remnants of past farm days, increasingly this is a land of Virginia juniper—one of the most successful colonizers of abandoned fields throughout much of southern New England. (You may also hear this tree called redcedar.) These trees provide nesting cover for a variety of birds, including owls, while the bluish berries—which are actually the tree's cones—form an important food source for other species of birds, such as hermit thrushes, bluebirds, cedar waxwings, and brown thrashers.

As you make your way around the loop trail, you'll pass many other kinds of trees and common shrubs, including shadbush, dogwood, sumac, oak, and a fair amount of poison ivy (see sidebar p. 85). Toward the north end of the loop is a sizable grove of sassafras, a medium-size tree with leathery leaves of different shapes, including one that looks like a mitten with a thumb and another that resembles a three-fingered glove. While today sassafras may seem unremarkable, it was in fact a serious factor in the European push to establish a colonial presence on the Atlantic coast. During colonial times, sassafras was highly touted as a blood tonic, a tea, and most notably as a treatment for syphilis. In early colonial days, as an export sassafras was second only to tobacco. Until a few decades ago, sassafras was still being used as an antiseptic in dentistry, as well as a flavoring in everything from root beer to toothpaste.

The highlight of this walk is a fine observation platform offering sweeping views of the salt meadows and tidal marsh. On any given day these areas may be busy with sharp-tailed and seaside sparrows, snowy egrets, various ducks, red-winged blackbirds, greater yellowlegs, willet, and ospreys, the last claiming the platform nests.

While even the colonists recognized the value of salt marshes as pasture, only recently have we come to appreciate the full value of these ecosystems. One of the greatest alterations to the marsh came after the Civil War, when returning soldiers brought malaria to Connecticut; in short order a wholesale effort was launched to drain or fill such wetlands as a means of controlling mosquito populations. Ditching of the marsh to drain off tidal water continued in Connecticut until 1985. Today the state still makes an effort to control mosquitoes, but does so most often through permanent deepwater ponds, created to provide habitat for native minnow species that live and feed on mosquito larvae.

Coastal salt marshes like the one here are highly productive systems. The vast majority of the plant material, or biomass, produced by the salt marsh every year is decomposed by bacteria, forming a nutrient-rich soup that feeds everything from small fish to crabs, snails to shellfish. These, in turn, feed hundreds of other species that live along the coast.

If you've got extra time on your hands, by all means take a stroll on the **Rocky Beach Trail,** which heads east from the nature center and winds for 0.25 mile (one way) to **Meig's Point,** eventually leading to a series of tide pools. ■

Northern Forest

Evergreens on the slopes of the White Mountains, New Hampshire

IT MUST HAVE BEEN AN INCREDIBLE EVENT: Great slabs of mile-thick glacial ice ground southward out of Canada, scouring the river channels of New England into U-shaped valleys, rounding and smoothing the sharp, craggy ridges of the Appalachian Mountains. Then, some 12,000 to 15,000 years ago, the glaciers pulled back to reveal a bare, wind-blasted landscape. Ever so slowly, new life appeared. First were the low-growing plants of the tundra: shrubs, mat vegetation, sedges.

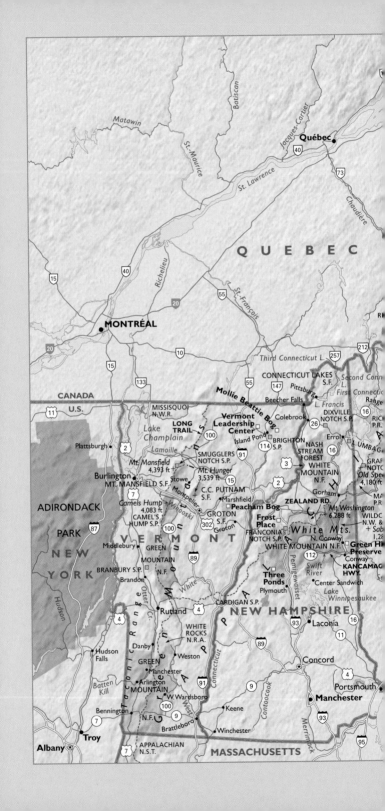

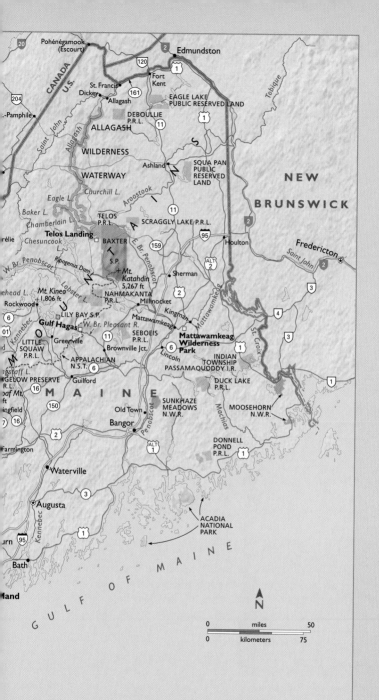

Cabin at Daicey Pond, Baxter State Park, Maine

Next came the conifers—spruce, and then fir, and later still, broadleaf trees such as aspen and birch, all in a wondrous, if rather fitful, march to reclaim the land.

When Europeans first began fanning out across what is now southeast New England, they often found themselves in open, park-like forests. Well to the north, though—in lands that extend into the Canadian provinces of New Brunswick, Quebec, and Ontario—trappers and explorers found a far more tangled land, a region laced with enormous sweeps of spruce and fir, with dense mats of shade-tolerant saplings at their feet. These were the boreal, or northern, woods, a word that comes from Boreas, the Greek god of the north wind. Here you did not travel with ease, sitting atop your horse or even riding in wagons, as you could in the south. In the boreal woods, travel even by foot was difficult.

That all changed in remarkably little time, as much of the northern forest was harvested for firewood and building materials, and cleared to make room for agriculture. Then, in the middle 1800s, people from rural New England took jobs in the cities, or moved farther inland to settle the rich farmlands of the Midwest, abandoning a great many farms and pastures. In the wake of that mass emigration, trees once again reclaimed the land.

In the warmer lowland valleys and the more southerly reaches of the region came an explosion of white pine, a tree whose seeds are adept at regenerating in abandoned fields and pastures, where they compete with mats of grass and forbs; the more fragile, less drought-resistant seeds of the hardwoods, on the other hand, do not compete well in such places. Meanwhile, the uplands, as well as some of the more northerly areas, saw a rebound of fir and spruce. So rapid was this new growth of conifers that it allowed another logging boom to begin at the end of the 19th century. Even more fierce than its predecessor, the boom continued for some 30 years, finally dying out in the 1920s.

With the tree harvest all but played out, the lands were once again abandoned. This time, however, it wasn't grassy fields that got left behind, as happened when the farmers moved on, but scarred, rutted patches of bare dirt from heavy logging. These conditions favored not conifers, but the seeds of hardwoods, which were quick to gain purchase on the bare ground. Thus, as you hike many of the trails of the northern forest today, you'll find yourself traversing not yawning sweeps of white pine or endless runs of spruce and fir, but limited conifer growth amid a wash of hardwoods. Were the land to remain largely free of harvesting, fire, and disease—and assuming the climate remained generally stable—conifers would again take center stage throughout northern New England.

One of the main characteristics of the northern forest is, of course, cool weather, which leads to lingering snow and in many places, saturated soils. (This part of New England is among the coldest regions for its latitude of any place in the world.) Everywhere are signs of how life responds to such chilly conditions. Conifers, for example, grow in streamlined shapes that shed the snow easily, while hardwoods such as birch and aspen are supple, able to bend nearly to the ground under blankets of snow without breaking. Many of the shrubs here are evergreen, so they don't waste energy setting leaves in little more than a four-month growing season. Wintering birds wear thick layers of feathers, while animals sport thick fur or spend much of the winter season in protected burrows.

This cool climate, combined with the relatively recent retreat of glaciers, means that the soils overlying the granitic rock of the northern woods tend to be thin, and not nearly so full of nutrients as soils farther south. The remarkable thing is that these woods, far from being sterile, are seasoned with blossoms in late spring through midsummer, especially in the more open areas of mixed forests.

Also intriguing is the abundance of ponds and bogs, each of which gives rise to its own special weave of life. Many of the water pockets you'll come across originated when large chunks of glacial ice broke off from the mother flow, coming to rest in a depression in the ground. Typically, these blocks were then buried by blankets of till and other debris and later melted, creating ponds. Ponds that were cut off from both groundwater and other external flows may have ended up stagnating, their oxygen all but used up by decaying plants and animals, their water growing more and more acidic. Without enough oxygen to fuel decomposition, plant and animal matter accumulated, eventually turning into mats of peat, sometimes 30 or even 40 feet thick.

Beyond the sweet spice of balsam fir, beyond the snort of moose and the loud whistle of a ruby-crowned kinglet on a nearby spruce, the northern forest is a place whose appeal defies description. In the end, all we can say for sure is that there is wildness here, something full of shadow and mystery, something that courses through our veins long after we have left the woods and made for home. ■

Baxter State Park

MAINE ■ 204,733 acres ■ North-central Maine, 18 miles north of Millinocket on park access road ■ Best months mid-May–mid-Oct., Dec.–March ■ Camping, hiking, backpacking, mountain climbing, canoeing, fishing, cross-country skiing, snowshoeing, bird-watching, wildlife viewing ■ Nonresident vehicle fee ■ No pets, RVs, or motorcycles. No vehicles over 9 feet high, 7 feet wide, or 22 feet long ■ Contact the park, 64 Balsam Dr., Millinocket, ME 04462; phone 207-723-5140. www.state.me.us/doc/parks.htm

BAXTER STATE PARK, sometimes called Maine's Yellowstone, is a testimony to the power of a single human being to affect the quality of people's lives for generations to come. In 1930, Percival Baxter, former governor of Maine, made a gift to the state of 6,000 acres on and around Mount Katahdin, the northern terminus of the 2,167-mile long Appalachian Trail. In the decades that followed, Baxter would bestow many more such parcels. The good governor's generous gifts, along with subsequent land purchases, resulted in a park that encompasses nearly 205,000 acres, or more than 300 square miles of some of the finest wild country in the Northeast.

Nearly as significant as the gift itself are the conditions under which the park is managed and funded. When the state accepted this land, officials were obliged to maintain it according to the wishes of the donor.

View of Mount Katahdin, Baxter State Park

Thus, with the exception of two parcels in the northern part of the park that are open to experimental forestry, most of the land was to remain essentially a wilderness, as "a sanctuary for wild birds and beasts." Recreation was allowed, but it would always take a back seat to the preservation of the resource. Thus the park imposes quotas on the number of people allowed into Baxter on any given day—a practice necessary in July and August, when the parking lot near Roaring Brook Campground is often full.

Although more than 90 percent of Baxter is forested, with a full complement of northern forest wildflowers, this is first and foremost a mountain park. Of 46 peaks and upland ridges, more than a third rise above 3,000 feet. This mix of high country not only offers unforgettable vistas but also provides countless opportunities to note the dramatic changes in plant life that come as one climbs in elevation. Several peaks —including Katahdin, which at 5,267 feet is Maine's highest—are actually treeless, covered by a fragile web of low-growing alpine vegetation. Indeed, from a biological point of view, walking from the lowest point in Baxter to the highest is roughly equivalent to making a journey from Maine to the Arctic tundra. Finally, evidence of the abrasive power of glaciers is everywhere. This is especially true just south of the Katahdin summit, where ice has carved the rock into a sharp, narrow ridge known as the Knife Edge.

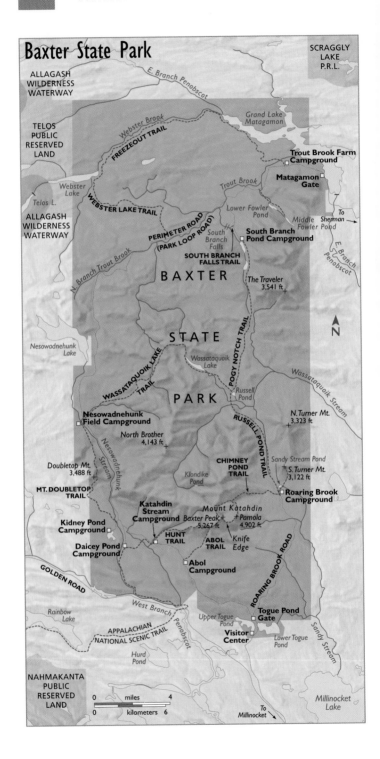

Baxter State Park

SCRAGGLY LAKE P.R.L.

ALLAGASH WILDERNESS WATERWAY

TELOS PUBLIC RESERVED LAND

E. Branch Penobscot

Grand Lake Matagamon

Webster Brook

FREEZEOUT TRAIL

Trout Brook Farm Campground

Trout Brook

Matagamon Gate

Webster Lake

WEBSTER LAKE TRAIL

Telos L.

Lower Fowler Pond

Middle Fowler Pond

To Sherman

ALLAGASH WILDERNESS WATERWAY

PERIMETER ROAD (PARK LOOP ROAD)

South Branch Falls

South Branch Pond Campground

SOUTH BRANCH FALLS TRAIL

N. Branch Trout Brook

BAXTER

The Traveler 3,541 ft

E. Branch Penobscot

Nesowadnehunk Lake

STATE

POGY NOTCH TRAIL

Wassataquoik Lake

Wassataquoik Stream

WASSATAQUOIK LAKE TRAIL

PARK

Russell Pond

N. Turner Mt. 3,323 ft

Nesowadnehunk Field Campground

RUSSELL POND TRAIL

North Brother 4,143 ft

CHIMNEY POND TRAIL

Sandy Stream Pond

S. Turner Mt. 3,122 ft

Doubletop Mt. 3,488 ft

Nesowadnehunk Stream

Klondike Pond

Roaring Brook Campground

MT. DOUBLETOP TRAIL

Katahdin Stream Campground

Mount Katahdin Baxter Peak 5,267 ft

Pamola 4,902 ft

Kidney Pond Campground

HUNT TRAIL

ABOL TRAIL

Knife Edge

ROARING BROOK ROAD

Daicey Pond Campground

Abol Campground

GOLDEN ROAD

West Branch Penobscot

Togue Pond Gate

Rainbow Lake

Upper Togue Pond

Visitor Center

Lower Togue Pond

APPALACHIAN NATIONAL SCENIC TRAIL

Hurd Pond

Sandy Stream

NAHMAKANTA PUBLIC RESERVED LAND

0   miles   4

0   kilometers   6

To Millinocket

Millinocket Lake

N

What to See and Do

An incredible array of recreational opportunities are available throughout the preserve, from hiking to canoeing to snowshoeing, depending on the season. Those wanting to savor the real Baxter should begin not at the crowded south entrance, where the masses line up each morning for a shot at climbing the great Katahdin, but at the northeast entrance at Matagamon Gate *(from Bangor, take I-95 N to the Sherman exit, then take Me.11 and 159 for 27 miles, following signs for the park)*. From there you can literally spend days working your way along the **perimeter road** past canoeing streams, swimming holes, and hiking trails before finally reaching the southern boundary of the park. (Be advised that for much of its length through the park, the perimeter road is a narrow, twisted dirt track where in places the modest speed limit of 20 miles an hour can seem way too fast.)

Once inside the park at Matagamon Gate, you are greeted by the lovely **Grand Lake Matagamon,** a sprawling body of water wrapped in a nearly perfect mix of boreal forest. This is the place for those fond of canoeing. (If you can start planning your trip to Baxter early, say in January or February, you stand a good chance of being able to reserve one of the fabulous canoe-in campsites located on the north shore of the lake.) One of the best put-in points for accessing the lake is at **Trout Brook,** located a short drive up the perimeter road from the gate at **Trout Brook Farm**

Campground. From there you'll be treated to a quiet quarter-mile paddle down a lovely stream, entering Grand Lake Matagamon west of **Hub Hall Cove.** Canoe rentals are also available at the campground.

Once into the lake, if energy levels and prevailing winds allow, paddle 6 miles toward the western shore, where you can park the canoe for a couple of hours and hike up the **Freezeout Trail** along Webster Brook—one of the great sauntering paths in all of Maine. (Bear in mind that big winds can come up on this lake, pinning you down for hours. Don't be caught unprepared.)

South Branch Falls Trail

As you make your way slowly along the perimeter road, you'll find another hiking opportunity presenting itself, roughly every 10 or 15 minutes, from the Fowler Ponds to Webster Lake to Doubletop Mountain.

One of my favorite walks in Baxter, which is especially good for families with younger children, is the half-mile-long South Branch Falls Trail. Follow the perimeter road for 9 miles from Grand Lake Matagamon, turn left onto South Branch Road, then follow that for 1.3 miles to a small parking area on the right.

The trail begins in a fairly young forest of beeches, beaked hazelnuts, red and striped maples, and white and yellow birches, with bracken, Canada mayflower, and bunchberry growing at their feet. The four-leaved bunchberry is a plant you'll see hugging moist ground throughout northern New England; in June it will greet you with beautiful four-petaled white flowers, which are followed later in the summer by red berries. Bunchberry is one of only two herbs in the dogwood family, all others being trees or shrubs. After a few minutes of easy walking you'll reach the bank of **South Branch Ponds Brook.** Head downstream a short distance, walking along tilted gray slabs of volcanic rock called traveler rhyolite, which lie in such a way that they create the lovely series of plunge pools and sluice channels known as **South Branch Falls.** When you're ready, simply turn and head back to the car.

Mount Katahdin

It was vast, Titanic, and such [scenery] as man never inhabits. Some part of the beholder, even some vital part, seems to escape through the loose grating of his ribs as he ascends. He is more alone than you can imagine …
    Henry David Thoreau
    The Maine Woods, 1864

For anyone who has seen milehigh **Mount Katahdin,** it would come as no surprise to be told by a folklorist that this mountain is wrapped in more myth and lore than perhaps any other peak in America. Rising virtually alone from a vast, undulating sweep of boreal forest, Katahdin commands the horizon from every direction, a granite monolith that practically shouts wildness through mile after mile of balsam-scented air. It is a force that has provoked a nearly constant stream of musings by writers and paintings by the hundreds, and it has left countless

adventurers unable to do anything but lace up their hiking boots and begin to climb.

The uplifting of this great mountain is the handiwork of glaciers, as is much of the dramatic scenery to be found on Katahdin, from the cirques on the east and northwest sides of the upper mountain to the lonely, cloudswept ravine that cradles **Klondike Pond.** You'll see the abrupt spine of granite known as the **Knife Edge,** which separates the peak called Pamola from the rest of the mountain, and the flat, glorious run of rock known as the **Tableland.** All of this is evidence of the time when the whole of New England was covered in ice that planed and gouged, scoured and polished the land.

For all the pleasures of climbing Katahdin, this is not a trek to be taken lightly. Routes for this allday journey average 10 miles round-trip—and gain roughly 4,000 feet of elevation. With much of the actual mileage above tree line, exposure to bad weather, especially in spring and fall, can be severe enough to threaten the lives of those not adequately outfitted. Be sure to let someone know your intended route, and use the sign-out sheets posted near the ranger cabins at most campgrounds.

The most direct route up Katahdin—and therefore one of the most heavily used—is the 7.6-mile (round-trip) **Abol Trail,** which departs from Abol Campground, makes a steep, rugged ascent up **Abol Slide** and the **Needle's Eye,** and finally comes out at the Tableland. You can also take the southwestern route from Katahdin Stream Campground

Canoeing, Baxter State Park

along the **Hunt Trail** (5 miles one way), which is the route along the Appalachian Trail. **Chimney Pond Trail** (3.3 miles one way) leaves from Roaring Brook Campground and offers an overnight stop at the base of Katahdin. From here you can continue to Pamola peak via the **Dudley Trail,** or to Baxter Peak, Katahdin's highest point, via **Cathedral** and **Saddle Trails;** you can also connect Pamola with Baxter on the magnificent but thoroughly exposed Knife Edge.

Sandy Stream Pond

If you're in the mood to stroll, another good family walk— not to mention a wonderful place to spot moose—is the trail to **Sandy Stream Pond.** (This is also a major departure point for Mount Katahdin, making it a perfect staging area if some members of the family are heading for the summit while others are not.) The path begins at the end of 8-mile-long **Roaring Brook Road,** which is a spur route off the perimeter road near **Togue Pond Gate,** at the southern border of the park.

A 3-mile loop begins in a classic slice of boreal forest, thick with the smell of balsam fir, the path crowded by red and striped maples, birches, sarsaparillas, hobblebushes, bluebead lilies, and snowberries. Later on in the walk, wetter, more open areas along the trail will serve an entirely different menu: rhodora, meadowsweet, and blueberry, to name but a few plants. In such places, especially very early in the morning and in late evening, you'll stand the best

chance of seeing moose, most of them busy gulping down some of the 40 to 50 pounds of greens they can consume in a day. Note that moose may look docile but can in fact be quite aggressive; as with all native animals, respect their wildness by not approaching too closely.

At just under a half mile, watch for a spur trail taking off to the left, running beside Sandy Stream Pond. Spectacular views of Mount Katahdin are available along this route, most notably two giant glacial cirques known as **Great** and **North Basins,** and just to the left of those, 4,902-foot **Pamola,** a peak named for a fierce god who has often been portrayed as half-man and half-eagle. Shunned by more powerful gods at Katahdin, the sacred meeting place of the creators, Pamola is said to have stomped off to take up residence on the peak that now bears his name.

Continue past South Turner Mountain Trail to the junction with the **Russell Pond Trail,** and turn left. (If you want a heartier hike, consider heading up **South Turner Mountain;** the path makes a tolerable climb of 1,600 feet over 2 miles, finishing with some of the most glorious views of Katahdin to be found anywhere in Baxter.) Russell Pond Trail will eventually take you back to the Sandy Stream Pond route, barely 0.1 mile from the parking area. Along the way it runs past a bog rich with pitcher plant, blueberry, elderberry, and Labrador tea, a favorite of 17th-century explorers who made a fragrant, rose-colored beverage from the leaves. ■

Allagash Wilderness Waterway

MAINE ■ 92 miles long ■ North-central Maine, access 15 miles northwest of Baxter State Park off Millinocket Lake Road ■ Best months May–early Oct. ■ Camping, canoeing ■ Day-use fee; camping fee ■ Contact North Maine Woods, P.O. Box 425, Ashland, ME 04732; phone 207-435-6213, www.north-mainewoods .org; or Maine Bureau of Parks and Lands, 106 Hogan Rd., Bangor, ME 04401; phone 207-941-4014, www.state.me.us/doc/prkslnds/alla.htm

CERTAIN NATURAL AREAS IN AMERICA serve us on more than one level. In an obvious way, they thrill the senses of those who take the trouble actually to visit them, people who will pause long enough to drink in the smell of the woods, who will listen at night to the sound of rain drumming on the tent, who can measure their aliveness by the racing of their hearts as a moose or a bear flushes from the stream bank. And yet these places can also satisfy from a distance. So powerful are their names and legends that the mere mention of them can ignite our imaginations though we stand a thousand miles away. They are places like the Allagash.

In addition to Allagash Stream and Allagash River, the Allagash Wilderness Waterway encompasses a string of huge lakes, including Churchill, Eagle, and Chamberlain. Strewn across these vast blue waters—some of which are more than 100 feet deep—is a medley of wood-lined inlets and marshes, rocky islands, and steep cliffs that provide a breathtaking landscape, especially during the fall. Besides the scenery, there is much to savor in the way of wildlife. You will often see eagles, as well as moose, ospreys, loons, and great blue herons.

It isn't that the Allagash Wilderness Waterway is without sign of human influence. Not even close. The bustle of logging is never far away, either through current operations, many of them taking place just beyond the waterway's 500-foot protective corridor; or in the haunting whisper of days long gone—old bridge ties sprouting moss or a 150-year-old steamboat boiler rusting in the woods. But when the citizens of Maine decided during the mid-1960s to protect this beautiful river—spending a fair amount of their own money to do so—they declared that along with the sheer commerce of the woods there would be a celebration of the web of living forest. (The Allagash was the first state-administered parcel of the National Wild and Scenic Rivers System.) Although today there are increasing concerns about encroachments on the integrity of the Allagash, from overflights to access roads to the silting of feeder streams, this river yet flashes with the spirit of a people wise enough to know the value of a resource before it was gone. As the great Supreme Court justice William O. Douglas said of the Allagash, "There are no hundred miles in America quite their equal."

One of the most common trips on the Allagash consists of a 7 to 10-day float from **Telos Landing,** near the northwest corner of Baxter

Following pages: Allagash Wilderness Waterway

Mist along the Allagash Wilderness Waterway

State Park (see pp. 94-100), to either West Twin Brook (92 miles), or 5 miles farther, to Allagash village, at the confluence with the **St. John River** (see p. 107). There are two Class II to Class III stretches, **Chase Rapids** and **Twin Brook Rapids,** as well as portages to contend with. For those who don't want to run Chase Rapids, portage service is available at scheduled times from the Waterway ranger office at Churchill Dam *(207-941-4014).* There are also many crossings of open water (nearly two-thirds of your trip will be on lakes), and hard winds can keep boaters pinned down for extended periods, especially from late morning to late afternoon. So even though this trip can be done in less than the recommended 7 to 10 days, it's important to have some flexibility in your schedule and to allow as much time as possible to cover the entire distance. Group size is strictly limited to 12 persons; larger groups must travel and camp separately.

Remember that this is a remote wilderness area, and go prepared. "Ice-out" comes late on northern Maine lakes, and trips should not begin before the last week in May. Although the canoe route through the waterway is not marked by signs, topographic maps will give you good navigational references. You can order them by mail from the U.S. Geological Survey *(USGS Distribution Section, Federal Center, Building 41, Box 25286, Denver, CO 80225)* or from the Natural Resources Information and Mapping Center *(22 State House Station, Augusta, ME 04333-0022).* Boaters who enjoy having topographic maps along will want all of the following: Chesuncook, Telos Lake, Churchill Lake, Umsaskis Lake, Round Pond, Allagash Falls, and Allagash.

If you plan on driving to your put-in on the Allagash, Norman Litalier *(Pelletier's Campground, St. Francis. 207-398-3187 or 207-834-6118)* will transport your vehicle to your final destination. Many people prefer to use an outfitter for this trip, and there are many to choose from. For starters, consider North Woods Ways *(Guilford. 207-997-3723),* Allagash

Guide Incorporated *(207-634-3748. www.allagashguide.com)*, Katahdin Outfitters *(800-862-2663)*, Maine Path and Paddle Guides *(207-892-3121. www.canoemaine.com)*, or Allagash Canoe Trips *(207-695-3668)*. A brochure highlighting the route, campsites, and other general information, called "Allagash Wilderness Waterway," as well as a pamphlet called "Allagash Wilderness Waterway: A Natural History Guide," are available from the Maine Bureau of Parks and Lands (see p. 101). ■

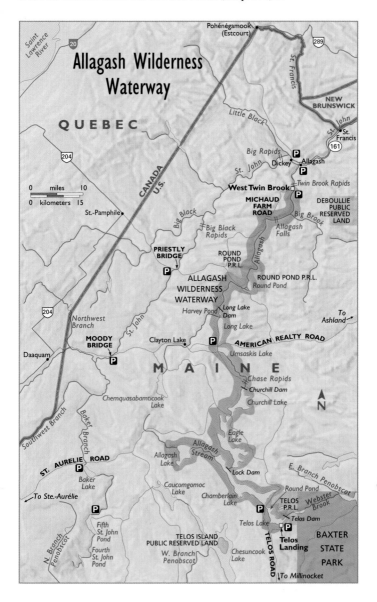

St. John River

MAINE ■ Northern Maine, near the Maine-Quebec border ■ Best water typically May–early June ■ Camping, kayaking, canoeing, wildlife viewing ■ Day-use fee ■ No supplies or services along the river ■ Contact the Nature Conservancy, 14 Maine St., Suite 401, Brunswick, ME 04011; phone 207-729-5181, www.tnc.org/maine; or North Maine Woods, P.O. Box 425, Ashland, ME 04732; phone 207-435-6213, www.northmainewoods.org

THE LONGEST, MOST REMOTE STRETCH OF WILD RIVER left in eastern America, the St. John River collects waters from the heart of the northern woods, a land of third-growth red, black, and white spruce, balsam fir, and hardwoods, as well as ponds and bogs beyond counting. These woods hold moose and coyotes, lynx and bobcats, and marten and mink. In late 1998, an extraordinary event in modern conservation history took place on lands bordering the upper St. John. That year, the Nature Conservancy committed some 35 million dollars to secure 185,000 acres along nearly 41 miles of the upper river—the single biggest purchase of land for conservation since former Governor Baxter donated the park that bears his name.

What to See and Do

If you have the hankering to feel as well as see the power of the boreal forest and its waters, this is the place to do it. Though most of the river is strong, continuous Class II water, there are two Class III sections, **Big Black Rapids** and **Big Rapids,** appropriate only for skilled boaters. Furthermore, water levels drop fast. The route from **Fourth St. John Pond** (accessible by floatplane) is often runnable only until the end of May. In many years, the run from **Baker Lake,** located 26.5 miles downstream, or farther downstream still, from the American Realty Road, is best done no later than early June. Seventy percent of the canoe traffic on this river occurs in the week around Memorial Day. (For other access points, see p.278.)

For water level information, call North Maine Woods, the group that manages public access on private forestlands, a day or two before your planned departure; the suggested minimum level for running the St. John is 3,000 cubic feet per second, as measured at the Dickey gauging station.

Boaters must register. If you're traveling by vehicle, you can do so at a checkpoint run by North Maine Woods. If you're flying into Baker Lake, your flying service should take care of registration.

Hiring a knowledgeable guide is a good idea. Consider North Woods Ways *(207-997-3723),* Katahdin Outfitters *(800-862-2663),* or Maine Path and Paddle Guides *(207-892-3121. www.canoemaine.com).* ■

White-water kayaking

Kingfield Loop Drive

MAINE ■ 115 miles ■ West-central Maine via Me. 16/27, Me. 4, Me. 142 ■
Late spring through early fall; after late Oct. be prepared for snow ■ Camping,
hiking, kayaking, canoeing, swimming, mountain biking, downhill skiing, wildlife
viewing, wildflower viewing ■ Contact the Sugarloaf Area Information Center,
R.R. 1, Box 2151, Carrabassett Valley, ME 04947; phone 207-235-2100

THIS SCENIC DRIVE—one of the finest in all of Maine—takes you through
well-watered mountain country that draws skiers in winter and hikers
and boaters in summer. The drive begins in the beautiful little village
of Kingfield: a friendly cluster of shops, a couple of wonderfully eclectic
museums, and the old Herbert Hotel *(207-265-2000),* with its stuffed
chairs, softly creaking wooden floors, and on most mornings, a dog
or two power-napping in the lobby. From Kingfield, journey north
through the **Carrabassett Valley** on Me. 16/27, where a lovely, high-
stepping river by the same name is a nearly constant companion. If
boating is in your blood, note that the **Carrabassett River** is runnable
by experienced kayakers on generally Class III water from a point roughly
10 miles north of Kingfield. Less experienced boaters, and those in open
canoes, are well served by a wonderful 6.5-mile stretch of Class I and II
water from below the dam in Kingfield to the wire bridge in New Portland.

About 12 miles north of Kingfield, 1 mile south of the main access
road to Sugarloaf ski area, is the **Sugarloaf Outdoor Center** *(207-237-
6830)* on the left. The center, part of Sugarloaf Mountain Resort, is an
excellent place to rent mountain bikes for rides on 4,237-foot **Sugarloaf
Mountain,** as well as for more mellow treks down a dirt track that
parallels the Carrabassett River, with more good swimming holes than
you can imagine. The resort is building a reputation for bringing
increased environmental awareness to its operations. In the summer of
1997, the regular staff was joined by an environmental steward, who has
made significant gains in basics such as waste reduction and recycling
(the resort's goal is to recycle 75 percent of all waste). Efforts are also
underway to adopt strict standards for Sugarloaf's golf course, earning
it certification as a National Audubon Cooperative Sanctuary—an effort
that includes wildlife management and education, as well as reducing the
use of pesticides in favor of an integrated pest-management program.

Bigelow Range

Farther north on Me. 16/27, fine views open up to the east through the
trees of the **Bigelow Range**—or "the Biggies," as the locals like to call
them—as well as an occasional glimpse to the west of magnificent glacial
cirques on Crocker Mountain. If hiking is on the agenda, you can gain
excellent foot access to the Biggies by walking north on the **Appalachian
Trail** to **Cranberry Peak;** the AT, as the trail is called, crosses Me. 16/27
just northwest of the village of Bigelow. You can also reach the AT northbound on a rough but quite navigable road to Stratton Brook Pond that

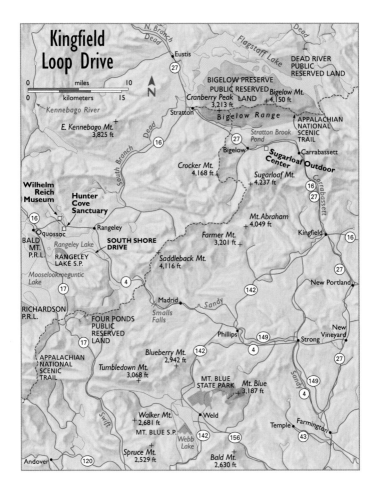

takes off to the right a mile farther up Me. 16/27, leading in another mile to a small parking area next to the trail. Starting from this point will take roughly 2 miles off what will otherwise be a 10-mile round-trip hike.

No matter which starting point you use, the trails begin in a boreal forest thick with the smell of balsam, the chirps and songs of thrushes, kinglets, and pine siskins, as well as the drum and flutter of spruce grouse. Within an hour you'll reach a junction with the **Bigelow Range Trail,** coming in from the left. If you turn left here, you'll go past lovely **Cranberry Pond,** and after a fairly sharp climb reach the summit of Cranberry Peak. A right at the Bigelow Range Trail intersection, on the other hand (which means continuing on the AT), will lead in about the same distance to a summit called **South Horn.** Both places rise above woods of red spruce and balsam, offering splendid views to the south of Sugarloaf Mountain (easily identified by the ski runs), as well as to the north, into the blue sprawl of **Flagstaff Lake.** This enormous lake is the result of a control dam at its northeast corner, which blocks the sluggish, twisted meander of the Dead River. Its relatively shallow depth makes for bad motorboating, which in turn makes for some very enjoyable canoeing.

Moose Country

Coming back down onto Me. 16/27 and continuing north, you'll find a convenient launch site in the town of Stratton. If you do decide to wet a paddle here, keep in mind that big winds can come up with little notice on this lake, trapping canoeists far from the dock.

Just past Stratton, bear left to stay on Me. 16, heading south. Great views of East Kennebago Mountain will be on your right. The streams along this stretch of the road—most notably, the South Branch Dead River—are much broader and more open than those of the Carrabassett Valley, the water choked in places with willow, making this absolutely perfect moose country. Only 50 or 60 years ago, the moose population in Maine had plummeted to a scant 2,000 animals. The animal's decline was due in large part to poaching, as well as to the loss of habitat from clear cutting. Thanks to careful management and regrowth, however, today the state's moose population is estimated at about 20,000. If you spot a moose, admire it from a distance; don't even think about approaching these big animals on foot. Moose can be extremely aggressive, especially with young nearby, and a 1,000-pound animal, fast as a horse with an enormously powerful kick, is hardly the kind of critter to be getting chummy with.

After 19 miles, you'll come to the tiny town of **Rangeley** (population 1,200), which sits at an altitude of 1,545 feet. For a refreshing pause in the Rangeley Lakes area (see pp. 115-16), stay on Me. 16 as it heads west. To continue the Kingfield loop drive, turn left (south) on Me. 4.

In 8 miles the road intersects the Appalachian Trail, which is moving ever closer to its terminus at Baxter State Park. Heading northeast as it crosses Me. 4, the trail begins a series of mountainous encounters: with **Saddleback** and **Farmer Mountains, Mount Abraham,** and Sugarloaf. Along this stretch of the AT, hikers are treated to some dramatic views of the western Maine uplands. In addition, wildlife is abundant, from deer to bear, as well as thrushes, kinglets, spruce grouse, and both pileated and downy woodpeckers.

Just before you cross the AT on Me. 4, you'll be joined by the beau-

Geology Lesson

The mountains of southwest Maine are a geological feast. Saddleback Mountain southeast of Rangeley, for instance has great slabs of granite. Sugarloaf, by contrast, consists of gabbro, a darker crystalline rock, without the quartz of granite. And at Mount Blue, intense heat in pockets of molten rock trapped miles beneath the surface transformed the surrounding soft sandstones and mudstones into more erosion-resistant metamorphic rock.

Hiking Mount Blue

tiful **Sandy River.** Experienced kayakers looking for a challengie can find it in a 5.5-mile-long stretch of the Sandy from the **Smalls Falls** scenic turnout along Me. 4 to the third Me. 4 bridge, 2 miles south of Madrid. This is Class II to Class IV water, with fallen trees, ledges, and waterfalls requiring a fair amount of scouting. A somewhat easier but still challeng-ing, trip in medium flows is a run of nearly the same length from the bridge 2 miles south of Madrid to Davenport Flats, a mile upstream from the town of Phillips. For more information consult the *AMC River Guide–Maine (800-262-4455 for book orders).* After spring runoff, regular dam releases during the week make weekdays the better choice for boating.

Mount Blue State Park

For a wonderful side trip from the loop drive, take the right turn onto Me. 142, about 5 miles after Madrid, and drive 10 miles to **Mount Blue State Park** *(Weld. 207-585-2261. www.state.me.us/doc/parks.htm; day-use fee).* At 5,021 acres, this is Maine's next largest state park, second only to Baxter. The main section of the park, located on the right side of the road, has a large campground, swimming beach on **Webb Lake,** and weekly nature programs throughout the summer (skiing and ice skating in the winter). If you want walking, hiking, and eye-popping scenery, continue

Following pages: Webb Lake, Mount Blue State Park

past the main entrance to the village of Weld and turn left onto Center Hill–Mount Blue Road, following signs for a portion of the park known as **Center Hill.** This hillside picnic area and half-mile self-guided nature trail offer a banquet of Maine scenery: a 180-degree wash of uplands, from **Bald Mountain** to **Spruce** and **Walker Mountains** in the southwest, to the blue shimmer of Webb Lake, to **Tumbledown** and **Blueberry Mountains** to the northwest. An interpretive brochure at the trailhead, produced with the Maine Audubon Society, offers a wealth of information about the cultural and natural history of the park.

If this short ramble leaves you in the mood for an even bigger dose of upland Maine, continue driving up the Center Hill–Mount Blue Road, following signs to the **Mount Blue** trailhead. (The final 2.5 miles is on a dirt road, a bit narrow and cobbly in places, but easily traversed by passenger cars.) Here you'll find a fairly steep but steady 1,800-foot climb, ending at a series of granite ledges poking out of a tattered blanket of spruce and fir. The views here are full of sky and timber and a crumpled blanket of uplands that seem to roll on forever into the far horizons.

To return to the drive, simply retrace your steps north on Me. 142 to Me. 4 and turn right. Just outside the town of Phillips, Me. 142 heads north again toward Kingfield. This is blue-highway traveling at its finest. You'll pass through young to middle-aged mixed woods interspersed with patches of potato fields and grazing cattle, as well as the occasional view out your left window of Mount Abraham and Farmer Mountain. ■

Lupines

In addition to offering fine views of Sugarloaf and East Kennebago Mountains, Me. 16/27 and many other northern woods roadsides in June will almost certainly be cradled by long runs of blue, pink, and red flower blooms on tall spikes. These are lupines, and so abundant are they from late spring through midsummer that they've become a key festival theme in small towns throughout western Maine and New Hampshire.

For all its beauty, lupine has some rather disagreeable associations. The flower takes its name from the Greek word *lupe,* meaning "grief," which may be a reference to the bitter taste of the seeds. Curiously, though the lupine plant has a reputation for being poisonous, it also has a long history as a food. The Roman statesman Pliny the Elder considered ingesting the plant a means to "brighten the mind and quicken the imagination." Meriwether Lewis and William Clark feasted on lupine root along the Columbia River with the Chinook Indians. (They thought it tasted like licorice.) In later years lupine was associated with the Latin word *lupus,* for "wolf," which is believed to refer not to the fact that the poisonous alkaloids of the plant are harmful to cattle, but to the notion that the plant swallowed up all the nutrients in the soil like a hungry wolf. In truth, lupine is a legume that fixes nitrogen to the soil, enriching the ground it grows on.

Boating at Rangeley Lake State Park

Rangeley Lakes Area

MAINE ■ West-central Maine via Me. 4 and Me. 142 ■ Camping, hiking, walking, boating, kayaking, canoeing, swimming, mountain biking, skiing, wildflower viewing ■ Contact Rangeley Lakes Region Chamber of Commerce, P.O. Box 317, Rangeley, ME 04970; phone 207-864-5364 or 800-685-2537. www.rangeleymaine.com

RANGELEY, LIKE MUCH of western Maine, has an abundance of recreational opportunities, from hiking to canoeing to bicycling. Far more significant, however, is the fact that on most days this area feels far off the beaten path, a place where being confounded by, say, a lack of directional signs ends up a pleasure because it offers a chance to stop at the corner store and talk to the locals, most of whom seem fond of sharing their back-yard. Centuries ago, the area's 111 lakes and ponds drew the Abnaki Indians, who set up hunting and fishing camps. Around the time of the Civil War, well-to-do "flatlanders" (anyone from south of New Hampshire) discovered the same attractions. Bring a bike or a boat or a pair of walking shoes, settle in for a day or two, and feel what it's like to fill your days with a sense of discovery.

Hunter Cove Sanctuary

If you're someone who appreciates little-known places, the **Hunter Cove Sanctuary** *(207-781-2330)*, 5 miles west of Rangeley along Me. 4, is a real find. As you come to the bottom of a large hill, you'll see a small parking area on the left. Managed by the Maine Audubon Society, this restful little preserve—its trails muddy in places and slightly overgrown, full of deer tracks and even the occasional pile of bear scat—has the look of a place meant more for wildlife than humans. A delightful trek is a counterclockwise walk along the **Red Trail,** which begins at the southwest corner of the parking lot near a picnic table and leads in roughly a half mile to

Hunter Cove on **Rangeley Lake.** (Canoeists can reach the sanctuary from a number of put-in points, including the launch at Rangeley Lake State Park, which lies across the lake directly to the south.) If you know ahead of time that you're coming to the area, order a copy of the Hunter Cove trail guide from the Maine Audubon Society *(118 US 1, Falmouth, ME 04105. 207-781-2330)*.

On the outbound portion of the walk, you'll see fine patches of wild-flowers, including bunchberry and Canada lily, tattered runs of hawk-weed in the open areas, and an exquisite collection of iris. The species of iris common in wet areas throughout the Northeast is often called blue flag; in this case "flag" doesn't refer to any sort of banner, but rather comes from the English flagge, for rush or reed. Notice how insects attracted to the plant can reach the colored sepals only by brushing against a stamen and stigma, thus helping to pollinate the plant. Hunter Cove itself is a wild, unkempt slice of shoreline. Volunteers have placed several crude log benches among the trees near the water; these are perfect for watching kingfishers, a variety of ducks, and ospreys.

Wilhelm Reich Museum and Preserve

If you happen to be in the area during the months of July and August, a pleasant interlude in the Rangeley area waits for you at the 175-acre Wilhelm Reich Museum and Preserve *(Dodge Pond Rd. via Me. 4. 207-864-3443. www.somtel.com/~wreich; preserve open year-round, observatory July-Aug. Wed.-Sun., Sept. Sun. only; adm. fee)*. The entrance is a short distance off Me. 4, at a sign that says "Orgonon." This historic property is dedicated to the life and work of scientist, inventor, and artist Wilhelm Reich (1897-1957), a bit of a Renaissance man who spent his life investigating human and natural biosystems.

The preserve contains a modest braid of self-guided trails with eclectic names such as "Trail of Thought," each running through a quilt of meadows and woodlands of white cedar; yellow, white and gray birch; eastern hemlock; speckled alder; quaking aspen; red oak; and white ash. The trails are open daily, and guided walks take off from the ticket office every Wednesday in July and August. Sunday afternoon workshops are held in the same months, covering topics from wildflowers to medicinal plants to ferns and mushrooms. The primary building on the property is the **Orgone Energy Observatory,** which contains a modest discovery center for children and a rooftop observatory with striking views of the tree-covered high country to the south and east.

Continuing counterclockwise around Rangeley Lake onto South Shore Drive, you'll find the entrance to 870-acre **Rangeley Lake State Park** *(207-864-3858. www.state.me.us/doc/prklands/rangeley.htm; day-use fee; camping fee)*. The park is a fine place for an early-morning canoe launch. Walkers will find an easy quarter-mile trail starting at the boat dock along the shore through birches, moosewood, maples and bead lilies. The path ends at a grassy swimming and picnic area, surely among the ten best places in New England to lie back with a good book and let summer roll on without you. ■

Canoeing calm waters

West Branch Penobscot River

MAINE ■ North-central Maine, northwest of Millinocket on Golden Rd.
■ Year-round ■ Camping, kayaking, canoeing ■ Day-use fee; camping fee
■ Contact North Maine Woods, P.O. Box 425, Ashland, ME 04732; phone 207-435-6213. www.northmainewoods.org

BEFORE THE COMING of private logging roads, the West Branch Penobscot River, located near Baxter State Park, was perhaps the most heavily traveled river in the state, providing backcountry travelers with access to the St. John, East Branch Penobscot, and Allagash Rivers. Today the West Branch Penobscot remains a beautiful waterway, at times flowing easy through a mosaic of wooded valleys and quiet lakes, at other times pounding with incredible fury over steep ledges and through rockbound gorges. Throughout it all are those splendid sensations of the North Woods—the call of chickadees and the smell of balsam fir, the soft whisper of striped and red maple leaves.

Canoeists of moderate ability can make a fine primitive trip from the Roll Dam Campsite north of Moosehead Lake to **Hannibal's Crossing.** The first day involves roughly 11 miles of paddling—9 miles to **Lobster Stream,** which comes in on the right side of the West Branch, then 2 miles upstream to any of several fine campsites on the west side of **Lobster Lake.** The remainder of the trip turns on an easy downstream paddle back to the West Branch, following that for another 2 miles to Hannibal's Crossing. More seasoned canoeists, preferably with lake experience, could turn this into a 47-mile-long trip (including the side trip to Lobster Lake) by following the West Branch to **Chesuncook Lake,** then heading southeast to a take-out at Ripogenus Dam.

Note that this trip is through private timber company lands, and permits are required. Outfitted trips on the West Branch are offered by North Woods Ways *(207-997-3723)*. ■

Mount Kineo

MAINE ■ North-central Maine on a peninsula in center of Moosehead Lake ■ Accessed by boat only ■ Best months June-Sept. ■ Hiking, canoeing ■ Contact Lily Bay State Park, HC 76, P.O. Box 425, Greenville, ME 04441; phone 207-287-3824 or 800-332-1501 (Maine). www.state.me.us/doc/parks.htm

THE LARGEST BODY OF FRESH WATER in New England, 74,890-acre **Moosehead Lake** is the point at which Maine's wilderness begins to thicken, a jumping-off point for boreal dreams that can stretch north for hundreds of miles, all the way into the dark woods of Quebec. For the biggest, fullest drink of Moosehead Lake possible, put in your canoe or kayak at the town of Rockwood—or if you're not so equipped, use the water taxi located there *(207-534-7333)*—and head east. Across a mile of open water you'll be approaching the dramatic southeastern face of Mount Kineo. (Boaters need to be aware that while this is a fairly short crossing, strong winds can come up with very little warning; keep a watchful eye on the weather.) From the southern shore of a narrow-necked peninsula, Mount Kineo's sheer cliffs rise abruptly, towering more than 800 feet above the lake.

The profile you see at Kineo is common to many of the peaks in this area. As glaciers moved south out of Canada, they rode up and over the northern slopes of the mountains, leaving them relatively smooth. At the same time, on the southern side of the summits, the ice tended to clutch and tear at the rock, creating the cliffs you see today. The native people of this area long prized the mountain for its cliffs of volcanic rhyolite, used to make weapons and tools. Some thought the mountain looked like a moose (see sidebar at left).

Roughly 4 miles of hiking trails thread the mountain. A shore trail rims the lower portion of the peninsula, passing under the cliff face. Three paths—the **Indian, Bridle,** and **North Trails**—lead upward to a watchtower at the summit. The blue-blazed Indian Trail hugs the cliff edge, so adults should keep a close eye on children. ■

The Giant Glooskap and the Moose

Early peoples spoke of Mount Kineo as the body of a moose killed by the giant Glooskap, one of the best-known and most celebrated creators of the Algonquian tribes. It was to Glooskap that the people had gone to complain about the size of the moose, which the giant had originally made so huge that it was impossible to hunt. Seeing their point, Glooskap called the enormous moose over, took it in his hands, and began to squeeze the animal down to a smaller size. When he finally stopped, the moose was more or less how we see it today—smaller, yes, but also rather knock-kneed and hump-shouldered, an ungainly looking creature, thanks to all that squeezing.

Purple coneflowers and black-eyed Susans

Lily Bay State Park

MAINE ■ 925 acres ■ North-central Maine, on the eastern shore of Moosehead Lake ■ Best months May–mid-Oct. ■ Camping, hiking, boating, canoeing, swimming, fishing, wildlife viewing, wildflower viewing ■ Day-use fee; camping fee ■ Reservations recommended for camping ■ Contact the park, HC 76, P.O. Box 425, Greenville, ME 04441; phone 207-287-3824 or 800-332-1501 (in Maine). www.state.me.us/doc/parks.htm

NESTLED ON THE EASTERN SHORE of **Moosehead Lake,** Lily Bay State Park is a fine departure point for those with a penchant for the water. A dawn, or even a moonlight, canoe trek in the protected bays along the ragged shore is sure to satisfy. "A gleaming silver platter at the end of the table," said Thoreau of Moosehead in 1846, on his way to Mount Katahdin. While the rest of the world was busy that year marveling at a host of breakthroughs in technology—from electric arc lights at the opera house in Paris to John Deere's new plow—Thoreau was busy reveling in something quite different. He imagined that the snowberry, trillium, bellwort, and aster he saw lining the shores of Moosehead "had a peculiarly wild and primitive look," that an evergreen just fallen across the trail, thick with cones, was "fuller of life than our trees in the most favorable conditions." Pieces of the wilds that so delighted Thoreau remain today, from the firs and the wildflowers to the kingfishers, wood peewees and olive-sided flycatchers.

Despite the timeless feel of the wilds at Moosehead, the lake has long been a center of intense logging, given that it is a catch basin for some 1,200 square miles of land. Before the days of steam-powered towing vessels, logs were dumped into the lake from points along the shore or from any of several inlet streams. They were then secured in massive clusters by wrapping them in a perimeter of logs, tied together lengthwise, called a boom.

To move those logs mile after mile down the lake was an incredible ordeal. It worked like this: Loggers tied rafts to the boom, then attached one end of a long rope to a winding device on the raft called a capstan. They carried the other end of the rope by boat in the direction of travel, attached an anchor to it, and dropped the anchor to the bottom of the lake. Relying on sheer muscle, the men would wind the capstan, thus slowly drawing the mass of logs toward the anchor point. Over and over, day after day they worked, until they finally reached the outlet.

Lily Bay State Park contains two campgrounds (Rowell Cove and Dunn Point) with 91 well-spaced campsites, many along the shore; group camping is available. A day-use area with a playground is near the Dunn Point campground, as is a fine swimming beach, cradled by white pines. Those who want to stroll can follow a 1.6-mile footpath along the shore. ■

Water grasses

Waterfall, Gulf Hagas

Gulf Hagas

MAINE ■ 5,000 acres ■ Central Maine, 26 miles south of Millinocket on Me. 11, then follow signs for Katahdin Iron Works ■ Best months mid-May–Sept. ■ Camping, hiking ■ Day-use fee; camping fee ■ No bicycles, horses, or ATVs ■ Contact North Maine Woods, P.O. Box 425, Ashland, ME 04732; phone 207-435-6213. www.northmainewoods.org

LOCATED JUST OFF THE **Appalachian Trail**—at this point only 81 miles from its terminus at Mount Katahdin—Gulf Hagas offers one of the great loop walks in all of Maine. The outbound portion of this 8-mile trek brushes elbows with an outstanding 3.5-mile-long gorge spiced with the thunder of five major waterfalls and rapids beyond counting. First protected voluntarily by timber companies, this area has been named a National Natural Landmark and is managed by North Maine Woods.

Before reaching the drama of the gorge, however, you are in for other pleasures, not the least of which is yet another national natural landmark, the Nature Conservancy's 35-acre **Hermitage Preserve** *(207-729-5181)*, reached early in the walk after wading the **West Branch Pleasant River.** The centerpiece of the Hermitage is a hushed grove of white pines, many 3 feet or more at their base and towering 130 feet in the air. It's sobering to consider that early explorers, who coveted the straight wood of the white pine for making ships' masts, would routinely find trees nearly twice as big as these.

After following the Appalachian Trail for 1.3 miles, you'll reach a path branching off to the left, into Gulf Hagas. Follow this across **Gulf Hagas Brook** and turn left to go downstream past **Screw Auger Falls** (another falls by the same name is at Grafton Notch State Park; see p. 124) and finally to the **West Branch Pleasant River** and the edge of the gorge. From here the trail skirts the gorge for several miles, eventually intersecting the Pleasant River Road, which serves as the route back to the Appalachian Trail. The outbound portion of this walk is fairly strenuous, the path lined with roots and rocks. Near the trail are many dangerous ledges and cliffs, so keep a close eye on children. ■

Mattawamkeag Wilderness Park

MAINE ■ 1,240 acres ■ Eastern Maine, 8 miles east of Mattawamkeag off US 2 ■ Open Mem. Day–mid-Oct. ■ Camping, hiking, kayaking ■ Day-use fee; camping fee ■ Contact the park, P.O. Box 5, Mattawamkeag, ME 04459; phone 888-724-2465. www.mwpark.com

NO MATTER HOW OFTEN I roam New England, I never cease to be amazed by how many unexpected delights are waiting around the next corner, hidden in a pocket of woods or halfway up a wind-blasted mountain. Mattawamkeag Wilderness Park is one of those surprises. The park campground, owned and run by the Town of Mattawamkeag, offers fishing, canoeing, and hiking on 15 miles of trails.

Central to the park is the **Mattawamkeag River,** cold and dark with tannin, slip-sliding across rhyolite rock shelves and past tattered runs of balsam, white pine, maple, and white and yellow birch. The river is on its way from a remote stretch of woodland far to the north to a meeting with the **Penobscot River,** just west of the park. It's a stretch of pure, unadulterated Maine.

If you're an experienced kayaker and have a hankering to run a wild north woods river, this might be the one for you. Paddlers can put in at Kingman and run 13 miles to the Penobscot, stopping at the park for an overnight at the campground; should the weather be foul, some sites contain Adirondack shelters. Keep in mind that there are Class III to Class IV rapids along this stretch, though most of the more difficult ones can be avoided by somewhat strenuous portages. A few miles downstream from the park are the rapids named **Upper** and **Lower Gordon Falls.** Remember that, as is the case on most rivers in New England, the level of the Mattawamkeag is controlled by dam releases upstream. To check current flows, contact the U.S. Geological Survey in Augusta *(207-622-8201)*. If you're not up for such a run on your own but would like to try the river, give Katahdin Outfitters in Millinocket a call *(800-862-2663)*.

Those in the mood for a refreshing walk should head straight for the picnic area below the park's campground. Here you'll find the beginning of the **River Trail,** which heads downstream a couple of miles to a beautiful section of Class IV rapids in Sleugundy Heater Gorge. ■

Yellow Birch

Early European explorers of the North Woods often returned home with tales of a great deciduous tree, sporting yellow, papery bark, growing to heights well over 100 feet. This was the yellow birch, and it soon became a favorite of craftsmen for making everything from sleighs to ships, wagon hubs to furniture. The yellow birch produces remarkable quantities of winged seed. Moreover, its seeds are capable of sprouting in a wide variety of habitats, from deep, wet woods to dried-out pastures.

Birches in Grafton Notch State Park

Grafton Notch State Park

MAINE ■ 3,192 acres ■ Western Maine, 8 miles north of Newry on Me. 26
■ Mid-May–Mid-Oct., trails open year-round ■ Hiking ■ Day-use fee
■ Contact the park, HC 61, P.O. Box 330, Newry, ME 04261; phone 207-824-2912. www.state.me.us/doc/parks.htm

IF YOU'VE SOMEHOW gotten the notion that the Maine high country is restricted to that lone giant, Mount Katahdin, there's good news: The far western reaches of the state are awash with steep, rugged mountain ridges and fast-stepping streams—the kind of country that leaves hikers open-mouthed in wonder. Grafton Notch State Park, formerly the site of a rough- and-ready lumber camp, is just such a place. In the lowlands you'll find short, easy family walks along the **Bear River** leading to two intriguing gorges. In the first, on the east end of the park, is one of Maine's two **Screw Auger Falls** (see p. 121), a wonderful corkscrew of slips and slides, carved in the bedrock over the course of thousands of years by torrents of water. If the weather is good you'll probably have lots of company. On a hot day, there are plenty of places where you can splash your feet in the water. Just over a mile farther up the road is a second gorge, at **Mother Walker Falls,** and in another mile, a pleasant quarter-mile trail on packed surfaces, leading to huge granite slabs at **Moose Cave.**

Given that New England isn't exactly rich with gorges, to have two of them within a mile of each other is extraordinary. Both serve as fine examples of how the amount of sunlight that reaches one patch of ground can (along with soil conditions) make one area far different from another just a few feet away.

By entering these narrow ravines, you'll leave behind the beeches, yellow birches, and maples of the Bear River Valley and enter a dark, mysterious land of shade-loving conifers, blankets of lichen, and, especially at **Moose Cave,** exquisite green gardens of moss. Such mosses, by the way, are considered to be among the first plants to have left the sea for life on land. If you study this moss with a hand lens, you'll notice a cluster of leaflike scales, each covered with a tough coating to prevent water loss. Because the sperm of the plant must swim to complete fertilization (both the sperm and the female reproductive organ are located near the tip of the plant), maintaining moisture is critical for reproduction. From this fertilization a filament and spore case will grow. Eventually that case breaks open and the spores scatter; those that land in a congenial spot will end up becoming new moss plants.

Nearby

If you have time, head south a few miles from Grafton Notch State Park to reach **Sabattus Mountain.** From the town of Center Lovell, just north of the intersection of Me. 5 and 5A, turn east onto Sabattus Road, then right in 1.5 miles on Sabattus Mountain Road.

There you'll find the 165-acre area, which offers a modest climb through a forest in various stages of succession, ending in less than a mile with a soaring view of the uplands of western Maine.

For energetic souls eager to reach loftier places, crossing midway through the park is the **Appalachian Trail,** 0.8 mile beyond the pull-off for Moose Cave. Heading southwest on the AT from this point will take you to **Old Speck Mountain,** in the Mahoosuc Range, Maine's third highest peak at 4,180 feet. Getting there requires a steep climb for a distance of 3.5 miles—first through a mix of hardwoods, then into thick blankets of spruce and fir. Finally, after scrambling up a beautiful brow of granite, you will arrive some 2,700 feet above the Bear River. The view from there is a symphony of forest and peaks, including the line of the Mahoosuc Range, dancing 20 miles to the south along the western border of Maine. ■

Canoeing in Connecticut Lakes State Forest

Connecticut Lakes

NEW HAMPSHIRE ■ North New Hampshire, off US 3 near the border with Quebec ■ Year-round ■ Camping, hiking, kayaking, canoeing, bird-watching ■ Contact New Hampshire's Connecticut Lakes Region, P.O. Box 400, Pittsburg, NH 03592; phone 603-538-7118. www.nhconnlakes.com

GIVEN THE TENS OF THOUSANDS of people who make pilgrimages to the high country of the White Mountains, the Connecticut Lakes country, just a short drive to the north, can on some days seem all but forgotten. Named for the four lakes that grace New Hampshire's northern notch, the area has no 4,000-foot peaks, flower-bedecked alpine parks, or cog railways waiting to haul you into the sky. And given the occasional lack of signs, finding your way around may leave you a bit dazed and confused. (In this part of New Hampshire, as in much of Maine and the Northeast Kingdom of Vermont, a copy of DeLorme's *Atlas and Gazetteer,* available at stores throughout the region, is a must.) Yet this is unmistakably the great boreal forest, a land of birch and balsam and alder and spruce, of black bears and bobcats, of cool, quiet backwaters, unbroken but for the plunge of the kingfishers and the comings and goings of beavers. Armed with nothing more than a canoe or a kayak on top of the car and a pair of good walking shoes on your feet, you'll find plenty to keep you busy.

What to See and Do

The Connecticut Lakes are great places for bird-watchers. During a visit in early July there was an absolute feast of neotropical migratory songbirds, including olive-sided flycatchers, purple finches, blackpoll and yellow-rumped warblers, Swainson's thrushes, redstarts, and ruby-crowned kinglets, as well as plenty of other feathered residents such as cedar waxwings, ruby-throated hummingbirds, great blue herons, bitterns and snipes.

Connecticut Lakes State Forest

Located in the **Connecticut Lakes State Forest** (*On the W side of US 3, 20 miles N of Pittsburg. 603-538-6965*), **Moose Falls** has several nice picnic sites, as well as 20 primitive campsites with fireplaces and a single canoe for rent beside a humble park manager's cottage. A bird diary, where birdwatchers can record their sightings, hangs in a box on the wall of the cottage. Great blue herons, bitterns, and snipes are often seen at nearby **Scott's Bog,** an altogether remote spot lying just to the east, where you can catch a surprising variety of wildlife. To get there, follow the dirt road that takes off on the east side of US 3, about a half mile south of the entrance to the Moose Falls Picnic Area. After 0.3 mile this route turns into a walking trail along **Scott Brook,** reaching the bog in 2 miles. (See the *New Hampshire Atlas and Gazetteer.*)

Canoeing

Exploring this part of New Hampshire is even better by canoe. You can use your paddles on **First, Second,** and **Third Connecticut Lakes,** as well as on **Lake Francis,** though on Francis especially, big winds can be a concern. There's no problem with that on **Moose Flowage,** however, which you get to from the west side of US 3, just north of the Moose Falls Picnic Area. The current is slow here, allowing you to travel north or south to your heart's content.

Beaver Ponds

You can get a short, but utterly out-in-the-boondocks taste of the North Woods by walking an old roadway taking off just south of the Canadian border, on the west side of US 3, beside a sign that says "Welcome to New Hampshire—The Granite State." The route weaves between forests and ponds thick with life, as well as long lines of hawkweed, daisy, self-heal, fireweed, and cow vetch. After only 0.3 mile of flat walking, you'll find one of the best abandoned beaver pond complexes you'll ever set eyes on. (A second good beaver pond lies another 0.2 mile down the trail.) The lodge of this complex is only 15 yards from the shore, and it is enormous. The U-shaped dam holding back the water braces the north side of the pond with a wall of sticks running for more than 150 feet.

One reason the beavers aren't using this spot anymore—at least for the time being—can be found in the fact that the border of the pond is no longer cradled by aspens or alders, the beavers' preferred source of food, but by a thick growth of conifers, which they don't care for at all. You can gnaw off an aspen once or twice or even three times, and it will come back as a sprout. But sooner or later, the underground energy required for such regrowth will be depleted, at which point conifers take over. The line where you see alders and aspens still growing, well back from the pond, represents the distance these beavers were willing to go to secure their food. Anytime you spot signs of past beaver activity in a pond

Loons

Common Loons

Admittedly, it's a thrill to see a loon close-up, trimmed out in its jet-black cap and checkerboard jacket. Yet even if you never actually lay eyes on one of these handsome birds, hearing a loon's call—either an unbridled laughing or a mournful yodel—is one of the most satisfying wildlife experiences in all of North America.

Loons are powerful swimmers and phenomenal divers (fishing boats have caught loons in their nets at depths of more than 200 feet!). This in part is because their large webbed feet are set well back on their bodies, an arrangement that makes the birds slow and clumsy on land. Not by accident, then, loon nests are always found near the edge of the water, either on islands or in protected areas on coves and headlands.

As part of an ongoing effort to protect the loon, a number of studies are under-way on lakes throughout northern New England. Biologists on New Hamp-shire's Umbagog Lake, for example, are gently netting the birds at night and analyzing blood samples for the presence of toxic elements and chemicals such as mercury, dioxins, and lead.

One of the greatest forces for loon protection in New England is the Loon Preservation Committee of the New Hampshire Audubon Society, which was formed in 1975 in response to dramatic declines in the state's loon populations. Through the work of this organization and others, we are at last getting not only basic information about loon behavior, but also a clearer understanding of what most threatens their survival. We now know, for example, that one of the main causes of loon decline is loss of habitat through shoreline development. Still other birds are threatened by changing water levels that affect nesting activity. To deal with this latter problem, the preser-vation committee is monitoring the construction and careful placement of floating nest platforms.

Nearby
Straddling the New Hampshire-
Maine border is the **Lake
Umbagog National
Wildlife Refuge** *(N.H. 16,
east of Errol. P.O. Box 240, Errol,
NH 03579. 603-482-3415).*
At the heart of the refuge is a
fantastic big-water environment, suitable for canoeing or
kayaking. But hikers will also
find peat bogs, alder swamps,
and spruce-fir thickets. Umbagog Lake, the westernmost lake
of the so-called Rangeley
Chain, is often touted as the
best breeding habitat in New
Hampshire for both ospreys
and common loons. In addition
to those species, look for bald
eagles, goldeneye, ring-necked
and black ducks, northern harriers, and woodcocks.

rimmed by spruce or fir, it's a sure sign that the beavers who once lived there basically ate themselves out of house and home.

Fourth Connecticut Lake

It's hard to imagine that this obscure little water pocket is the beginning of the Connecticut River, one of the greatest water-ways in all America. Reaching it entails a 1.7-mile loop hike that requires climbing 400 feet in just 0.6 mile—an effort perhaps best reserved for dyed-in-the-wool nature fanatics.

The path takes off behind the American Customs Office on US 3, in a 78-acre area owned by the Nature Conservancy *(603-224-5853)*. Park in the lot across the highway from the check station. There's a sign-in sheet inside the mud porch of the customs office—registration is required. The walk

Barn, Dixville Notch area

leaves from behind the customs office at the edge of a mowed area.

As you start to climb uphill from the lawn of the customs office, you'll be entering the quietest of worlds, a place of bunchberry and wood sorrel blossoms and meadow rue, pine and spruce and red maple (some of it thrashed by the ice storm of 1998; see p. 193), fragrant water and pond lilies, and always the tracks and scat of bear and moose. This walk, which includes a trail around the lake itself, is well suited for connoisseurs of boreal ponds —especially those who love birds. Show up early in the morning with your binoculars, put on some bug spray, and settle in to look for yellow-bellied flycatchers, Lincoln's sparrows, boreal chickadees, ruby- crowned kinglets, and black-backed woodpeckers. ■

Dixville Notch State Park

NEW HAMPSHIRE ■ 127 acres ■ Northern New Hampshire, 7 miles east of Colebrook on N.H. 26 ■ Year-round ■ Hiking, mountain biking, bird-watching ■ Contact the park, P.O. Box 1856, Concord, NH 03302; phone 603-323-2087. www.nhparks.state.nh.us

THOSE TRAVELING ON N.H. 26 will go through Dixville Notch State Park, which embraces the most northern of New Hampshire's famous notches, or mountain passes. The eastern portion of the park is particularly rough and rugged, a tossed and tattered mix of swift-running streams, red spruce and balsam fir forests, and sheer cliffs of metamorphic and sedimentary rock that have proven remarkably resistant to erosion. This passageway rises from a low point of 1,500 feet to a high point of nearly 2,000 feet. The east-west orientation of **Dixville Notch** allows winds to blast through with remarkable intensity. This has a lot to do with the modest size of the trees in the upper reaches of the notch; many of them look far more stunted than an elevation of 1,990 feet would lead you to expect.

A spectacular view awaits you at the end of a fairly modest hike along **Table Rock Trail** to **Table Rock,** which climbs 760 feet over about 0.75 mile. (Note that this trail contains steep drop-offs.) The trailhead is located on N.H. 26, about a half mile west of the Balsams Resort. The hotel maintains an information booth (603-255-3400. Open most days mid-June–Columbus Day) across the highway from the resort, with hiking and other travel information.

Those with less time or energy can get a peek at the kind of magic that goes on here on the short **Waterfall Walk,** which takes off from the back of a wayside picnic area, located on the north side of the highway just inside the eastern boundary of the park. On the same side of the highway, just outside the boundary, is a watchable wildlife area with a small, kid-friendly interpretive trail. Although this path leads walkers to an interpretive platform elbow to elbow with a noisy highway, it's a good place for a close look at birds and at a forest in different stages of succession. ■

White Mountain National Forest

NEW HAMPSHIRE ■ 800,000 acres ■ North-central New Hampshire
■ Year-round ■ Camping, hiking, backpacking, mountain climbing, biking
■ Contact the Appalachian Mountain Club/Forest Service visitor center, P.O.
Box 298, Gorham, NH 03581; phone 603-466-2721 or 877-444-6777 (camping
reservations). www.fs.fed.us/r9/white

TRYING TO SUM UP THE White Mountains of New Hampshire is like trying
to sum up a great painting, or the sound of a Mozart symphony. There is
simply nowhere else in New England with a more intoxicating sprawl of
hidden nooks, flower-bedecked woodland streams, or soaring, wind-
blasted summits than the Whites. This is big country, lavish but tough,
one minute full of the sublime and the next full of bluster. The White

Kancamagus Overlook, White Mountain National Forest

Mountains are what is left after erosion wore down what was a much higher, even more dramatic mountain range. The geologic tale of these mountains is incredibly complex—a drama that begins with sedimentary rock being folded and broken by uplift into a chaotic jumble. In addition to later periods of folding and uplifting, tremendous quantities of molten rock welled up at various times from deep in the earth, yet failed to break the surface. Over eons, this magma cooled slowly into granite and other related rocks. Sometimes this same rock was heated again, metamorphosing into marble, slate, and schist. As various forms of erosion worked their magic, the sedimentary rocks were worn away, leaving the hard tumble of granite and metamorphic rocks you see today.

Forty-three peaks in the White Mountains are 4,000 feet or higher, while seven rise above 5,000 feet. The Presidential Range—which includes Mount Jefferson, Mount Adams, Mount Madison, and Mount

Washington—is a favorite spot for hikers. As you make your way up from the lower portions of the White Mountains, roughly below 2,000 feet, you first find yourself wrapped in a classic slice of northern hardwood forest, dominated by yellow birch, beech, and sugar maple. At higher elevations, these are slowly replaced by conifers such as red spruce and balsam, as well as scattered patches of paper birch and mountain ash, the trees growing ever smaller the higher you climb. Beyond timberline, which generally appears around 4,400 to 4,600 feet, are the same tundra-type plant communities—sedges, lichens, mosses, and various dwarf shrubs—usually found along the extreme northern edges of Canada and into Greenland. Plants in the White Mountains must contend with some of the fiercest, windiest weather in the world. Temperatures on the 6,288-foot summit of Mount Washington have plummeted to minus 47°F; in 1934 the wind there reached an incredible 231 miles an hour—highest wind speed ever recorded on Earth.

What to See and Do

Given the extent of this region, covering all the recreational opportunities that await you is next to impossible. Other attractions in the area are described on the pages that follow, including Franconia Notch (see pp. 135-38), the Kancamagus Highway (see pp. 139-41), and Robert Frost's farm (see p. 142).

Indeed, of all the regions in New England, the White Mountains area is probably best to approach with help from additional resources. When in doubt, turn to the Appalachian Mountain Club (617-523-0651; White Mountain Trail information and weather, 603-466-2725; reservations 604-466-2727. outdoors.org). You may also want to refer to the following books: Hiking New Hampshire by Larry Pletcher (Falcon Press), AMC White Mountain Guide: Hiking Trails in the White Mountains National Forest (AMC Books), and Hiker's Guide to the Mountains of New Hampshire by Jared Gange (Huntington Graphics).

Airline and Tuckerman Ravine Trails

Two of the more strenuous hikes I'll mention here are the Airline Trail to **Mount Adams** (total vertical 4,500 feet) and the Tuckerman Ravine Trail to **Mount Washington** (total vertical 4,270 feet). The trailhead for the Airline Trail, roughly 5 miles west of Gorham on the north side of the mountains on US 2, is served by the Appalachian Mountain Club's shuttle service (603-466-2725). You can reach the trailhead for the Tuckerman Ravine Trail on the east side of the mountains, at the AMC's Pinkham Notch Visitor Center on N.H. 16.

Zealand Road Walks

The **Zealand Road,** located on the south side of US 302, east of Twin Mountain, leads to a wonderful variety of easy to moderate walking opportunities on the west side of the White Mountains. These are more suitable to families, or to those simply wanting to taste

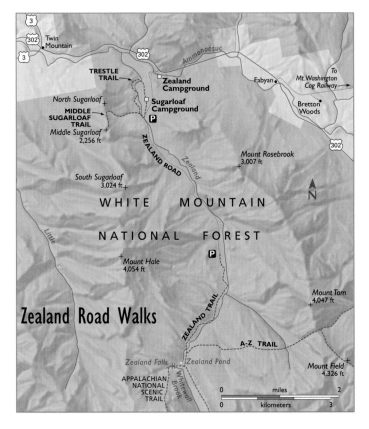

this country without launching a major climb.

That this area is today a place of such beauty is a testament to the power of the New England forest to rebound after an alarming level of abuse. By the end of the 19th century, extensive logging by lumber baron J. E. Henry had rendered the Zealand Valley an utter wasteland, full of twisted slash piles and ravaged by fires thought to have been started by Henry's locomotives. Henry, who owned the largest tract of New Hampshire forest ever controlled by one man—10,000 acres, much of it prime virgin timber—was not one to grow sentimental about a patch of woods. "I never seen the tree yet," he said at 77, "that didn't mean a damn sight more to me goin' under the saw than it did standin' on a mountain." It was in large part the public outcry over his ruthless exploitation of the Zealand Valley that led to the establishment of the White Mountain National Forest.

Trestle Trail and Middle Sugarloaf Trail

To find the trailhead for these two pleasant ambles, travel east from Twin Mountain on US 302 for 3 miles and turn right onto Zealand

Road. In 0.6 mile you'll reach a parking area on the right.

The Trestle Trail is an easy walk of 1.1 miles through a mix of maples, firs, and birches, along with trailside gardens of bluebead lily, Canada mayflower, bracken fern and bunchberry. At 0.2 mile into the walk, you'll come to the intersection with the Middle Sugarloaf Trail; continue straight, and at the next crossing of a north-south trail, 0.3 mile later, go straight again. Another ten minutes of walking will take you to a footbridge over the beautiful **Zealand River,** built in almost exactly the same spot where one of J. E. Henry's trestle bridges was located more than a hundred years ago. Once over the bridge stay left, follow yellow blazes to the campground loop road, and turn right. The Trestle Trail takes off again in less than a quarter mile, reaching the parking area after a quick run through blueberry, raspberry, and bracken fern.

For a longer hike, requiring a modest climb but paying off in a view that stretches all the way from the Green Mountains of Vermont to mighty Mount Washington, leave from the same trailhead and go instead to **Middle Sugarloaf.** Although this is an uphill affair from roughly 0.2 mile to the summit at 1.4 miles, it's a pleasant trek through a fairly young forest with undergrowth of sheep laurel, blueberry, hobblebush, and sarsaparilla. The elevation gain on this walk isn't enough to leave all the hardwoods behind for conifers, but you'll nonetheless notice subtle changes. There will be fewer hemlocks and beeches

higher up, and more white birches, spruces, and firs, as well as a sudden appearance of mountain ash.

Zealand Pond

Although at 5.5 miles round trip this is the longest of our Zealand Road walks, it not only traverses fairly gentle terrain, but ends with a flourish at beautiful **Zealand Falls,** fresh in from a dizzy drop along the flanks of **Mount Hale.** To reach the trailhead, follow Zealand Road to its end, about 3 miles past the trailhead for the Trestle and Middle Sugarloaf Trails.

This path is also interesting for the diversity of vegetation, much of which is thanks to the local beavers. What would normally be just another slice of northern forest—spruces, firs, red maples, and birches—has been transformed into chains of water pockets ringed with alder, tall meadow rue, and wild raisin.

You're likely to spy the characteristic mounds that beavers call home. Beaver lodges are built with a mix of sticks and mud and then excavated from underneath. A lodge may have more than one entrance, but will typically have only one living chamber—a lower level, for dining, and an upper level lined with wood chips, which serves as a sleeping area. If the food supply is good, lodges may be extended each year; some have grown to over 400 square feet.

At 2.4 miles you'll cross the A-Z Trail, and in another 0.25 mile you come to a spur trail leading to the edge of enchanting Zealand Pond, where our walk ends. Backtrack the way you came to return to the parking area. ∎

Moose crossing

Franconia Notch State Park

NEW HAMPSHIRE ■ 6,440 acres ■ White Mountain National Forest, central New Hampshire on I-93 between Lincoln and Franconia ■ Year-round ■ Camping, hiking, biking ■ Contact the park, US 3, Franconia, NH 03580; phone 603-823-5563 or 603-271-3628 (camping reservations). www.nhparks.state.nh.us

FRANCONIA NOTCH RUNS for 8 miles between the Franconia and Kinsman mountain ranges. Everywhere you look are cliffs and talus slopes and trees hanging on by their toenails, the upper reaches soaring more than 2,000 feet above the pass. Paralleling the road is the bright flash of the **Pemigewasset River** and, high above the shimmer of **Profile Lake,** the famous frost-sculpted **Old Man of the Mountain**—long the symbol of New Hampshire. Trails offer everything from quiet lakes, easily reached, to thigh-burning climbs to the tundra. Little wonder that **Franconia Notch** has been a favorite of travelers since stagecoach days.

What to See and Do

You may as well begin your visit to Franconia Notch State Park with one of its best-known attractions: **The Flume Gorge** *(mid-May–mid-Oct.; adm. fee).* Coming north on I-93, which becomes the Franconia Notch Parkway, leave the thoroughfare at Parkway Exit 1 and follow the signs to The Flume Gorge. Be forewarned: This is one of the most visited parts of the park. It is also one of the most

White Birch

Not by happenstance did New Hampshire residents end up choosing white, or paper birch as their state tree. Indeed, what could be a more perfect symbol of a New Englander than a tough, scrappy tree like this one—a pioneer on lands burned or cut, able to bend under blankets of ice and the blow of winds, among the most elegant survivors of cold climates to be found anywhere in North America.

On a more practical note, early lumbermen laid strips of birch bark under the cedar shingles of their bunkhouse roofs, thus waterproofing them. Paper birch was a staple of life for Native American people, who sewed sheets of the bark together with spruce roots and laid them on frames for wigwams. They also employed a somewhat similar process, sheathing the sewn pieces of bark with cedar planks, to make what were arguably the world's most perfect canoes. Canoe builders were sold on white birch—not just for its incredible strength and flexibility, which allowed the vessels to hold up on rockbound streams or in ocean waves—but also because birch didn't absorb water, unlike canoe barks such as hickory, chestnut, and elm used in other parts of the country. A birchbark canoe might survive a decade of regular use, whereas boats made of other barks had far more limited life spans.

Many people, especially young children, feel an almost irresistible urge to peel birch bark off the tree. Yet even in remote places, such as in the backwoods of the national forests, you should only do so from fallen trees. Bark stripped from a live tree does not grow back again, but is instead replaced by black, clotted rings.

White birches

beautiful—the perfect first stop, especially for those coming into the park from the south.

Get oriented at the **Flume Visitor Center,** which has some fascinating natural and cultural exhibits, then head out behind the center (skipping the shuttle bus unless you really need it), following signs through the woods to the **Flume Trail.** Shortly after crossing a covered bridge across the Pemigewasset River, you'll spot a small cabin with still more exhibits. After this, the real fun begins, as the path enters what was 200 million years ago a solid piece of granite lying deep in the earth. At some point, a vertical fracture occurred, and molten basalt, or magma, flowed into the crack, spreading it; eventually, the magma cooled and hardened. Millions of years of erosion wore away the earth above it, exposing the rock to the patient fingers of ice and rain and wind. The basalt, which was softer than the surrounding granite, wore away at a faster rate— especially at the end of the glacial period, when **Flume Creek** was supercharged with torrents of meltwater.

This 2-mile trail, which in places consists of a boardwalk anchored to the sheer sides of the gorge, will lead you through some 800 feet of 90-foot-high walls, hung with a bewitching garden of leaf lichens, wood sorrels, and tiny ferns. Once you reach the outstanding **Avalanche Falls,** instead of returning via a path that parallels the gorge, continue on a trail toward a beautiful feature called the Pool, on the Pemigewasset River. From there make your way back to the visitor center via the **Wildwood Trail,** which provides good views of Liberty Peak and Flume Mountain.

It's easy to see why this outstanding area attracted many of America's most prominent writers, including Hawthorne, Emerson, and Thoreau. On the other hand, it also lured the not-so-prominent, such as the local character Professor John Merrill, who in the late 1800s spent his days rowing his boat in circles around the Pool, happily spouting his philosophy of the universe.

Lonesome Lake

A lovely place for an early morning walk is the trail to Lonesome Lake. Heading north on the Franconia Notch Parkway from the Flume Visitor Cener, exit at the Lafayette Campground; trailhead parking is on your left, shortly after leaving the parkway.

When the weather is cool, a 1,000-foot climb over a little less than 1.5 miles of trail seems like exactly the right thing to do. After a pleasant trek through a northern hardwood forest, you'll reach an intersection with **Cascade Brook Trail.** If you just want to touch the shoreline and turn around, you can follow the Lonesome Lake Trail. But a more enjoyable option is to take the Cascade Brook Trail along the lake, then make a right turn on the **Fishin' Jimmy Trail.** A short distance past this junction is **Lonesome Lake Hut,** a fantastic abode with a view that will set your head spinning. This is one of many huts managed by and available for rent through the

Appalachian Mountain Club (604-466-2727).

Returning from your trek to Lonesome Lake, take a few minutes to walk through the large grassy area next to the campground, where a number of interpretive signs help orient you to the mountains that rise to the east, across the parkway. Visible from this point are the shoulders of Mount Lafayette and Mount Lincoln. Little Haystack is there too, complete with **Shining Rock,** a steep slab of granite some 800 feet long and 200 feet high with sheets of springwater running across its face.

If all this leaves you hungry to get up into that country, you can do so on a trail called **Falling Waters,** located right across the parkway (through the pedestrian underpass), leading to the **Franconia Ridge Trail.** This is part of the Appalachian Trail and one of the most popular hiking trails in all the White Mountains. If you have to climb a mountain, it would be hard to imagine a more stunning way to do it, passing **Stairs, Swiftwater,** and **Cloudland falls,** as well as the face of Shining Rock. Keep in mind that this trail is steep, and often wet; allow two-and-a-half to three hours to reach the ridge.

Biking

Finally, while it comes with a hum of traffic from the nearby parkway, the paved recreation trail running the length of Franconia Notch is nonetheless a wonderful place for bikers. If you don't have your own bicycles, you can rent them at the state park. You can also get maps of the parkway at the visitor center. ▪

Waterfalls along the Falling Waters Trail, Franconia Notch State Park

Swimming hole on the Swift River

Kancamagus Highway

NEW HAMPSHIRE ■ 34.5 miles ■ White Mountain National Forest, central New Hampshire along N.H. 112 between Conway and Lincoln ■ Best months May-Sept. Roads crowded on fall foliage weekends ■ Camping, hiking, wildflower viewing ■ Contact Saco Ranger District, White Mountain National Forest, 33 Kancamagus Hwy., Conway, NH 03818; phone 603-447-2166. www.fs.fed.us/r9/white

THE KANCAMAGUS HIGHWAY, first opened in 1959, is one of the most enjoyable roads in all of New England, and that's saying a lot. Along this National Forest Scenic Byway are beautiful forests and serene ponds, breakneck rivers and spectacular views, engaging historic sites, and enough walking paths to wear out a set of hiking boots.

Immediately after turning east off N.H. 16 you'll see the Saco Ranger District and Information Center of the White Mountain National Forest. If you need maps or a break, or want to plan a trek into the backcountry, this is the place to go for help. Near the ranger district office (as well as at the other end of the Kancamagus Highway, just east of the I-93/N.H. 112 exchange), are signboards indicating vacancies in the campgrounds along the route.

What to See and Do

Along much of this route you'll have as company the beautiful **Swift River**. In most places it's a bright, confident river, making headlong flings over endless runs of boulders, gathering itself here and there in deep, clear pools that seem custom-made for fishing and swimming. Rising from the banks of the Swift River along the lower stretches of the drive are exquisite runs of white birches, shimmering against the dark of the forest. One Penobscot story tells of star-crossed lovers long ago who, forbidden to be together, died of despair. Upon their death the conjure man, feeling sorry for them, turned them into birch trees. Their children are growing in the forest today. Birch is one of the few naturally clumping trees in the forest. When you see multiple trunks on other species, it's nearly always a sign of a past cutting, or of fire.

Boulder Loop Trail

This easy to moderate 2.9-mile round-trip hike comes 6 miles west of the Saco ranger station. Turn right off the highway and go through the covered bridge to

Kancamagus

The scenic highway is named for a Penacook chief of the late 1600s. Sadly, although Kancamagus (The Fearless One) went to great lengths to be a friend to the English, he was lied to and mistreated at every turn. In the end he led the Penacook on their last uprising against the English settlers. Bloodied and disheartened, he retreated with his people to St. Frances, Quebec.

Kancamagus was the grandson of Passaconaway (Child of the Bear), who united the more than 17 tribes of central New England into the Penacook. Legend says that when Passaconaway died, he rose into the sky from the summit of Mount Washington in a sled pulled by wolves.

the parking lot on the right; the trailhead is opposite the parking lot. You'll be rewarded during this gradual climb (with some steep pitches) with excellent views of Mount Chocorua and the Swift River Valley.

At 6.7 miles, a spectacular falls and a nice spot for a swim in the Swift River, is Lower Falls. But if that doesn't tempt you to get out of the car for a few deep breaths, you can do so a couple of miles down the road in the **Rocky Gorge Scenic Area,** which has a small one-way auto road next to the Swift River and a short strolling path of about 0.2 miles. From here the road continues to climb, offering at 11 miles a chance to hike for real on **Bolles Trail** (8 miles round trip).

Rail 'n' River Trail

A couple of miles later, right after Jigger Johnson Campground, is a nice mix of history and nature at the **Passaconaway Historic Site.** Beside the historic **Russell-Colbath House,** which includes a medicinal plant garden with sage, mint, and comfrey, is a half-mile round-trip walk called **Rail 'n' River,** beginning along the old railroad bed of the Bartlett and Albany Railroad.

The path—which is accessible to wheelchairs and lined with benches—traverses a forest of maples, hemlocks, birches, spruces, and white pines. The area once contained some of the finest white pines in the White Mountains, many of them so big it took teams of 40 to 80 oxen to drag them out of the woods. The path also brushes elbows with the Swift River, here not swift at all, but quiet, nut-colored, and shining in the sun.

Mount Washington Cog Railway

Church Pond Trail

More good trails follow farther down the Kancamagus Highway, ranging from short and easy to long and challenging, including Olivarian Brook, Sawyer Pond Trail, and Church Pond. The Church Pond Trail, which takes off from between sites 18 and 19 in the Passaconaway Campground, is especially interesting in that it offers a close-up view of a peat bog sprouting rich mats of Labrador tea, black spruce, small cranberry, leatherleaf, and laurel.

As you make your way over **Kancamagus Pass,** the size and composition of the forest will have changed dramatically, and fabulous views will open into a rugged tumble of peaks, including Mount Garfield, Mount Bond, Whitewall Mountain, Mount Hale, and North Twin Mountain.

Mount Bond

If you've come to the Kancamagus to gain access to the mountains to the north, a truly dramatic way to do it is by way of a 20-mile round trip to **Mount Bond.** This is not a trek to be taken lightly. The ambitious hike begins on the **Lincoln Woods Trail** (31 miles from where you turned off N.H. 16), departing from the north side of the highway several miles west of Big Rock Campground. The path hits Franconia Brook Campsite at 2.8 miles, crosses the **Pemigewasset River,** and turns east on the **Wilderness Trail**—all over fairly flat terrain. At 4.7 miles, near the camp 16 tentsite, the route heads north on the **Bondcliff Trail,** and the real climbing begins. The last mile of this hike is along a magnificent open ridgeline, as good as it gets when it comes to views, but no place to be in bad weather. ■

Shaded woods, New Hampshire

Frost Place

NEW HAMPSHIRE ■ Central New Hampshire, on Ridge Rd. off N.H. 116 in Franconia ■ July–Columbus Day Wed.-Mon., weekends only Mem. Day–June ■ Walking, wildflower viewing ■ Adm. fee ■ Contact the farm, P.O. Box 74, Franconia, NH 03580; phone 603-823-5510. www.frostplace.com

WHEN YOU'VE STOOD IN LINE one too many times for ice cream in North Conway, or cruised around much too long for a parking space at the Flume, get in the car and regain your composure with a slice of woodland trail and a little poetry at the farm of one of America's favorite sons. It was here in the shadow of the Franconia Mountains that Robert Frost wrote two of his most enduring poetry collections:

New Hampshire and *Mountain Interval.*

Start your visit with a tour of Frost's house. Walk the porch where he sat with his bare feet stuck through the morning glory vines, perhaps even then living a line he wrote in 1954: "what you want, what you're hanging around in the world waiting for, is something to occur to you." Best of all, behind the house is a half-mile trail through a wonderful sampling of woodland, busy with milkweed, jack-in-the-pulpit, jewelweed, birch, sugar maple, and balsam fir—all of it laced with snippets of Frost's poetry, set in exactly the right places along the trail. ■

Three Ponds Trail

NEW HAMPSHIRE ■ White Mountain National Forest, central New Hampshire, 3 miles west of West Plymouth off N.H. 25 ■ Year-round ■ Hiking, wildflower viewing ■ Contact the Appalachian Mountain Club/Forest Service visitor center, P.O. Box 298, Gorham, NH 03581; phone 603-466-2721. www.fs.fed.us/r9/white

THIS DELIGHTFUL WALK gives a sense of the rich, yet subtle beauty that exists in the White Mountain National Forest off the wind-blasted summits of the Presidentials. Follow the sign for Stinson Lake Trailhead; the path begins a half mile north of the lake, on the west side. After 0.1 mile, the trail is marked with yellow blazes. The walk takes you through a place of falling streams and beaver ponds, of horsetail and sensitive and marsh ferns, of self-heal and bluebead lily, Indian cucumbers and large mats of sarsaparilla (once used in a drink by the same name—sometimes referred to as a "root beer").

By the time you've logged 20 or 30 minutes of walking, crossing a bridge over **Sucker Brook**, there is barely any part of the path not within sight and sound of water. At 1.5 miles the trail reaches the first in a braid of beaver ponds; evidence of the trees they've taken is everywhere, etched by their sharp incisors on the stumps of birch. Ten minutes' more walking and you'll find yourself at the middle member of **Three Ponds.** Follow a right branch of the trail here to climb a hill to yet another one of the ponds, or be content on the shore of this one. ■

Nearby
If you'd like to spend more time in the eastern White Mountains, you may want to walk the **Black Cap Trail** in the **Green Hills Preserve** *(N of North Conway off N.H. 16 on Hurricane Mountain Rd. 603-356-8833).*

You'll see signs for the trail on the right side of the road, which is a narrow, steep route, not suitable for large vehicles or those with trailers. The trail is an easy walk, beginning on state lands and leading in 1.1 miles to a Nature Conservancy preserve with splendid views of the White Mountains. You'll start out in a lovely coniferous woods, but soon enter a forest of beech, maple and white birch.

Green Mountain National Forest, South Half Drive

VERMONT ■ 75 miles ■ Southern Vermont ■ Spring through fall; color peaks in early to mid-Oct. Some roads closed in winter ■ Camping, hiking, kayaking, canoeing, swimming, fishing, downhill skiing, cross-country skiing ■ Contact the national forest, 231 N. Main St., Rutland, VT 05701; phone 802-747-6700. www.fs.fed.us/r9/gmfl/

DESPITE HAVING been cut over no fewer than three times, the Green Mountain National Forest includes a diversity of landscapes ranging from the rugged, exposed heights of Mount Abraham to the quiet, secluded hollows of Lye Brook Wilderness. Within these 231,131 acres, you'll find everything from hemlocks to hardwoods, red-spotted newts to peregrine falcons to black bears. Stretching over nearly two-thirds the length of Vermont, the forest is divided into two sections, a north unit (see pp. 154-59) and a south unit, which extends from the Vermont-Massachusetts border to Vt. 140 in the town of Wallingford.

The following loop drive in the south half of the forest will lead you to a splendid mix of trails, streams, mountain vistas, even swimming holes, not to mention a fine collection of enchanting villages—former textile towns that are today sprinkled with inns, art galleries, clapboard churches, and antique stores by the dozen. While the trails are perfect for day walks, nearly all lead to more extensive hiking opportunities. Note that roughly half of the loop drive—which wends through West Wardsboro, East Arlington, Danby, and Weston—consists of rather narrow dirt roads, not well suited to large recreational vehicles or to cars pulling trailers.

Begin the drive in the little village of West Wardsboro, on a road leading from Vt. 100 to Stratton Mountain Ski Area. When you first turn west from Vt. 100, roughly a half mile south of the West Wardsboro Post Office, a weathered, faded street sign identifies your route as Arlington Stratton Road. However, as is typical in rural New England, the actual name of roads around here may depend both on whom you ask and where you happen to be at the time. Officially this road is known alternately as Arlington Road and Kelly Stand Road before reaching East Arlington. (This has nothing to do with any plot to confound tourists and everything to do with the fact that for a long time the only people who were interested pretty much knew where they were going anyway.)

From this intersection our route climbs steadily through a long run of woods for 6 miles, at which point the pavement ends. Just beyond this, on the left, is the turnoff for Grout Pond, a perfect stop for those wanting to stretch their legs and walk the shoreline of one of southern Vermont's most beautiful and accessible pockets of water.

Emerald Lake State Park

Grout Pond

Grout Pond is a summer kind of place. In some sections it's cradled by beeches and balsams and sugar maples, in others by a thick weave of flowering ground plants, from whorled wood aster and self-heal to

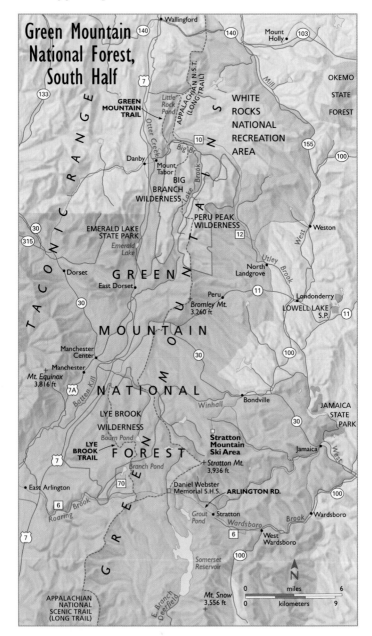

Green Mountain National Forest, South Half

OKEMO STATE FOREST

WHITE ROCKS NATIONAL RECREATION AREA

GREEN MOUNTAIN TRAIL

Little Rock Pond

APPALACHIAN N.S.T. (LONG TRAIL)

Wallingford

Mount Holly

Danby

Mount Tabor

BIG BRANCH WILDERNESS

Otter Creek

Big Br.

PERU PEAK WILDERNESS

Weston

EMERALD LAKE STATE PARK

Emerald Lake

Dorset

East Dorset

North Landgrove

Utley Brook

West River

Peru

Bromley Mt. 3,260 ft

Londonderry

LOWELL LAKE S.P.

GREEN MOUNTAIN

Manchester Center

Manchester

Mt. Equinox 3,816 ft

Batten Kill

NATIONAL

Winhall

Bondville

JAMAICA STATE PARK

LYE BROOK WILDERNESS

Bourn Pond

LYE BROOK TRAIL

FOREST

Branch Pond

Stratton Mountain Ski Area

Stratton Mt. 3,936 ft

Jamaica

East Arlington

Roaring Brook

Daniel Webster Memorial S.H.S.

ARLINGTON RD.

Grout Pond

Stratton

Wardsboro Brook

Wardsboro

West Wardsboro

Somerset Reservoir

Mt. Snow 3,556 ft

E. Branch Deerfield

APPALACHIAN NATIONAL SCENIC TRAIL (LONG TRAIL)

N

miles   0   6
kilometers   0   9

TACONIC RANGE

GREEN MOUNTAIN NATIONAL FOREST

bunchberry, wood sorrel, and red-berried elder. If you're in the mood for a good stroll, you could do no better than to follow the roadway on the north end of the water, which leads to a network of trails that will take you on a 2.9-mile walk clockwise around the pond. (Bear right at each of several trail intersections along the way.)

Grout Pond, Green Mountain National Forest

Early on, several side trails lead to a handful of picnic areas. (Be forewarned that eating your picnic in peace may require a generous dose of bug spray or whatever concoction you have on hand to fend off New England's official bird, the mosquito.) Along the path are fine views of Mount Snow to the southeast and Stratton Mountain to the north. Both of these areas offer a full range of summer activities, including high-speed gondola rides to the summits.

As you round the wetlands on the southeast corner of the lake, notice the birdhouses scattered about the shore. These are nesting boxes for wood ducks, one of Vermont's most remarkable waterfowl. Unlike most other ducks, wood ducks are quite content to live in places without much ground cover, assuming there are suitable nesting cavities. Not that wood ducks are the only ones fond of these box nests; over the years managers have found in them everything from mice to bees to flying squirrels.

Along the shore of Grout Pond is also a variety of the region's more interesting plants. Get out the field guides and see if you can find mountain maple and ironwood (both have buds that are a favorite of the many ruffed grouse that live here), as well as mountain holly, withe rod, self-heal, and jewelweed.

Daniel Webster Memorial State Historical Marker

Leave Grout Pond by retracing your route back out to Arlington Road. On the way, you'll pass a turnoff to a small historical marker on the right, noting the place where that consummate orator, Daniel Webster, gave a rousing speech to 15,000 people at the Whig convention of July 1840. Not bad for someone who, as a kid, was so shy that when called to speak to his classmates at Exeter Academy, he found himself too petrified even to get out of his seat.

The mixed hardwood forest along this road is still fairly young, the latest of many to have grown here since the area was settled 300 years ago. Each year these branches lean out into the road a little farther, reaching for

Following pages: Fog on Vermont farm

Day Hike on the Road to East Arlington

If not everyone in your group wants to walk, send the hikers on a terrific one-way, 10-mile trip from the southwest corner of Bourn Pond down the **Lye Brook Trail** to Glen Road in the town of East Manchester, where the rest of the group can pick them up. To reach the pickup point from Branch Pond, return to US 7 North. Follow this to Manchester; go east onto Vt. 11 and 30, then right onto East Manchester Road and left onto Glen Road. Follow the signs to Lye Brook Wilderness; pickup is at the end of a spur road on the right.

the sunlight, in some places locking arms to create a tunnel of leaves to shade you in the summer and thrill you with their colors in the fall.

The next chance for a leg stretch comes at Forest Road 70, on the right at just over 11 miles from Vt. 100. Follow this for 2.4 miles to a small parking area at **Branch Pond.** If you have a canoe, waste no time portaging it down 0.2 mile of forested pathway to the shore. In summer this lovely little pond is fringed with the blooms of flowering raspberry, sheep laurel, pond lilies, and, in June, blue flag iris, not to mention common woodland plants including wood sorrel, bead lily, Canada mayflower, and ferns beyond counting.

If you're more in the mood for walking than boating, put on your hiking boots and head up the trail directly opposite the one to Branch Pond. Following this will lead you in 2.6 miles to **Bourn Pond,** a remote water pocket in the **Lye Brook Wilderness.** A camping shelter there is available on a first-come, first-served basis.

Back on the main road again, all too soon you'll begin descending past the shouts of **Roaring Brook,** as well as past some exquisite gardens of hay-scented and interrupted ferns. Pavement comes again 6.4 miles from the turnoff to Branch Pond and 17 miles from where the trip began at Vt. 100.

As you leave the forest, watch for signs to US 7 and follow that north toward Manchester, passing through the **Batten Kill River Valley,** framed on one side by the **Green Mountains** and on the other by the larger, younger **Taconic Range.** One theory in the debate over the Taconics' origins (see p. 214) holds that the they were formed 500 million years ago, when the enormous mass of what was then Europe and Africa moved west, sweeping up chains of offshore volcanic islands as it collided with North America and plastering the islands onto the continent—creating the Taconics in Vermont and putting volcanic rocks in New Hampshire.

Winding along the base of these "crunch mountains," as geologists call them, the **Batten Kill** is an exceptionally good fly-fishing stream. For information, supplies, or guides contact Angler's Exchange in Manchester Center *(802-362-4296),* Orvis Company in Manchester *(802-362-3622),* or Brookside Angler, also in Manchester *(802-362-3538).* If you're traveling with your kayak or canoe, two stretches of the Batten Kill are worth your attention. The first is a 7.5-mile, Class I to Class II trip from the bridge in Manchester to the US 7 bridge in Arlington. The second trek extends the first, continuing on Class I water to the New York state line, at N.Y. 313.

Emerald Lake State Park

Located on the west side of US 7, approximately 7 miles north of Manchester, is tiny Emerald Lake State Park *(65 Emerald Lake Ln., East Dorset. 802-362-1655 summer, 802-483-2001 winter, or 800-658-1622. Mid-May–Columbus Day; day-use fee).* While not exactly wild, this is a perfect place for road-weary travelers to spend a couple of hours recharging their batteries. Directly north of the entrance station, at the top of a mowed hill, you'll find a half-mile nature hike that has numbered stops keyed to an interpretive brochure.

As the trail enters the woods, what it loses in views it more than makes up for in vegetation: a middle-aged mixed hardwood forest, the feet of the trees planted in maidenhair, lady, interrupted, sensitive, and Christmas fern, not to mention a host of forest wildflowers. In the last stretch of the walk, right before joining the paved pathway leading to the beach, look along the path for a small ground plant known as herb

Water lilies

Birches

Robert. Though no one seems to remember exactly which Robert this plant was meant to honor—likely candidates include everyone from a 12th-century duke to Robert Goodfellow, also known as Robin Hood—because of its high tannin content herb Robert was long used as a compress to stop bleeding. Unlike many forest wildflowers, which bloom early in the spring before the trees put on their leaves and thus block the sunlight, herb Robert wears its clusters of pink to purple blooms from May all the way to October.

At the paved path take a right, top a small hill, and descend onto a pleasant little beach. Here you can swim or rent a canoe, rowboat, or paddlewheel boat and cruise the ragged fringes of Emerald Lake, the green uplands of the Taconics rising to the southwest like a sweet summer dream. To return to your car, take the path around the beach past a small nature museum to the parking area.

White Rocks National Recreation Area

The driving tour continues north from Emerald Lake State Park on US 7 for 4.4 miles. In the village of Danby make a right turn, following signs for Mount Tabor. (This is actually Forest Road 10, which we'll be following for roughly 13 miles.) Just minutes after leaving US 7 you'll enter the **White Rocks National Recreation Area** *(Manchester Ranger District, Vt. 11 and 30. 802-362-2307)*. Cross a bridge over beautiful **Big Branch;** upstream from this bridge are some wonderful places to soak your feet, eat lunch, or even settle in with a good book. Yet another great opportunity for all of the above comes 2.7 miles from US 7 at a picnic area on the right, offering glimpses through the trees into a remarkably rugged slice of the Green Mountains.

A short distance past this picnic area is the trailhead for **Little Rock Pond.** This 4-mile round-trip hike traces the meanders of **Little Black Brook** through a mix of hardwoods, rich with the sounds of vireo and wood thrush. Framing the trail is a blend of viburnum, strawberry, meadow rue, false Solomon's seal, and wood sorrel. Little Rock Pond itself is as close to perfect as a pond gets, especially if you're inclined to do a bit of swimming. Alternatively, you can extend your walk by following the trail around the entire pond, which adds roughly a mile. You can also get back to Forest Road 10 a mile west of the parking area by hiking the **Green Mountain Trail,** which takes off from the northeast corner of the pond. Note that this latter option adds roughly 2 miles to your trek, much of it over rougher terrain than you covered on the way in.

Once back in the car, continue east on Forest Road 10. The road drops down to join beautiful **Utley Brook** and leaves the national forest 13 miles from Danby. Less than a mile later is a T-intersection. Make a left and drive another 0.3 mile to yet another T-junction, where you'll turn left again, following the signs for Weston. In Weston you'll rejoin Vt. 100, roughly 30 miles north of where the drive began in West Wardsboro. ■

Green Mountain
National Forest, North Half

VERMONT ■ 144,000 acres ■ Central Vermont, bordered by US 7, US 4, Vt. 100, and Vt. 17 ■ Year-round ■ Camping, hiking, walking, canoeing, swimming, fishing, mountain biking, downhill skiing, cross-country skiing ■ Contact the national forest, 231 N. Main St., Rutland, VT 05701; phone 802-747-6700. www.fs.fed.us/r9/gmfl/

THE NORTHERN SECTION of the Green Mountain National Forest spans 144,076 acres, but a favorite part of this vast area is the region called Moosalamoo, located between the western ridge of the Green Mountains and Lake Dunmore. You may never have heard of Moosalamoo, but those who find it don't soon forget it. More than 20,000 acres are being managed for wildlife and recreation by a cooperative effort among federal, state, corporate, and private landholders. It's among the best examples in all New England of what people can do when they attempt to

Silver Lake

build a vision of stewardship that serves nature and commerce alike. Moosalamoo is a large, contiguous habitat that is home to a variety of animals, from moose and bear to bobcat and weasel. In the spring the forest floor is a carpet of woodland wildflowers, which give way later in the season to purple asters, goldenrod, and ripening grasses just before the spectacular autumn foliage display. The air of Moosalamoo is the playground of hawks, which ride the thermals of the Green Mountains, and of recently reestablished peregrine falcons that nest on the Great Cliffs of Mount Horrid and Rattlesnake Cliffs.

What to See and Do

There are almost endless opportunities for excellent outdoor recreation here. Walking and hiking trails abound, as do areas for mountain biking, canoeing, swimming, cross-country skiing, blueberry picking, primitive and improved camping, inn-to-inn walking (complete with shuttle services for gear), fly-fishing, and interpretive walks and talks throughout the summer. For more

Canada Mayflower

For much of the early summer, hikers on moist, shady trails throughout New England's northern hardwoods will have as company the delicate blooms of the Canada mayflower. Easily recognized by its spike of white, star-shaped flowers sitting on short, often zigzag stems, this member of the lily family spreads by underground runners. Under the right conditions—acidic soil being chief among them—you may find yourself walking through large mats of this plant, one bloom after another, lending a certain cheeriness to what might otherwise be rather somber woods.

information, visit the area's website (www.moosalamoo.com). For information on inn-to-inn hiking, contact Country Inns Along the Trail (802-247-3300).

The name Moosalamoo is thought by some to mean "place of the shining fish." Local tales suggest that native people once gazed down into the waters of Silver Lake, or perhaps Lake Dunmore, from this mountain, and watched those shining fish— more than likely landlocked salmon—rolling in the surface waters, thousands of them flashing in the sun.

Silver Lake

A fitting place to start your tour of Moosalamoo is Silver Lake (from FR 32 about 1.5 miles, left on FR 27). A shimmering jewel in a quiet fold of mixed hardwoods, Silver Lake is a place of trout and grouse and loons. It's been set aside by the Forest Service as a primitive recreation site closed to motor vehicles—the reason being, as the sign at the parking area on Forest Road 27 proudly proclaims, "to provide the quiet and solitude so rare in our daily lives." From this parking area, walkers can reach the lake via a 0.6 mile stroll on the **Goshen Trail**, while canoeists can make a long, though well-graded portage down the old forest road. At the northeast end of the lake a number of camping sites are available on a first-come, first-served basis. There is also a picnic area here.

Archaeological evidence suggests that Silver Lake was long used as a winter encampment for native peoples. Artifacts have been found along the shore, and two dugout canoes, each several hundred years old, lie on the cold, dark bottom of the lake. While the two-track road on the east side of the lake is open to both foot and bike travel, the rather rugged trail on the west side is for foot travel only.

It's well worth your while to make a trek around the lake, especially if you've done your homework and secured one of the interpretive guides linked to numbered posts, available from the Green Mountain National Forest office in Middlebury (802-388-4362) as well as the Brandon Area Chamber of Commerce (802-247-6401). On the south and east end of the lake is a mix of bracken and polypody ferns and hobblebush,

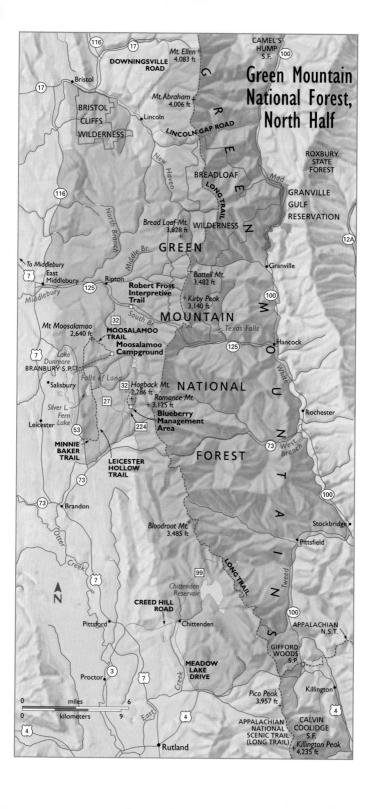

Green Mountain
National Forest,
North Half

CAMEL'S HUMP S.F.

100

116

17

DOWNINGSVILLE ROAD

Mt. Ellen 4,083 ft

Bristol

17

Mt. Abraham 4,006 ft

Lincoln

BRISTOL CLIFFS WILDERNESS

LINCOLN GAP ROAD

ROXBURY STATE FOREST

116

BREADLOAF

New Haven

GRANVILLE GULF RESERVATION

Mad

12A

LONG TRAIL

Bread Loaf Mt. 3,828 ft

WILDERNESS

GREEN

North Branch

Middle Br.

To Middlebury

7

East Middlebury

Granville

Battell Mt. 3,482 ft

125

Ripton

Robert Frost Interpretive Trail

Kirby Peak 3,140 ft

100

Middlebury

South Br.

MOUNTAIN

32

Mt Moosalamoo 2,640 ft

MOOSALAMOO TRAIL

Texas Falls

Hancock

125

MOUNTAINS

Moosalamoo Campground

7

Lake Dunmore

BRANBURY S.P.

Falls of Lana

32

Hogback Mt. 2,286 ft

NATIONAL

White

Salisbury

27

Romance Mt. 3,125 ft

Rochester

Silver L.

Fern Lake

53

224

Blueberry Management Area

73

West Branch

Leicester

MINNIE BAKER TRAIL

FOREST

100

LEICESTER HOLLOW TRAIL

73

73

Brandon

Stockbridge

Bloodroot Mt. 3,485 ft

Pittsfield

Otter Creek

7

99

LONG TRAIL

Tweed

Chittenden Reservoir

100

CREED HILL ROAD

N

Pittsford

Chittenden

APPALACHIAN N.S.T.

GIFFORD WOODS S.P.

3

7

MEADOW LAKE DRIVE

Proctor

Creek

Pico Peak 3,957 ft

Killington

0   miles   6

0   kilometers   9

East

4

APPALACHIAN NATIONAL SCENIC TRAIL (LONG TRAIL)

CALVIN COOLIDGE S.F.

4

Killington Peak 4,235 ft

4

Rutland

all clustered around the feet of a beautiful middle-aged forest of hemlock and birch. You'll also see here the small ground plant known as wintergreen, long popular as a pain reliever and used much as aspirin is today.

You can also make a fine, 9-mile-long mountain-bike trip by connecting the **Minnie Baker Trail,** which takes off from Vt. 53 south of **Fern Lake,** to the **Leicester Hollow Trail.** Head north on the Leicester Hollow Trail to the north side of Silver Lake, where you'll join the **Silver Lake Trail,** which will take you back to Vt. 53 near the entrance to Branbury State Park (see p. 161).

Mount Moosalamoo

There are certainly higher mountains in these parts than **Mount Moosalamoo,** and many with more expansive views. Yet few have the combination of a perfectly graded incline, the haunting beauty of a middle-aged mixed hardwood forest, an almost perfect woodland stream, and, on the back side of the mountain, an excellent chance to catch glimpses of that magnificent raptor, the peregrine falcon—among the fastest of fliers, and not so long ago brought to the edge of extinction by pesticides.

The perfect way to experience this beauty is along a 7-mile walk that begins near the Moosalamoo campground. From the intersection of Vt. 125 and Forest Road 32, head south on Forest Road 32 for 3.2 miles, turning west at a sign for Moosalamoo Campground. The **Moosalamoo Trail** begins at a parking area on the right, just outside the entrance to the campground. (Sections adjacent to this downslope walking route are closed between mid-March and early August to protect nesting peregrine falcons.)

As you start up the mountain, the trail is easy enough to follow in a long series of switchbacks past gardens of bead lily, Canada mayflower, fern, and wood sorrel. At the summit a small spur trail takes off to the left, quickly leading

Red-Spotted Newt

One of the friendliest faces in the New England woods belongs to a fascinating salamander known as the red-spotted newt. Admittedly, part of the attraction stems from the many lives this little critter leads. After spending its first several months in a shallow pool, the newt puts on a beautiful skin of orange and crawls out to live as a land dweller for anywhere from one to three years. When it comes time to breed, the male newt goes through yet another change, trading his orange skin for green, and then returns to water where he finds a mate. The female newt lays more than 15 eggs, which she attaches to the leaf or stem of a water plant.

Be aware that although newts are poisonous only to those who eat them (the orange color may be a keep-away warning to hungry predators), it's best not to handle them, as their skin is thin and easily damaged.

Forest reflections

to a yawning view of a wild-looking view of a wild-looking slice of Vermont countryside. The trip down is by way of the **Oak Ridge Trail,** which at one point bears left onto another path, called the **Rattlesnake Cliffs Trail.**

One caveat: At the base of the mountain is an intersection with a path leading to the Falls of Lana and Branbury State Park, as well as our route, the **North Branch Trail.** Be aware that the North Branch Trail crosses the stream only 20 or 30 yards after this intersection. If you miss this crossing, you could easily find yourself turned around and heading right back up the mountain!

The return to Moosalamoo Campground is gentle, much of it along a beautiful mountain stream in a narrow ravine filled with boulders carried here thousands of years ago on tongues of glacial ice—a massive jumble that produces a symphony of cascades and waterfalls and plunge pools.

This latter stretch of the hike is a good place to spot the wood sorrel, with its three bright green leaves and solitary white and reddish flowers. In the British Isles, where wood sorrel is also native, some say that it is in fact the true shamrock made famous by St. Patrick, who used the three-part leaves to explain the doctrine of the Trinity to the Celts. In a more practical vein, wood sorrel was used for a time to treat fever and nausea. It was also used as a diuretic for kidney and bladder infections. Today it has its fans among herbalists, most of whom prescribe it as a lotion for treating skin infections. ■

Robert Frost Interpretive Trail

If there's one writer whose life and work are a nearly perfect mirror of the moods of New England—at once harsh and sublime, sometimes dark and sometimes full of light, some days frantic and some days spinning out like a quiet, fragile dream—it would have to be the late poet laureate of Vermont, Robert Frost. There are a number of recreation sites named for Frost scattered about New England, from former residences in northern and southern New Hampshire to an extended recreation trail near the Connecticut River in central Massachusetts. In truth, all have something special to offer. But the 1-mile Robert Frost Interpretive Trail (E of Ripton on Vt. 125) in the Green Mountains, a stone's throw from Middlebury College, seems just the right mix of woodland and fields, thicket and sunlight. Many of the trees and plants wear name tags and a trailside map will help you identify the high, crumpled peaks lying to the north and east:

Bread Loaf, Battell, Kirby Peak, and Burnt Hill. There are boardwalks, bridges, benches, and, perhaps best of all, wooden posts holding excerpts from some of Frost's best loved works, including "The Secret Sits," "The Road Not Taken," "Winter Eden," and "Hardwood Groves." Many of them seem to be planted in exactly the right spot.

As is true throughout much of Moosalamoo country, this trail offers a chance to become familiar with a surprising variety of habitats, dry to moist to marsh. That, of course, in turn gives rise to a range of plant life from white pines and red spruces to beaked hazelnuts and black cherries, meadowsweets to black-eyed Susans, lowbush blueberries to bunchberries. In fact, this easy walk, perfect for small children, would be an excellent first stop for those looking to build a working knowledge of Vermont flora. In addition, the abundance of "edge zones"—places where two habitats, such as field and forest, come together—makes this a fine spot for bird-watching.

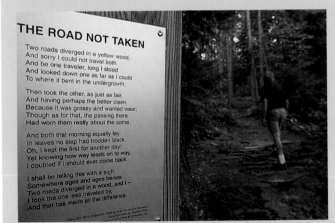

Robert Frost Interpretive Trail

Campsite, Branbury State Park

Branbury State Park

VERMONT ■ 69 acres ■ Central Vermont, 11 miles south of Middlebury off US 7 on Vt. 53 ■ Open mid-May–Columbus Day ■ Camping, hiking, swimming, biking ■ Day-use fee ■ Contact the park, 3570 Lake Dunmore Rd, Salisbury, VT 05733; phone 802-247-5925 (summer), 802-483-2001 (winter), or 800-658-1622. www.state.vt.us/anr/fpr/parks/branbury

WITH ITS GRASSY, SUN-WASHED day-use areas, splendid beach, nature trail, and access to some rather nice biking and hiking routes, Branbury State Park has long been a favorite of people throughout Vermont. This is a state park in the classic sense, something you might have come up with as a kid if you had been given a chance to design a place for whiling away the long, sweet days of summer. Over the years Branbury has had many incarnations—as a farm, a guesthouse, a summer boy's camp, even as a private beach—before becoming a state park. It was just down the road, incidentally, in the town of Brandon, that Stephen A. Douglas, the "little giant" who went on to debate Abraham Lincoln in Illinois, was born in 1813.

Those interested in getting a better sense of the forest that surrounds **Lake Dunmore** would do well to start out on the gentle quarter-mile nature trail, which takes off across the road from the contact station beside camp 41. This restful walk, much of it through an exceptionally fine hemlock forest, includes occasional glimpses of Lake Dunmore shimmering between the trunks of the big trees. Those in the mood for a somewhat longer walk, yet one manageable even by kids, should check out the side trail leading off the nature path to the **Falls of Lana.** If along the way you happen upon a bird or plant you have questions about, look for answers at the park's small nature center, located near the beach just west of the basketball court, or attend the variety of walks and other programs offered by the park naturalist throughout the summer. ■

Blueberry Management Area

VERMONT ■ 100 acres ■ Central Vermont, 5 miles northeast of Forest Dale via Vt 73, FR 32, and FR 224 ■ Blueberries peak in late July–early Aug. ■ Hiking, bird-watching, wildflower viewing ■ Contact Middlebury Ranger District, Green Mountain National Forest, RD 4, Box 1260, Middlebury, VT 05753; phone 802-388-4362. www.fs.fed.us/r9/gmfl/

THE FOREST SERVICE KEEPS THIS loose collection of plots free of timber by regular burning—thus rendering them perfect for growing lowbush blueberries. As it happens, this is a process that mirrors closely what native people throughout New England did for hundreds of years. The best way to enjoy the management area is to take a serene, woodland ramble that offers a nice mix of forests and views and, for those visiting in July and August, the ultimate reward of the unforgettable pleasures of fresh blueberries.

Park your car at the edge of the management area and continue walking up the same Forest Road 224 for a couple of hundred yards to a post on your left marked with the number 25. **Hogback Mountain Trail** begins here, spinning a 3-mile circle around the small rise of land just to the south known as **Hogback Mountain.** The trail slips quietly into a pleasant forest of birches, hemlocks, striped and red maples, and, at toe level, nice mats of fern, clubmoss, and Canada mayflower.

If you're here a month or so too early for blueberries, you can at least console yourself with Canada mayflower's sweet-scented spikes of white, star-shaped flowers that carpet the forest floor in early to mid-June (see p. 156). Curiously, mayflowers can emerge as plants with one, two, or three leaves, yet only the ones with three leaves actually bloom. If you miss the blueberry fest because you get here too late, the mayflowers will still be here for you, this time wearing the ruby red fruits that are a favorite of local grouse.

On your right during the first part of this walk are nice views of an uplift known as Romance Mountain. This soon fades from sight, though, leaving you to the woods. Birders should be alert for black-throated blue and blackburnian warblers, as well as scarlet tanagers. Although there are more than 200 species of tanagers in the tropics—nearly all with males sporting brilliant plumage—only four ever make it north of the Mexican border: the hepatic, summer, western, and scarlet, and all four are merely summer visitors.

As you make your way through the forest, you'll come across several intersections with numbered trails. These are connecting links to an outstanding network of groomed ski trails maintained by the Blueberry Hill Inn *(802-247-6735 or 800-448-0707)*; the trails are also great for mountain biking. After bearing left on the trail at each intersection, in just under 3 miles you'll reach a large open area filled not only with blueberries, but with a feast of great views to the west and north.■

Blueberries

Blueberries

Blueberries as big as the end
of your thumb,
Real sky-blue, and heavy, and
ready to drum
In the cavernous pail of the
first one to come!
   "Blueberries," Robert Frost

One of my favorite images of Thoreau has him trudging through face-slapping scrub on the upper reaches of Mount Katahdin, his companions bone weary and near collapse, finding heart in the discovery of blueberries. "Such patches afforded a grateful repast, and served to bait the tired party forward. When any lagged behind, the cry of 'blueberries' was most effectual to bring them up." Just as anyone who visits New England must at some point sit down to a plate of pancakes and maple syrup, so must the summertime lover of the outdoors commit to discovering a sun-drenched patch of ground flush with blueberries.

Everyone, it would seem, loves these members of the heath family. Songbirds, bears, and small mammals eat the berries, deer eat the twigs, and rabbits eat the foliage. There are many species of blueberry, but in New England they are classified either as lowbush, which grow to heights of 10 to 20 inches, or highbush, which are from 3 to 15 feet tall. Lowbush species are found in dry, sandy, or rocky soil, blooming in late June and July. Highbush varieties tend to grow in in nearly the opposite conditions—swampy places and in moist thickets, blooming in late July and August.

Mount Mansfield

VERMONT ■ North-central Vermont, 7 miles north of Stowe on Vt. 108
■ Toll road to summit open late May-Oct. ■ Camping, hiking, downhill skiing,
cross-country skiing, bird-watching, wildflower viewing ■ Contact Stowe
Information Center, P.O. Box 1320, Stowe VT 05672; phone 802-253-7321
or 800-247-8693

HIGH-COUNTRY THEOREM number one: The thrill one feels on reaching the
summit of a high peak is directly proportional to the quality of the landscape visible from the summit. Given that Mount Mansfield offers the
chance to drink from an absolute sea of tree-covered uplands, from New
York to Quebec to New Hampshire, with ponds and lakes and rivers fresh
and flashing in the sun, walking atop the summit is about as thrilling as
it gets. As you savor the view, bear in mind that some 400 acres along the
ridgeline are part of the **Mount Mansfield Natural Area,** which harbors
the largest expanse of alpine tundra in the state. This fragile community,
along with the adjacent subalpine heath krummholz and several alpine
bogs, contains some of the rarest plants in Vermont. In these harsh
conditions, it can take between 500 and 1,000 years to make a single inch
of soil, so as you walk this area, please stay on trails or on exposed rocks.

If you want to make your way to the summit of Mansfield in your
car via the toll road, try to allow enough time for all or part of a 3-mile
round-trip walk along the **Long Trail,** from the summit house (located
near the Nose) to the Chin. The summit house by the upper parking
area, as well as the trails themselves, are staffed throughout the summer
by the Green Mountain Club *(802-244-7037),* one of the best outdoors
organizations in all New England.

The 1.5-mile walk from **the Nose** to **the Chin** (at 4,393 feet, the
highest point in Vermont) is generally over undulating terrain, first
through a tight squeeze of firs, and then across a sweep of alpine tundra.
The views to the west along the way range across Lake Champlain and
into the Adirondack Mountains of New York. Trailside are gardens of
mountain sandwort, alpine bilberry, black crowberry, and mountain
cranberry. The small size of these plants' leaves and the way the plants
tend to grow close to the ground help to reduce damage from the fierce
winds. Also, the leaves are often thick, with waxy coatings, to minimize
water loss. (You might not think water would be an issue here, what with
all the rain and snow. But quick runoff into this rocky ground, along with
the highly acidic soil, leaves plants little to work with.)

Serious hikers can climb to the summit via a number of trails. One leaves
from Vt. 108 at **Smugglers Notch State Park** *(Between Stowe and Jefferson-
ville on Vt. 108. 802-253-4014. www.state.vt.us/anr/fpr/parks; mid-May–
Columbus Day),* another from **Underhill State Park** *(15 miles E of Essex
Junction via Vt. 15 and Town Rd. 802-899-3022. www.state.vt.us/anr/fpr/parks;
mid-May–Columbus Day; day-use fee, steep entrance, no trailers).* ■

Hikers, Mount Mansfield

Kettle Lake seen from Camels Hump

Other Peaks Nearby
Camels Hump

People set on bagging Vermont's highest peaks have to include Camels Hump—a mountain recognizable by its double-humped profiles—located some 25 miles south of Mount Mansfield. The mountain has been known by several names: In the 1600s it was called *lion couchant* ("crouching lion") by Samuel de Champlain's explorers. In the 1780s it went by the unflattering moniker of Camels Rump before finally being designated Camels Hump.

From Waterbury, cross the Winoocki River and head west on River Road for 5 miles. Turn left onto Camels Hump Road and park just beyond the Monroe Ranger Station. From here you can make a long but rewarding day hike of roughly 7.4 miles, with an elevation gain of 2,600 feet. This distance reflects a loop walk that begins with an ascent on the historic **Monroe Trail;** on meeting the Long Trail turn left to gain the summit and then continue on the Long Trail south off the peak to the intersection with the **Dean Trail,** where you make another left. In a mile the Dean Trail rejoins the Monroe Trail; turn right to return to the parking lot. Primitive camping is allowed in the lower elevations of Camels Hump, and at the Long Trail lodges and shelters *(Green Mountain Club. 802-244-7037).*

Mount Hunger

The view from the high rock slabs and crooked ridges of Mount Hunger *(southeast of Mount Mansfield in C.C. Putnam State Forest off Vt. 100 near Waterbury Center. 802-244-7103. Mid-May–Columbus Day)* is among the most inspiring in the state. The moderately difficult trail gains 2,300 feet in just under 2 miles, and blueberries are abundant. Gaze across the lush Waterville Valley to Mount Mansfield and the Stowe area. Looking east on a clear day, you'll see the White Mountains of New Hampshire.

Northeast Kingdom

VERMONT ■ 2,000 sq. miles ■ Northeast Vermont, north of St. Johnsbury to the Canadian border ■ Best seasons summer and fall ■ Camping, hiking, guided walks, boating, canoeing, mountain biking, bird-watching, wildflower viewing ■ Contact Northeast Kingdom Travel and Tourism Association, P.O. Box 355, Island Pond, VT 05846; phone 802-525-4386 or 888-884-8001. www.vtnek.com

THEY CALL THIS AREA THE KINGDOM, and somehow the name fits. As one resident put it, this is the "the essence of old Vermont." Made up of three counties and covering 2,000 square miles, the Kingdom has 117 square miles of public forest parkland, 1,500 square miles of private forested land, 35,575 acres of public lakes and ponds, and almost 4000 miles of public rivers and streams. Black bear, deer, and moose claim the kingdom as their natural habitat, as do the once-endangered peregrine falcon and many other species of birds, animals and fish.

There is, happily, not the polish evident in other, far busier places in New England—the shine that comes from dressing up for guests instead of simply keeping on your old, comfortable shoes and inviting people to sit a spell, maybe join you as you go about your day. Such an attitude seems to fit especially well in this rugged land, this world of black spruce bogs and tannin-stained rivers, of dirt roads and woods growing fatter with every passing year. In the Northeast Kingdom, suddenly there's more road between villages, more valley between the mountains, more creeks to cross before reaching the river.

What to See and Do
Brighton State Park

A perfect example of the Kingdom's laid-back warmth lies just a few skips of a flat stone from the town of Island Pond at Brighton State Park (*Off Vt. 114. 802-723-4360 summer, 802-476-0170 winter. www.vtstateparks.com; May–Columbus Day; day-use and camping fees*). You'll reach the park's beach first; the campground and hiking trails are farther down the road, on the right.

The park has few whistles and bells, but everything you need for an encounter with the natural world is here. The campground is well-kept and the sites spacious, and many have shelters if it rains. Within an easy walk are rowboats and canoes to rent and a **nature center,** started years ago by Charles Johnson, one of the most gifted naturalists in New England. You can enjoy a half-mile self-guided nature trail, and additional footpaths wind through the woods that surround **Spectacle Pond.** Best of all is a full slate of guided activities throughout the summer, from morning canoe treks to bog walks to bird-watching.

This area is a perfect place to begin acquainting yourself with the

Following pages: Camels Hump

Spiderweb

players of the boreal forest. Throughout your wanderings here you'll brush elbows with an assortment of trees, many of which you'll run into time and again in your travels across northern Vermont, New Hampshire, and Maine.

See if you can identify firs, red spruces, sugar and red maples, white cedars, white birches, and aspens. Along with those will come the birds and other animals that have learned to use this particular niche: boreal chickadees; ruby-crowned kinglets; spruce grouse; blackburnian, yellow-rumped,

blackpoll, black-throated green, Tennessee, and magnolia warblers; Swainson's thrushes; as well as moose, fishers, lynx, beavers, red squirrels, and marten.

Although birch and aspens do very well in this country on disturbed sites, in most places their days are numbered. This is ultimately a land of conifers—trees that are especially well adapted to such climates, both because being evergreen keeps them from having to sprout new leaves against a short growing season, and also because their conical shape is effective in allowing them to shed snow. Notice in places thick with spruce and fir how little light reaches the ground, even in the middle of the day. That condition, combined with highly acidic, nutrient-poor soil, makes for a sparse understory. Those plants that make it in the boreal woods tend to do so in open areas. These include starflower, wintergreen, bunchberry, goldthread, twinflower, shinleaf, and Canada mayflower—all of which you can see right here in Brighton State Park.

Mollie Beattie Bog

New England's fondness for a landscape without signs reaches its apex at Mollie Beattie Bog *(E of Island Pond, N of Vt. 105; contact Silvio O. Conte National Fish and Wildlife Refuge. 802-723-4398),* a new boardwalk site constructed in honor of the former Commissioner of Vermont Forests, Parks, and Recreation, and later the director of the U.S. Fish and Wildlife Service.

A walk through Mollie Beattie is not for those looking for a workout. Still, its 76 acres—part of an extensive system of bogs and evergreen swamps known locally as **Yellow Bog**—provide a small window into one of the most overlooked yet critical ecosystems in northern New England. Yellow Bog alone supports a number of rare plants, including coast sedge, and contains breeding populations of spruce grouse, boreal chickadees, black-backed woodpeckers, and three-toed woodpeckers. This is also home to the southern bog lemming, a vole-like creature that

lives and travels in tunnels excavated in the bog mat. One sure sign of the southern bog lemming's presence is small piles of sedge stems, about an inch long, clipped and stacked in piles near their runways.

This is an odd-looking world of dark, skinny trees with wet feet, spring peepers and insect-eating plants, laurel and leatherleaf, dragon- and damselflies. Yet something Mollie Beattie herself once said seems especially appropriate here: "All these unlovable species with funny names are connected to a system, and human beings are a part of that system. And if the system is in trouble, so are we." What the walk lacks in length (it's only 75 yards long) it makes up for in interpretation. Fine displays outline the workings of the bog

Nearby

West of Brighton State Park, on the other side of I-91, you'll find the **Vermont Leadership Center** *(1331 Ten Mile Square Rd., East Charleston, VT 05833. 802-723-6551. www.sover.net/~VLC; fee for events).* Located in the Clyde River Valley, VLC is the brainchild of Bill Manning, former president of Sterling College. The leadership center offers a range of courses, from canoe classes to birding walks, loon seminars, hiking trips, and extended camps for kids 6-11 and 12-16. Limited canoe rentals are available. Call the center for programming and directions.

community, while a number of other panels identify many of the common resident plants. At the end of the boardwalk are still more displays, with information about animals ranging from moose to grouse to snowshoe hares.

For all the water in places like this, it is largely so acidic as to be unusable by plants. Much as in desert environments, the plants that can make it here are those that manage to conserve water. The sedges you see have narrow leaves, thus reducing evaporation. Sphagnum mosses have cells that essentially function as water-storage containers. Labrador tea, bog rosemary, and leatherleaf have thick, firm leaves and woody stems, all of which help the plant retain water. As unspectacular as such environments might seem at first, if you keep still for a time, the unique thrum of life here will show itself to you: the smell of peat and spruce, the drone of flies, the buzz of boreal chickadees and the drum of male grouse, with cedar waxwings flashing against the dark stands of timber. ■

Maple Sugarin'

Part of what makes New England so unforgettable turns on that certain sweet time in the fall, when the sap stops flowing and the leaves of the sugar maple turn a riot of red and orange. But another part turns on exactly the opposite event —the March thaw, when the sap starts flowing again, heralding the beginning of the sugarin' season. Vermont alone taps roughly a million trees a year, producing a half million gallons of syrup, making it America's number one producer.

For the most part, only mature trees—those roughly 40 years old or more— are used for maple-syrup production. Metal taps inserted into the tree are used to collect the sap, which in spring is on its way out to the cambium layer, leaf buds, even to the roots. The sap is then heated in large metal evaporator pans. This thin, watery liquid—about 3 percent sugar at the start —moves through a series of compartments in the evaporator pans, becoming increasingly concentrated, finally arriving at a pour-off valve. By the time it runs out of that valve, the sugar content of the sap has increased more than 20-fold, which is why it takes on average some 40 gallons of sap to make a single gallon of syrup. In one season the average tree will produce in two taps about 20 gallons of sap, which will boil down to half a gallon of maple syrup, or four pounds of maple sugar. In what seems like the equivalent of big fish stories, however, tales from the 1800s talk about the occasional tree that produced ten times that amount.

"Sugaring off" celebrations were once among the biggest social events of the year throughout much of New England's sugar-bush country. The main event involved cooking down the syrup to a sticky, gooey sugar, which was eaten as is or dribbled on packed snow. Most such parties included a tub of sour pickles for those in need of something to cut the sweetness.

Osmore Pond, Groton State Forest

Groton State Forest

VERMONT ■ 25,000 acres ■ Northeast Vermont, 25 miles northeast of Barre along Vt. 232 between US 2 and US 302 ■ Best months June-Oct. ■ Camping, hiking, mountain biking, bird-watching, wildlife viewing, wildflower viewing ■ Contact District 4 office, 324 N. Main St., Barre, VT 05641; phone 802-476-0170. www.anr.state.vt.us

AT 25,000 ACRES, encompassing six state parks, Groton State Forest is the second largest state landholding in Vermont. It has risen from the ashes of a massive fire in the early 1900s to become a virtual garden of birches, balsams, spruces, red maples and tamaracks, with a mix of hay-scented and wood ferns, wintergreen, and bunchberry scattered across the forest floor. Those out and about early in the morning or late in the evening may catch sight not only of a wide variety of birds—including loons, nuthatches, finches, chickadees, and various warblers—but an abundance of mammals, including moose, deer, black bears, fishers, and mink.

What to See and Do

One way to tour the area is by mountain bike along the **Montpelier & Wells River Trail,** which has a number of access points along Vt. 232. This abandoned railroad bed, acquired by the state of Vermont in 1957, covers roughly 17 miles from Marsh-field to Groton. Along the way it winds through splendid forests and past quiet lakes, and if you want to stop, views of the surrounding uplands make it worthwhile. The Montpelier & Wells River Trail is the longest of several such multiuse trails in the forest, each of which is marked with orange diamonds. Be aware, however, that this particular bed is also used as an automobile access road to the lakeside dwellings between Marshfield and Lanesboro stations.

First-time visitors to Groton State Forest would do well to start out at the Groton Nature Center *(Boulder Beach Rd. 802-476-0170. Mid-May–Columbus Day)* and then make the pleasant half-mile walk around the nature trail that takes off beside the center. The trail has numbered posts keyed to an interpretive brochure that is available at the nature center and Stillwater State Park *(Boulder Beach Rd. 802-476-0170).*

Peacham Bog

From the nature center at Groton State Forest you can set off for Peacham Bog, one of my favorite bog walks in all of New England. This 4.8-mile round-trip amble begins in a flush of tamarack, the feathery-looking conifer that goes

against conifer custom, its needles turning from green to gold in the fall and dropping off, then returning in a fresh layer in the spring. (If you see bare tamarack trees in the summer, they have probably been killed by infestations of an insect known as the larch sawfly.) This tree is usually found growing in moist, acidic soils; starflower, clintonia, and cinnamon fern, which like the same conditions, are usually nearby.

At a little over a half mile, the trail passes cuts in the forest that were made in 1984. These cuts don't just sport smaller, younger versions of what's growing in the surrounding forest; rather, they are made up of very different species. While young birch and maples are starting to show themselves, there's also raspberry, blackberry, and pin cherry. These latter plants are the pioneers, usually rushing in to set up shop immediately after a major disturbance such as cutting or fire. Assuming there isn't another disturbance anytime soon, over the next several years the birches will gain the upper hand here. Though the shadows cast by their leaves will make life difficult for sun-loving shrubs such as raspberry, conditions will be exactly right for plants that do well in the shade, such as balsam firs.

This walk passes through a nice collection of ferns: wood-fern, hay-scented, and cinnamon, among others. Ferns reproduce by means of spores, which are often held in cases that appear as rust-colored lines or tiny dots on the underside of the fronds. The cases are covered by thin

Hay-scented ferns

protective shields that break open when it's time for the spores to be released. Fern spores are so light and tough that some scientists believe they may be transported from one continent to another in the jet stream.

Another 15 minutes of easy walking and you'll have traded the world of ferns for that of bogs. Peacham Bog, to be exact —a fascinating mix of sedge, rhodora, leatherleaf, rosemary, sphagnum, and black spruce, all doing just fine with their toes planted in water that has a pH slightly higher than vinegar. In recent years forest managers have erected a wonderful observation platform from which to view Peacham Bog. This was done in part because bogs are incredibly fragile. With that in mind, it's important that you confine your travel to this observation area and the trails leading up to it. ■

Lower New England

Gilson Pond, New Hampshire

OF ALL THE WOODS that rise from the lands east of the
Mississippi, few are more stirring, more full of chirp and
nap and texture than those of the northern Piedmont. In
New England they are stitched into the valleys and swales
of Connecticut, Massachusetts, and part of Rhode Island.
They spill over into extreme southern Maine, as well as
into the midsections of New Hampshire and Vermont.
These are the trees of our dreams: sugar maples turning
scarlet with the snap of fall; silent stands of beech, gray

and silky in the light of a winter moon; hemlock, dark and shaggy; huddles of white and red pine; the leathery leaves of white oak, twisting in the warm summer wind.

While lands to the north and those at higher elevations are marked by hardy conifers and the graceful forms of aspen and birch, the gentler conditions of these lower regions allow for a rich mixture of trees and plants. Adding in no small measure to the enchantment of these forests is the fact that the canopies tend to be somewhat patchier than those of woodlands to the north. This more open canopy, in turn, allows more sunlight to reach the ground, which affords a rich understory of shrubs and vines and ground covers. In these woods it is possible to mark the passing of the seasons by the sequence of blooms that trail at your feet. In early spring you'll find hepatica, trillium, spring beauty, and Canada mayflower, which yield in a few weeks to dogtooth violet and foamflower. Then come the less showy blooms of wild ginger and jack-in-the-pulpit. Even in summer, when the leaves of the trees are blocking the light, there are yet blooms to be found—harebell and iris and a wonderful variety of orchids. And then another burst of blossoms arrives, these reminding us that fall is not far away. Mid- to late summer is the time of whorled and white wood asters, of woodland sunflowers and rattlesnake root, and in the fields, daisies and goldenrod beyond the counting.

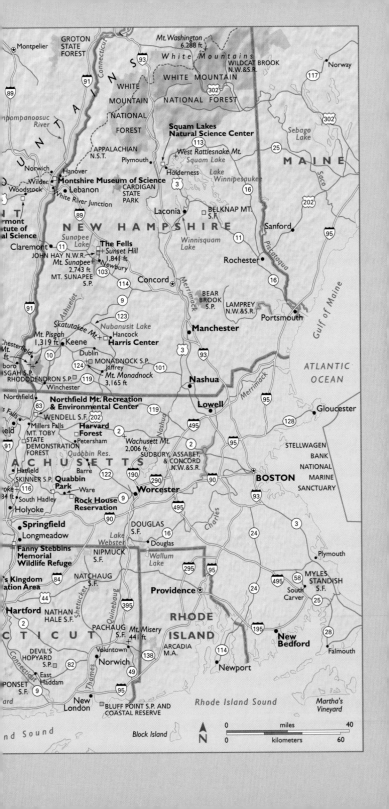

Montpelier

GROTON
STATE
FOREST

Mt. Washington
6,288 ft

White Mountains

WILDCAT BROOK
N.W.&S.R.

Norway

117

WHITE MOUNTAIN

WHITE

MOUNTAIN

NATIONAL FOREST

302

302

Sebago
Lake

M A I N E

Squam Lakes
Natural Science Center

West Rattlesnake Mt.
Squam Lake

25

Saco

APPALACHIAN
N.S.T.

Plymouth

Holderness

3

Norwich
Hanover
Wilder
Woodstock
Lebanon
White River Junction

CARDIGAN
STATE
PARK

Lake
Winnipesaukee

16

202

95

Montshire Museum of Science

N E W   H A M P S H I R E

Sanford

89

Laconia

BELKNAP MT.
S.F.

Sunapee
Lake

Winnisquam
Lake

11

Rochester

16

rmont
stitute of
al Science

JOHN HAY N.W.R.
Mt. Sunapee
2,743 ft
MT. SUNAPEE
S.P.

The Fells
Sunset Hill
1,841 ft
Newbury

103

202

Claremont

11

114

Concord

Portsmouth

Gulf of Maine

91

9

Merrimack

BEAR
BROOK
S.P.

LAMPREY
N.W.&S.R.

123

Nubanusit Lake

Skatutakee Mt.

Hancock

Manchester

ATLANTIC

OCEAN

Mt. Pisgah
1,319 ft

Keene

Dublin

Harris Center

3

93

hesterfield
Mt.
ft

10

124

MONADNOCK S.P.

Mt. Monadnock
3,165 ft

101

boro
SGAH S.P.
RHODODENDRON S.P.

119

Jaffrey

Winchester

Nashua

Northfield

63

Northfield Mt. Recreation
& Environmental Center

119

Lowell

495

s Falls

91

ield

WENDELL S.F.

202

Millers Falls
MT. TOBY
STATE
DEMONSTRATION
FOREST

Harvard
Forest

Petersham

2

Wachusett Mt.
2,006 ft

Quabbin Res.

SUDBURY, ASSABET,
& CONCORD
N.W.&S.R.

2

95

Merrimack

128

Gloucester

STELLWAGEN

BANK

NATIONAL

MARINE

SANCTUARY

Hatfield

SKINNER S.P.
oke
116
34 ft
South Hadley

Holyoke

Quabbin
Park

Barre

122

Ware

190

290

90

BOSTON

93

M A S S A C H U S E T T S

Worcester

Springfield

Longmeadow

Rock House
Reservation

9

90

495

Charles

24

3

Fanny Stebbins
Memorial
Wildlife Refuge

's Kingdom
ation Area

84

44

NIPMUCK
S.F.

NATCHAUG
S.F.

Lake
Webster

DOUGLAS
S.F.

16

Douglas

Wallum
Lake

295

95

Plymouth

MYLES
STANDISH
S.F.

58

Hartford

2

NATHAN
HALE S.F.

Quinebaug

Shetucket

PACHAUG
S.F.

395

Providence

24

South
Carver

25

C T I C U T

DEVIL'S
HOPYARD
S.P.

82

Voluntown

Mt. Misery
441 ft

R H O D E

ISLAND

ARCADIA
M.A.

138

114

195

New
Bedford

28

Falmouth

PONSET
S.F.
ard

9

East
Haddam

Norwich

49

Connecticut

New
London

BLUFF POINT S.P. AND
COASTAL RESERVE

95

Newport

Rhode Island Sound

Martha's
Vineyard

nd Sound

Block Island

N

0   miles   40

0   kilometers   60

Connecticut produce

It was in large part the sprawl of woods across this lovely, crumpled slice of New England that allowed early settlers to survive here at all. For starters, these forests were home to an incredibly rich collection of wildlife—deer, moose, bears, and enormous flocks of turkeys, the latter taken, at least at first, with little more effort than that of stepping outside the front door and pulling the trigger. Furthermore, because of the critical role these woods played as watersheds, retaining both rainfall and snowmelt, they contributed to an outstanding web of inland fisheries. In addition to food, the thick woods provided firewood beyond the ability of most new settlers to comprehend. Given the shortage of timber at the time in England and in much of Europe, people who had an abundant supply of firewood for cooking and for building fires in the winter may have felt as if they had reached the status of nobility.

Beyond providing such basics, these woodlands also yielded everything from shingles and clapboards to fence rails and poles, tar and pitch, tannin and turpentine. Lumbermen, as well as those simply clearing the land for agriculture, had the enormous luxury of using only the clearest, choicest trees, burning the rest or leaving them to rot. It was for this reason that the forests would become the foundation of the early New England economy. Masts, pitch, and clapboards went to England, while timber and boards sailed off to the sugar producers of the West Indies. New England businesses sent oak barrel staves to winemakers on Madeira while building entire ships for Portugal and Spain. During the mid-1600s a single shipment of timber from New England could be sold in southern Europe for more than five times the cost of acquiring it. Not surprisingly, then, many of the early fortunes made in the New World came about as a result of trading in trees.

Settlers also took down countless trees when it came time to make charcoal for fueling the blast furnaces of the Revolutionary War. That,

Swans, Mount Everett State Reservation

combined with the lucrative timber trade and the clearing of land for farming, thoroughly transformed the landscape. In very little time the region changed from one almost completely covered by forest to one nearly bereft of trees. Only in the last century has the forest begun to retake its historic area. Although the woodlands you see here today are far different in both stature and composition from those that existed in the early colonial period, in general you will find that the paths you explore today are more fully cradled by trees than they were at any other time during the past 300 years.

Similar soils and vegetation link the forests of southern New England to woodlands as far south as West Virginia. Yet the region is by no means homogeneous. In fact, in the northern reaches of this ecoregion—beneath, say, the uplands of central Vermont and New Hampshire—this is truly a transitional woodland: the southernmost range for many trees from the north, and the northernmost range for trees from the south. It has been estimated that close to a hundred woody plants reach their limits in this region—trees in number and variety enough to satisfy even the most discriminating lover of the woods.

As you explore this region, take special note of the extent to which plants react to specific conditions, or niches. Wind your way along a trail in central New England from the south side of a hill or mountain to the north side, for example, and the plants (and, therefore, the birds and animals) can change considerably. You may find the north side of the mountain favoring varieties that thrive in slightly cooler temperatures and additional moisture. In the same way, because the air becomes cooler the higher you climb, the plants that you'll find growing on the tops of Mounts Greylock, Monadnock, Sunapee, and dozens of other peaks in New England will be far different from the more mixed deciduous woods growing at their feet. ■

Squam Lakes Natural Science Center

NEW HAMPSHIRE ■ 200 acres ■ Central New Hampshire, 10 miles east of Plymouth at the junction of US 3 and N.H. 113 ■ May-Oct. ■ Hiking, boat tour, bird-watching, wildlife viewing ■ Adm. fee ■ Contact the center, P.O. Box 173, Holderness, NH 03245; phone 603-968-7194. www.nhnature.org

IN AN AGE OF INCREASING CONCERN ABOUT the welfare of animals in confinement, the Squam Lakes Natural Science Center (until recently called the Science Center of New Hampshire) is an inspiration. Located on New Hampshire's second biggest lake, the science center offers habitats for orphaned and wounded native animals—otters, bobcats, and black bears—that are unable to survive in the wild. Not only are the wildlife areas well tended, but the center's educational offerings are top-notch and the staff's level of enthusiasm is downright catching. While a lot of locals may think of this science center, with its engaging, interactive style, as the ideal place to take kids, it's a sure bet for adults as well. What you learn here, from how bobcats capture their food to what the musky, skunklike odor of a fox says to other animals (along with dozens of other animal messages), will only make your forays into those places where these animals still run free all the more enjoyable.

Just as impressive is the strong effort this center makes to put these animals in context, to link them to the larger world so essential to the survival of their species. After you've had a chance to visit the live animal habitats, you can see the kinds of places where many of those creatures live by taking a walk along the self-guided **Forest Trail;** or, as an alternative, you can make the relatively easy hike to the summit of **Mount Fayal,** where you'll be rewarded with sweeping views of **Squam Lake** and the surrounding countryside. The center also puts a premium on hands-on exhibits. At a special display on soils, for example, you will learn that five handfuls of dirt can contain more animals than there are humans on Earth—a point driven home at a microscope station, where you can see many of those creatures for yourself. When you're done exploring, take a moment to recover in **Kirkwood Gardens,** a three-acre, low-maintenance area located on the grounds of the Holderness Inn, and see how effective the plantings are at attracting birds, bees, and butterflies.

Besides a full range of daily live animal programs, the center sponsors an array of lectures and special events *(some require reservations)*. Are you looking for something the whole family will enjoy? How about an insect search party? A loon cruise? Bird-watching on 28-foot pontoon boats? Learning about the mysteries that lurk underwater in the center's aqua lab? Call the center for the latest offerings, or visit their web site. ■

Northern saw-whet owl

West Rattlesnake Mountain: Bridal Path Trail

NEW HAMPSHIRE ■ 2 miles round-trip ■ Central New Hampshire, 6 miles east of Holderness on N.H. 113 ■ Year-round ■ Hiking ■ Contact Squam Lakes Association, P.O. Box 204, Holderness, NH 03245; phone 603-968-7336

Queen Anne's lace

WHEN YOU'VE FINISHED hobnobbing with otters and orchids at the Squam Lakes Natural Science Center, venture northeast a few miles to take in West Rattlesnake Mountain. From its gentle summit you can watch the colors of the setting sun reflected in the waters of **Squam Lake.** The trailhead for an easy trek to the top is located on the right, a half mile beyond Pine Nurst Road, with parking on the left 50 yards above. This hike, appropriate for almost any age of hiker, takes you through a gnarly forest of sugar maples, oaks, and birches. (Note that the ledges on the summit are precipitous—keep a close eye on young children.) If time and energy allow, continue less than a mile on the challenging **Ridge Trail** from the summit of West Rattlesnake to **East Rattlesnake Mountain,** crossing the saddle between the two mountains.

From this elevated perch, the view of Squam Lake—and on a clear day, the view of **Lake Winnipesaukee** as well—is simply breathtaking, the kind of image that will be burned into your daydreams for months, if not for years to come. ■

Nearby

Just a few miles from the waters of Squam Lake, you'll find the **Belknap Mountain State Forest** *(From N.H. 11A, right on Belknap Mountain Rd, left on Carriage Rd. 603-271-3254. Trail closed at night; road not suitable for large vehicles).* If you have time, this 1,321-acre slice of wildlands is well worth a visit. From the trailhead on Carriage Road, a climb of 700 feet in less than 1 mile on the **Red Trail** leads you to a sweeping view of the countryside. On a clear day you can see as far as Vermont, the White Mountains of New Hampshire, and on to Maine. In the hills to the west shimmers beautiful Winnisquam Lake. Damage from the 1998 ice storm (see p. 193) is quite visible along various sections of the trail.

Bullfrog

Montshire Museum of Science

VERMONT ■ 110 acres ■ East-central Vermont, across the Connecticut River from Hanover, New Hampshire ■ Year-round ■ Walking, kayaking, canoeing, wildflower viewing, museum exhibits ■ Adm. fee ■ Contact the museum, 1 Montshire Rd., Norwich, VT 05055; phone 802-649-2200. www.montshire.net

WHEN DARTMOUTH COLLEGE decided to close its natural history museum, a determined group of area educators managed to acquire many of the collections. In a heroic effort to keep them close at hand, the educators ended up displaying these items in Hanover, New Hampshire, in the rather humble surroundings of a former bowling alley. No more. Many of these treasures, and so much more, have crossed the Connecticut River into Vermont and found a home in one of the best hands-on science museums around. Like the Vermont Institute of Natural Science in Woodstock (see p. 187), the Montshire Museum of Science has a fine network of interpretive trails crisscrossing its more than 100 acres of woodland. What's more, you'll discover that the interactive theme of the museum has been carried into the forest in some remarkably imaginative ways.

Start inside the museum, where after strolling around you can work your way to the third-floor "Tower." There an elevated outdoor walkway leads across the entrance road to a large deck on the side of a wooded hill. This platform is ringed with interpretive panels that focus on everything from nutrient cycling to why the woods are rich with flowers in early spring to what causes leaves to change colors in the fall. The museum has written guides linked to numbered posts along the trails, as well as pamphᵒlets explaining various science topics that you can take with you while you stroll the paths.

Mushroom

If you leave the far side of the deck and enter the woods you'll come to a T-intersection, with a large map of the Montshire trail system. From here you can pretty much wander at will, though you may want to take a left onto the mile-long **Ridge Trail.** At just under a half mile you'll come to an intersection with the **Hazen Trail,** which leaves Montshire property and parallels the **Connecticut River** to the town of Wilder, about a mile away. (The main attraction of the Hazen Trail—a sweeping view of the Connecticut River—comes about halfway to Wilder.)

To continue on Montshire's Ridge Trail, bear left at this intersection. The center's trail system takes you through a typical slice of upland beech-maple forest. What isn't typical are the clever ways the trail allows you to get to know the trees. In one place, for example, a rope leads from one kind of tree to another, allowing you to follow the path with your eyes closed and become familiar with individual trees by feeling their bark. Elsewhere, side paths head off to sites where you can explore everything from moss to wood frogs. Still farther down the trail are stairs leading to a small elevated platform sandwiched between four large hardwoods—a tree house of sorts—as well as a stop where you can use a hand lens to explore the strange world of tree lichens and liverworts.

The Ridge Trail will take you back toward the museum. Instead of simply heading for your car, however, just before reaching the parking area look for a short, bright little detour called the **Wildflower Trail.** This path winds past some lovely fern and moss gardens, and in spring and early summer it takes you on a pleasant walk through nice clusters of classic New England wildflowers and blooming shrubs. Once back at the museum, head past the children's play area to a backwater along the Connecticut River. From here you can either retrace your steps to the museum parking area, or continue back up to the Ridge Trail where you began the walk.

The Montshire museum is a partner in a relatively new and thoroughly ambitious project known as the **Silvio O. Conte National Fish and Wildlife Refuge,** which includes land throughout the 7.2-million-acre Connecticut River Watershed. There is an exhibit devoted to this project just inside the main entrance to the museum. Not only is this extensive refuge designed to help protect a large portion of the watershed, but its planners are working closely with cities and towns of the region to develop ways of growing without compromising the life of the river. If successful, the Silvio O. Conte National Fish and Wildlife Refuge may one day be thought of as one of the more remarkable chapters in the history of conservation partnerships.

Connecticut River

The scenes along the stretch of the Connecticut River at and above the Montshire Museum of Science are less wild than bucolic, and near Hanover even a little suburban. But in general, the roughly 6 miles of river from the unimproved Vermont State Ramp along Old Vt. 132 on the **Ompompanoosuc River** to the Lebanon Town Landing on the Connecticut River in New Hampshire, above **Wilder Dam,** is a very pleasant canoe or kayak trip. Here you'll find quiet parks and woodlands and fields, combined with classic New England townscapes, including the stately old campus of Dartmouth College. As you near the college you'll see an increasing number of people on the river training in sculls and canoes, and in the fall, actually racing; be courteous and give them a wide berth. Rentals and river access can be had in Hanover through Dartmouth's Ledyard Canoe Club *(Robinson Hall. 603-643-6709. Mid-May–mid-Oct.).*

Farther above Hanover there are many splendid flat-water to quick-water sections of the Connecticut River. If you'd like more information, consult *The Complete Boating Guide to the Connecticut River*, available through the Connecticut River Watershed Council *(1 Ferry St., East-hampton, MA 01027. 413-529-9500).* ∎

Vermont Institute of Natural Science

VERMONT ∎ 78 acres ∎ East-central Vermont, in Woodstock ∎ Daily May-Oct., Nov.-April Mon.-Sat. ∎ Hiking, walking, bird-watching ∎ Adm. fee ∎ Contact the institute, 27023 Church Hill Rd., Woodstock, VT 05091; phone 802-457-2779. www.vinsweb.org

THE VERMONT INSTITUTE OF NATURAL SCIENCE (also known as VINS) is a stellar example of the kind of vibrant organization that thrives in New England. Around its main office, located outside the beautiful village of Woodstock, you'll find acres of grounds dappled with marsh and woods, much of it crisscrossed by nature trails. Programming includes more top-notch hikes, talks, and programs than you can shake a walking stick at; in short, VINS should be on every nature lover's list of must-see places. A prime attraction is the Vermont Raptor Center, a clinic and school where wildlife rehabilitators treat and release injured eagles, hawks, owls, and falcons; permanently disabled birds often become part of education pro-grams for schools and community groups.

Call ahead to find out what's coming up, especially since some of the outings are by reservation *(fee)*. Even arriving on a whim, you may see birds being banded, and you can tour the raptor center as well as walk the institute's self-guided interpretive trails. What you learn at VINS will do much to light the landscape in your travels through New England. ∎

John Hay National Wildlife Refuge

NEW HAMPSHIRE ■ 164 acres ■ West-central New Hampshire, 2 miles north of Newbury on N.H. 103A ■ Year-round ■ Hiking, wildlife viewing ■ Adm. fee ■ Contact the refuge, P.O. Box 276, Newbury, NH 03255; phone 603-763-4789. www.thefells.org

THIS ENCHANTING SLICE of the **Sunapee Lake** shoreline includes the former summerhouse and grounds of John Hay, who was Abraham Lincoln's secretary and ambassador to Great Britain as well as secretary of state under Presidents William McKinley and Theodore Roosevelt—and was also a talented poet and essayist. Hay's grandson, John, who had the good fortune to spend summers here as a child, went on to become one of New England's most notable naturalists and authors. The self-

Sunapee Lake, John Hay National Wildlife Refuge

guided **John Hay II Forest Ecology Trail,** which includes nearly half a mile of walking along Sunapee Lake, was created to honor the younger Hay. This path offers one of the best opportunities in the area to understand the transitional woodlands typical of this part of New Hampshire —a region of the state where southern hardwoods meet and mix with members of the northern boreal forest.

The focus here is on a portion of the preserve known as **The Fells,** so-called by the Hay family because of the land's similarity to the rolling upland pastures of England that have long worn that name. From the parking area and visitor center at the entrance, a quarter-mile-long road *(closed to all vehicles except shuttle buses)* leads through the woods to the main house, today rimmed by several gardens containing perennials, shrub roses, even a rock garden with a surprising variety of alpine plants. The **Hay House** remains open to visitors on weekends and holidays from

Memorial Day to Columbus Day. It is also the setting for a variety of nature classes, including some excellent conservation-related offerings by those stalwart champions of New Hampshire's natural resources, the Society for the Protection of New Hampshire Forests.

The John Hay II Forest Ecology Trail takes off next to the rock garden; an interpretive guide is pegged to numbered stops along the mile-long path. Among the trees on this walk are runs of white, or paper, birch as well as scattered clumps of red spruce, a tree most at home in cooler climates well to the north. You'll also see some fine white pines—the tree that King George of England tried so hard to keep out of the hands of the colonists, wanting them held in reserve as mast trees for his majesty's Royal Navy. Rounding out the mix are hemlock, beech, striped maple, aspen, sugar maple, red maple, and yellow birch. While not an old-growth forest per se, there are definitely a few old-timers at The Fells. Some of the sugar maples here probably started growing around the time of the Civil War; one of the hemlocks at interpretive stop 18 along the shores of Sunapee Lake is older still, possibly having poked its head out of the dirt before the Pilgrims first set foot on the beaches of Massachusetts.

Despite having roughly 1,100 homes along 30 miles of shoreline, as well as being the drainage for the runoff of six towns spread across 55 square miles, Sunapee Lake continues to be one of the cleanest large lakes in New England. That's no accident. The fact that people still refer to Sunapee as one of the jewels of New Hampshire is thanks in large part to the dogged efforts of the hundred-year-old Lake Sunapee Protective Association, which supports everything from volunteer water-quality monitoring efforts to shoreland protection ordinances.

Sunset Hill

If you have a little extra time, before leaving The Fells walk from the parking lot across N.H. 103A to a trail that takes you for roughly 1 mile to the top of Sunset Hill. Along the way you'll be passing through a forest of beeches, the nuts of which are an important food source to local black bears, just as they once were to great flocks of the now extinct passenger pigeon. The cracks you see in the smooth gray bark of the beech tree are due to a fungus spread by an insect known as the beech scale. The seriousness of this blight remains to be seen, but a similar fungal blight went through the beech forests of northern New England in the early part of the 20th century. By the time that disease had run its course, nearly a quarter of all the beech trees in that region had been destroyed.

Atop 1,841-foot-high Sunset Hill is a cluster of granite ledges, exposed by erosion after heavy sheep grazing during the late 1800s. To the west are wonderful views of Sunapee Lake, and beyond that, graceful Mount Sunapee, a remnant of erosion-resistant bedrock that geologists refer to as a monadnock. In addition to being a choice spot for catching the setting sun, Sunset Hill is spectacular in autumn, when Sunapee's woodlands are bedecked in color. ∎

Treetop view of the Harris Center

Harris Center

NEW HAMPSHIRE ■ 9,000 acres ■ Southwest New Hampshire, 20 miles east of Keene off N.H. 123 ■ Year-round ■ Hiking, guided walks, orienteering, canoeing, bird-watching, wildflower viewing ■ Contact the center, 341 King's Hwy., Hancock, NH 03449; phone 603-525-3394. www.harriscenter.org

NO MATTER WHAT YOUR AGE OR INTEREST, in few places is it easier to find hands-on opportunities to unlock the mysteries of the natural world —from birdlife to animal tracks, edible plants to pond ecology—than in rural New England. The Harris Center offers just these sorts of opportunities. Founded in 1970 by Eleanor Briggs and friends, who managed to buy back from developers the land that once held Eleanor's grandparents' vacation home, the Harris Center has become one of the finest nature centers in the region. (Harris, by the way, was the name of Eleanor's cat.) Much of the energy of the Harris Center is focused on programs for schoolchildren; in a typical year the center offers hands-on science experiences to some 4,000 grade-school and high-school students. However, there's also a full slate of outdoor activities open to adults and families. For instance, at the center you can try out orienteering, climbs of **Mount Pisgah,** canoeing trips on the **Tully River,** bird surveys, journeys to bat caves, or hikes in the **Wildcat Hollow Wilderness.** If you know ahead of time that your travels will take you close to southwest New Hampshire, give the center a call and see about signing up for any of the dozens of activities that are offered year-round throughout New Hampshire and eastern Vermont.

Alarmed by the feverish pace of development during the mid-1980s, the Harris Center helped to launch a remarkable grassroots effort to create what they call a regional wildlife supersanctuary. With help from many donors and partner organizations, the regional sanctuary has now grown to a patchwork of about 9,000 acres—the majority of it on private lands—thoughtfully stitched together to provide the kinds of corridors and natural habitats many native animals need if they are to survive in the face of expanding development. Besides being critical to far-ranging

Striped maple, Harris Center

species like bobcat, bear, and moose, these clustered woodland spaces are also proving an important habitat for a number of migratory song-birds, including the black-throated blue warbler, Canada warbler, and blackburnian warbler.

What to See and Do

Even if you don't have time to take part in an organized trek, you might enjoy a spur-of-the-moment stop to explore some of the trails commonly used in Harris Center activities. Particularly engaging is the modest 4-mile round-trip hike to **Skatutakee Mountain,** which rises through a varied mix of hemlock, sugar maple, white pine, and red spruce to a blueberry-covered summit (best picking is early August). The trail offers fabulous views of

Crotched, Pack Monadnock, and **Monadnock** mountains. Try the wonderful loop walk that leads up the mountain on the **Harriskat Trail** (marked with white rectangles that are painted onto the trees), then descends on the **Thumbs Up Trail,** finally making a right turn back toward the parking lot via the **Thumbs Down Trail.**

In addition to glorious views, this walk offers incredible variety, especially on the back side of Skatutakee Mountain. Shortly after leaving the summit and meeting the Thumbs Up Trail, the path enters an absolute fantasy garden of bunchberry, club moss and ferns, with enormous boulders (glacial erratics) and handfuls of wildflowers scattered along the trail at nearly every bend. This short section, as much as any other trail within 100 miles of here, reveals the kind of unexpected magic to be found in these out-of-the-way pockets of the New England forest.

In the moist, shady parts of this walk, scan the brushy areas for a tiny brown bird with a buff-colored chest. This is a type of thrush known as a veery. While veeries can be hard to spot, there's no missing their song—a sweet, flutey downward spiral that can stop hikers in their tracks. In the fall the veery migrates all the way to South America, traveling mostly at night, using sharp whistles to keep in touch with the rest of the flock.

Lower down you'll pass **Jocks Pond,** its shore lined with stately beeches and white pines, clusters of hobblebush and Indian cucumber growing nearby. This latter plant —recognizable by the whorl of five to nine leaves on the stem and a greenish flower that looks like a large spider—was prized by Native Americans of the area, who used the root both as a medicine and as a source of food. (It does indeed smell and taste somewhat like a cucumber.)

Canoeing

You'll find excellent flat-water canoeing and kayaking at **Spoon-wood Pond,** within a 15-minute drive of the Harris Center (*King's*

Hwy. to N.H. 123, then to Hancock Town Landing at Nubanusit Lake. Canoe rentals at the center). Paddle north (to your right, as you stand at the dock looking at the lake) for roughly 2 miles until you reach a dam—this is the outlet of Spoon-wood Pond. Portage around the dam and continue paddling on into the pond. It's a restful and surprisingly clear body of water, free of both motorized boats and onshore development. Nearby **Willard Pond** also provides enjoyable canoeing. To reach it, drive to the **dePierrefeu-Willard Pond Wildlife Sanctuary** (*N.H. 123 to Willard Pond Rd. 603-224-9909. www.nhaudubon.org*), managed by the Audubon Society. ∎

The Ice Storm of 1998

In early January 1998, a series of slow-moving, back-to-back storms rolled across parts of New England, New York, and eastern Canada, producing large amounts of freezing rain. By the time the storms had passed, much of the region was trapped in up to 3 inches of ice. This ice storm, followed by cold weather, snow, and wind, turned out to be the worst one in New England's history. In all, the ice damaged 18 million acres of forest. Estimated long-term economic losses were more than one billion dollars. As you hike in New England, you'll still see evidence of this storm. You'll also see how forests begin to recover after such a calamity.

Mount Monadnock

NEW HAMPSHIRE ■ 5,000 acres ■ Southwest New Hampshire, off N.H. 124 near Jaffrey via Upper Jaffrey Rd. ■ Year-round ■ Camping, hiking ■ Adm. fee; camping fee ■ No pets ■ Contact Monadnock State Park, P.O. Box 181, Jaffrey, NH 03452; phone 603-532-8862. www.nhparks.state.nh.us

MOVE OVER MOUNT GREYLOCK and Cadillac Mountain. Scoot over, Katahdin and Washington. Recent numbers suggest that there is per-haps no other peak in New England—in fact, few other peaks in the world—with more hikers trudging to the top than Mount Monadnock (officially, Grand Monadnock). You may never meet a more loyal group of local climbers than those who make their way up and down this mountain; one party of 80-year-old men has been rendezvousing weekly near the summit for more than a decade. These gents are in good company. Monadnock was also the favorite mountain of some impressive nature gourmands, including Ralph Waldo Emerson and Henry David Thoreau. Many local farmers, on the other hand, regarded the upper mountain as worthless, since it was unfit for grazing. Those attitudes shifted a bit when the area began to be more popular with tourists. By the 1820s the town of Jaffrey was pleased to find itself having to license "fountains of rejuvenation" where alcohol was sold. The fountains soon became a line of shanties stretching from the high-way all the way to the summit.

For the Algonquian tribes that once inhabited this area, the name "monadnock" meant greatest, or unrivaled, mountain. In modern times, it has gained a more earthbound meaning. As a geological term, it refers to a mountain fashioned of erosion-resistant bedrock, tough enough to withstand the forces that long ago leveled its neighbors. From the top of 3,165-foot Mount Monadnock—which was designated a national natural landmark in 1987—you can spot two smaller monadnocks: **Pack Monadnock** to the east, and **Wachusett Mountain** to the south in northern Massachusetts.

If you come to this mountain on a clear day, you'll have the opportunity to sample scenery from all six New England states. Happily, there is no road to the top of Mount Monadnock; some 20 miles of trails surround the peak, most on its southern flank, where they depart from **Monadnock State Park** *(603-532-8862)*. If this is your first time in the area, these southern routes are a good choice. They will give you a chance—ideally before your climb—to stroll through the park's **Ecocenter,** which has a collection of displays that shows you're about to climb not just a moun-tain, but a piece of American history.

The **White Cross Trail** is a good choice for your first time up, being slightly less steep and more varied than the nearby **White Dot.** At 4.5 miles long and with elevation gains of 1,900 feet, trails like the White Cross are hardly a walk in the park, yet tens of thousands of people of all

Mist on Mount Monadnock

ages climb Mount Monadnock every year; for children especially the mountain's rock-bound summit is a fantastic place for exploration. If you want to try a less used and significantly longer trek, you could do no better than the 9-mile round-trip on the **Pumpelly Trail,** which begins about 12 miles east of Keene, near Dublin Lake. *(N.H. 101 to Lake Rd. Trail begins at SE corner of Dublin Lake. Parking is limited.)*

No matter how you reach the top, Monadnock offers a number of fine opportunities to see the variety of habitats that can exist on a single mountain. Near the base you'll encounter a forest of red oak, sugar maple, yellow birch, and white ash—some of the main players in New England's fall color show—but by the summit the trees have grown small, stunted by the poor soils of the higher elevations. Above 2,500 feet, for example, the red spruce may be no higher than your chest. Nevertheless, all around you will be a wealth of mountaintop survivors, including chokecherry, rhodora, mountain cranberry, and winterberry.

Although today the summit of Monadnock is bare, before 1800 it was covered in a bristly growth of mature spruces. Some of these burned in a fire, while others were taken out by a hurricane in 1815. Much of the remaining vegetation burned, according to local lore, when the summit was set on fire to drive out wolves that were taking refuge there and making nightly raids on sheep farms below. With that fire came not only the end of the trees, but of the soil that held them. (While there is no record of a healthy wolf ever having attacked a human, they were thoroughly despised in this region, as elsewhere. One history of Jaffrey reports the killing of the last wolf on Mount Monadnock in 1820. The creature was reputedly a thoroughly demonic fellow that "drank the sheep's blood and tasted only the best parts.") ■

Hiker, Mount. Monadnock

Hemlocks, Pisgah State Park

Pisgah State Park

NEW HAMPSHIRE ■ 13,421 acres ■ Southwest New Hampshire, 13 miles south of Keene off N.H. 10 ■ Year-round. Visitor center is staffed by volunteers and operates on an irregular schedule ■ Hiking, guided walks, canoeing, mountain biking, bird-watching ■ Contact the park, P.O. Box 242, Winchester, NH 03470; phone 603-239-8153. www.nhparks.state.nh.us

DESPITE THE FACT THAT Pisgah State Park is the largest tract of undeveloped land in southern New Hampshire, incorporating an entire watershed that empties into the beautiful **Ashuelot River,** most travelers bypass it altogether, aiming instead for the high peaks of the White Mountains. What they miss is a medley of forest and stream, cut by a considerable web of trails and roads, many suitable for travel by mountain bike.

A new visitor center, located on Old Chesterfield Road, will help you get oriented, which is a very good idea given the size of the park and the number of unmarked and unmaintained roads. The visitor center is also the central place for a variety of good, if somewhat irregular interpretive activities, including mushroom walks, geology explorations, classes on wild edible foods, bird-watching expeditions, and canoe trips on **Pisgah Reservoir.** Pisgah, happily, is a rather rough and ready park—its trails and roads can occasionally be flooded by beaver dams—so be prepared and keep your hiking plans flexible. Before you set out into its interior, check with the park office for current conditions in the area and look for park maps at information boards and at the main trailheads.

What to See and Do

You'll find great hiking and biking in the state park, some of it departing immediately from the visitor center.

Biking

Though the road from the visitor center north to **Fullam Pond** is typically open to vehicles, it makes a great 40-minute ride on a mountain bike, the route lined in striped maple, hemlock, gray and yellow birch, and witch hazel. For a much longer ride of roughly 21 miles, a good trek for advanced riders, continue north past the west side of Fullam Pond on Old Chesterfield Road to the north end of the park, where at a Y-intersection you'll veer right, exiting at a parking area on Horseshoe Road. From the parking lot, you'll leave the park, riding on local roads for the next 12 miles. Follow Horseshoe Road

Hale Pond, Pisgah State Park

to Old Chesterfield Road (note that this is a different Old Chesterfield Road from the one on your previous route) and turn right. Make another right in under 3 miles onto Tuttle Road, then right again on Old Swanzey Road. Next you'll pass the intersection with Zinn Road, which takes off to the left; stay right, and proceed for roughly 1.5 miles, turning right on an unmarked road with a wooden sign pointing to Pisgah.

This rather rough track will take you south to the park boundary, where you'll pick up Beal's Road. Follow this west (it becomes the **Fullam Pond Trail**) to the **Nash Trail,** and turn left. Follow this back to the dirt road you started on, at a point roughly 3 miles north of the visitor center.

Hiking

The western third of the preserve is a hiker's delight. Start near **Kilburn Pond** (*N.H. 63 S of Chesterfield to Kilburn Rd.*). The orange-blazed **Pisgah Ridge Trail** leading away from the gate near the highway is the walking road of our dreams: quiet, rich, with a lovely weave of hemlock, mountain maple, red oak, beech, and birch. At about 0.7 mile, at the bottom of a small hill, is the **Kilburn Loop Trail,** taking off to the right and leading around Kilburn Pond. A wonderful walk, full of the mysteries of wet places, it returns to the main trail a short distance to the east and makes a fine addition to a climb of **Mount Pisgah.** The main trail is also the place to see a number of young sprouts of the American chestnut, once among the most common

Chestnut Blight
About the time an American chestnut tree reaches 10 to 20 feet in height, a fungus (*Endothia parasitica*) begins girdling its trunk, blocking the flow of water and nutrients and killing the tree. Today, nearly a hundred years after the blight reached North America from Asia, there is still no cure. A few chestnuts have survived, apparently by encapsulating the fungus so it can't spread around the tree. Scientists are crossbreeding these trees with Chinese chestnuts in hopes of creating a resistant strain that can re-enter the wild.

trees in the country. Within its vast range, one out of four trees once was a chestnut. But the species fell victim to an Asian fungus that arrived in 1904. By 1950, the fungus, spread by a native beetle, had killed nearly every canopy chestnut in New England. Any young trees you might see today are sprouts from the root crown collars of fallen trees, but even these are affected by the blight and rarely reach reproduction age.

At a point roughly 2 miles along the trail, near the summit of Pisgah, a series of ledges offers wonderful views: **Bear Mountain** to the west and, to the east, the main portion of the park, cradled in wave after wave of timber. This is a grand spot for sitting and feeding your imagination —and if it's July, your stomach as well, on a feast of blueberries. ∎

Rhododendron State Park

NEW HAMPSHIRE ■ 2,725 acres ■ Southwest New Hampshire, 25 miles southeast of Keene off N.H. 119 ■ Daily mid-June–Labor Day, weekends mid-May–mid-June, closed rest of year. Flowers blossom mid-July ■ Walking, wild-flower viewing ■ Contact the park, P.O. Box 181, Jaffrey, NH 03452; phone 603-532-8862. www.nhparks.state.nh.us

In the southern Appalachians, rhododendrons often form enormous, far-reaching thickets that can snare the off-trail hiker. This far north, however, the plants grow mostly in isolated patches. At the Rhododendron State Park, the 0.6-mile-long trail through what is the largest patch of wild-growing rhododendron in New England thus is absolutely idyllic. In places the branches entwine overhead and in mid-July form long, quiet tunnels of white blossoms.

Even when the rhododendrons aren't blooming this is a wonderful walk, thanks not only to fine stands of white pine, yellow birch, hemlock and maple, but also to a fine little side loop called the **Wildflower Trail,** where a number of plants have been identified. This is an exceptionally good opportunity to learn some of the most common ground plants in southern New England, including foamflower, shinleaf, princes pine, lady's slipper, Solomon's seal, bleeding heart, bluebead lily, Indian cucumber, wild sarsaparilla, Canada mayflower, hobblebush, jack-in-the-pulpit, partridgeberry, white wood aster, and New York fern. For those looking for a heartier trek, note that the **Little Monadnock Trail** joins this nature path about 0.4 mile into the walk, and will in 1.1 miles carry you to the 1,883-foot peak of that fine climb.

Rhododendrons

The leaves and flowers of all 23 North American species of rhododendron are poisonous, but this did not keep the plants from becoming prized possessions for enthusiasts around the world. During the 1700s, botanists sent cuttings of American rhododendrons back to Europe for planting in major gardens. When various Asian species came along, the American species fell out of favor in Europe, but remain a favorite in yards and gardens throughout eastern America.

The beautiful old house you might have noticed on the way in is known as the **Old Patch Place**, named for Revolutionary war veteran Capt. Samuel Patch, who built it in the late 1790s. In later years the house and surrounding land passed through a number of owners, and in 1901 the title passed to Levi Fuller, a sawmill owner who planned to launch a logging operation here. It was then that botanist Mare Lee Ware stepped in. In 1903 she was able to purchase the original 300-acre tract, which she sold to the Appalachian Mountain Club for the grand sum of $1.00. Her only stipulation was that the area around the rhododendrons be protected and stay forever open to the public. ■

Flat-water canoeing

Mount Toby State Demonstration Forest

MASSACHUSETTS ■ 755 acres ■ North-central Massachusetts, 6 miles south of Millers Falls off Mass. 63 ■ Year-round ■ Hiking, walking, kayaking, canoeing ■ Contact the Department of Natural Resources Management, University of Massachusetts, Amherst, MA 01003; phone 413-545-2665

THERE IS NO INTERPRETATION on **Mount Toby.** There are no interpretive signs or brochures, no naturalists to bring the woods alive with awe-inspiring stories of snakes and spiders and salamanders. Not even the trail junctions are marked with signs. Nevertheless, Mount Toby contains one of the most interesting, diverse forests in all of Massachusetts, and that's saying a lot. The modest climb on an old carriage road, not to mention a lazy float in **Cranberry Pond,** are the kinds of outings you wish for when the chaos of the office or the rumble of traffic starts to weigh you down. Whether you come here for the chance to bone up on your knowledge of trees, or just to walk away the blues, Toby will remind you just how enchanting a forest can be.

If you're inclined to climb to the summit of Mount Toby (though be forewarned, there really isn't much of a view), a good route is a roughly 5-mile round-trip hike via an old carriage road marked with blue blazes. The woods along this route, much of which is managed by the University of Massachusetts Department of Natural Resources Management, are simply incredible. The forest is old enough to have been pruned of its lower branches, and thus offers deep views into wonderful stands of red oak and white pine, as well as into black birch, sugar maple, beech, white oak, striped maple, and paper birch.

If you happen to have a canoe or kayak with you, you can have a splendid little outing by paddling around Cranberry Pond, keeping an eye out for a fine mix of birdlife. Then beach the canoe on the west shore and follow any of several spur trails that run from the pond to the blue-blazed walking road described above. Walk up the road for a way and breathe in all the delights of this exquisite woodland. ■

Boating on the Connecticut River, Northfield Mountain REC

Northfield Mountain Recreation and Environmental Center

MASSACHUSETTS ■ 2,000 acres ■ North-central Massachusetts, 15 miles east of Greenfield on Mass. 63 ■ Daily Dec.-April, Wed.-Sun. May-Nov. ■ Camping, hiking, guided walks, orienteering, boating, canoeing, mountain biking, cross-country skiing, bird-watching, wildflower viewing ■ Fees for camping, skiing, and rentals ■ Contact the center, 99 Millers Falls Rd., Northfield, MA 01360; phone 413-659-3714 or 800-859-2960. www.nu.com/Northfield

BUT FOR A FEW POWER-LINE CORRIDORS, you could almost forget that Northfield Mountain is first and foremost a power facility, pumping water from the **Connecticut River** into a 300-acre reservoir high above. There it is released into a generating plant hidden in the mountain. What you're more likely to notice are the 25 miles of well-maintained trails open to hikers, mountain bikers, and skiers, not to mention the availability of an orienteering course, canoe rentals, and drive-in and paddle-in campgrounds. Furthermore, the center boasts a lineup of outdoor programs ranging from canoeing courses and identifying edible plants to wildflower and wildlife walks, bat-watching, stargazing, blueberry hikes, and eagle-watching. The Northfield Mountain power station had to provide these recreational facilities as part of a deal with the Federal Energy Regulatory Commission in order to be licensed, but it would be hard to deny that they've gone the extra mile.

If, as a hiker, the thought of power-line corridors bothers you, Northfield Mountain can still serve as a good place for securing canoe shuttles and equipment, as well as for heading out with biologists and other experts to learn more about the environment of southern New England. For families with kids, the mile-long **Hidden Quarry Nature Trail,** which has 15 interpretive stops, is worth a try. If you want a longer walk, try the upper **Rose Ledge Foot Trail,** which has an abundance of birdlife. Finally, this is a good area for mountain biking. However, as some of the routes are on grassy lanes, be careful if you are riding in wet weather.

Boating

Northfield Mountain offers canoe rentals *(413-863-9300. Reservations required)* as well as a shuttle service to three drop points 5.5, 14, and 20 miles upriver. You can also rent canoes and camping gear from Eastern Mountain Sports *(413-584-3554)* in Hadley. Canoeists may want to try out the **Connecticut River Water Trail,** part of the **Connecticut River Greenway State Park** *(413-586-8706)*. This route takes you along a 12-mile segment of the Connecticut River from Turners Falls to Hatfield.

By the time the Connecticut River reaches the Northfield area, it has run just over 200 miles. Whereas at its headwaters it was 2,551 feet above sea level, here it is barely 200 feet. In this flatter terrain the river looks more subdued, meandering through the landscape in wide, graceful curves. Soon after leaving Northfield it passes through French King Gorge and then briefly flows to the northwest—the only such change in direction along the river's entire 409-mile length. ∎

Finding the Animals

The forested environs of Northfield Mountain provide sustenance for a wide variety of creatures. Wildlife-watchers should consider participating in the plant interpretive activities here, since knowing the plants is the first step in knowing where to find the animals. Grouse and woodcocks, for instance, are fond of the seeds of cinquefoil, while muskrat can often be found among fragrant water lilies. Pheasants like wild carrots and partridgeberries, while many songbirds are attracted to the seeds of various asters.

Harvard Forest

MASSACHUSETTS ■ 3,000 acres ■ Central Massachusetts, 3 miles north of Petersham on Mass. 32 ■ Year-round ■ Hiking, walking ■ Contact the forest, P.O. Box 65, Petersham, MA 01366; phone **978-724-3302.** www.lternet.edu/hfr/mus.html.

WHEN IT COMES TO the natural history of the woods, Harvard Forest is one of the best educational experiences in the country. Invest an afternoon here, in the oldest continuously studied ecosystem in America, and you may never look at the forests of New England in the same way again.

The ideal visit to Harvard Forest would include a couple of hours in the **Fisher Museum** *(Closed weekends Nov.-April),* which features some intriguing forest history. In the lower level, an outstanding series of dioramas portrays the evolution of the New England landscape (audio-tape guide available). Follow this with a 1.5-mile walk on the **Black Gum Trail,** guided by a somewhat eclectic interpretive brochure, and then, if time allows, walk the 0.75-mile-long **John Sanderson Farm Trail.** Both trails take off from behind the museum.

The land containing the Harvard Forest was given to the university in 1907 and has since nearly doubled in size to 3,000 acres. Throughout its long history, the forest has been a place for research into the biology and historical use of the New England woods. In 1988 the National Science Foundation chose Harvard Forest as one of 17 sites across the country that would participate in its Long Term Ecological Research Program. After more than 80 years of intense research here—much of it based on an ecosystem approach, long before ecosystems were cool—scientists are beginning to knit together ideas about the effect of human activities on

the environment. Indeed, if there is a theme to the Harvard research facility, it is the attempt to better understand the relationship between human activity, environmental change, and natural disturbances. In one fascinating experiment, researchers simulated the blow-down of a hurricane in one section of the forest, toppling trees in a single direction as if driven down by the winds. In another area, they simulated human activity, most notably the effects of acid rain and global warming. The results strongly suggest that forests may be far more stressed by human-initiated events, such as pollution, than they are from natural ones. ■

Harvard Forest

Sunset, Mount Greylock

Greenfield to Mount Greylock Drive

MASSACHUSETTS ■ 40 miles ■ Northwest Massachusetts, west from Greenfield along Mass. 2 ■ Spring-fall. Notch Road closed mid-Oct.–mid-May ■ Camping, hiking, walking, guided walks, boating, kayaking, fishing, bird-watching, wildlife viewing, wildflower viewing ■ Contact the information center in Shelburne Falls, 75 Bridge St., Shelburne Falls, MA 01370; phone 413-625-2544. www.shelburnefalls.com

IF YOU STOOD ACROSS THE ROOM and tossed a dart at a map of western Massachusetts, chances are it would land on a place rich with natural beauty. Along this route, spanning 40 miles of roadway, you'll find more than enough to keep you busy for several days: running rivers, bird-watching, exploring old-growth forests, and scrambling around on the top of one of the most famous peaks in all of New England. Greenfield, starting point for the drive, lies in the Pioneer Valley at the intersection of I-91 and Mass.2. Eons ago, the valley floor was the bed of glacial Lake

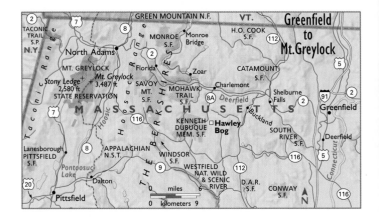

Hitchcock, which left rich sedimentary deposits—ideal soil for growing crops. Draining through this ancient deposit, the Connecticut River, and its tributaries the Deerfield, the Green, and the Falls, fostered Atlantic salmon and shad and brown and rainbow trout. Thus naturally blessed, the valley was coveted—and fought over—by all who came to know it. Indeed, Mass. 2 parallels the historic Mohawk Trail, thought to have been blazed during the 1600s not by the Mohawk for which it is named but by the Pocumtuck of the Connecticut River Valley. The Pocumtuck forged this passage to what is now extreme eastern New York State to gain access to their arch enemies, the Mohawk. Caught in the middle were the Dutch, who after much effort managed to get the two nations to agree to a treaty. Unfortunately, even as Mohawk Prince Saheda was traveling along the trail to put his mark on the agreement, he was murdered by Pocumtuck warriors. The Mohawk, fueled by rage, came east en masse and for all practical purposes destroyed the Pocumtuck Nation.

Over time the Mohawk Trail became an increasingly popular route among European travelers, who used it to reach the Hudson River. An effort is underway to establish a multiuse trail that will parallel the original route as closely as possible, stretching 100 miles from the Connecticut River to the Hudson. Portions are already completed, including a fine 8.25-mile section between Deerfield and Shelburne. Maps are available from the village information center in Shelburne Falls.

As you head west on Mass. 2 from Greenfield, the road offers just the right amount of twists and gallop, all framed by a sweet crumple of wooded hills. In 11 miles you'll come to Shelburne Falls, a town noted for its "Bridge of Flowers." In 1929 a 400-foot-long former trolley bridge across the Deerfield River was transformed into a stunning flower garden. Today the bridge is tended by the Shelburne Falls Women's Club, which manages more than 500 varieties of plantings, assuring blooms of one sort or another for much of the year, from tulips in spring to chrysanthemums in the fall.

A few hundred yards down the river from the bridge, just below a

Deerfield River

A sight that's likely to ignite a boater's fancy along this drive is the Deerfield River, fast-dancing its way from the Hoosac Range to the Connecticut River. The most frequently boated part of the Deerfield is a 17-mile free-flowing section from Fife Brook Dam in the town of Florida to the No. 4 Dam in Buckland. It's a splendid stretch of Class II to Class III white water, rife with herons and hawks, eagles and ospreys, as well as enough trout to keep those with fly rods happy for hours on end. Another stretch known as the Monroe Bridge Dryway, near the town of Monroe Bridge, is Class II to Class IV and is available for boating following special dam releases 32 days of the year.

Like many New England rivers, the Deerfield is a place where boating is closely tied to controlled water releases from upstream dams. In 1993 the New England Power Company (now Pacific Gas and Electric) and a coalition of white-water boating groups came up with a plan that provided for more than a hundred days a year of scheduled water releases on the lower Deerfield. (You'll notice the yellow and black traffic signs warning fishermen of sudden dangerous changes in water levels.) Before the scheduled releases, the river's unpredictable water levels kept the average number of "user days" to only 200 a year. Since the 1993 agreement, good white water is available throughout the summer, and user days have increased to 35,000 per year— including 17,000 by commercial rafters. *(For the current release schedule contact the Flow Phone 888-356-3663. www.kayak.com/kayak/schedule.html)*

Although on peak days the water will be full of rafters and kayakers, the Deerfield's banks are unmarred by development. You'll find the river itself has kept its wild and remote character.

White-water kayaking, Deerfield River

Following pages: Sunset view, Mount Greylock

Hiker and dog, Mohawk Trail State Forest

small hydroelectric facility, is one of the most intriguing geological areas in New England. Here in the granite river bed lie more than 50 potholes, ranging from 6 inches to more than 12 yards in diameter. The holes were scoured into the marbled, multi-colored rock by the action of whirling stones during high water at the end of the last glacial age. The resulting jumble of circular cups and slots and chasms is truly fascinating, making this a highly popular site for visiting geology students.

Hawley Bog

Continuing west on Mass.2, just past the town of Charlemont, you'll find Mass. 8A on your left, with a sign for Windsor and Hawley. What the sign doesn't reveal is that this is the way to **Hawley Bog** *(contact the Nature Conservancy. 617-423-2545)*, which used to be known as Cranberry Bog. Stay on Mass. 8A until it crosses the Deerfield River and then a set of railroad tracks. At the T-intersection bear left (do not follow Mass. 8A). In just over 0.1 mile, take a right on East Hawley Road; you'll reach the trailhead for Hawley Bog in 4 miles. The tiny parking area is on the right (look for a white rock with a bronze plaque marking the first Church of Hawley). This area is a fragile place, so if there isn't enough room to park, save your visit for another day.

Two trails depart from here: The one on the left, marked by an orange Nature Conservancy sign, leads to Hawley Bog; the other path, to the right, leads into the Kenneth Dubuque Memorial State Forest (see below).

Hawley Bog is one of the highest acid bogs in the state. It was most likely formed from a small stream that was blocked long ago, creating a small lake. From that point, low temperatures and short growing seasons helped set the stage for what you see today—a virtual garden of cranberry, Labrador tea, bladderworts, rose pogonias, round-leaf sundew, and pitcher plants. Around the edges of the bog are wet to moist areas, sporting fringed orchids, irises, mountain laurel, and hemlock.

After walking less than a half mile of dirt pathway, past an interesting interpretive display, you'll find a boardwalk out into the bog itself (please stay on the walkway). From here you can get a sense not only of the smell and feel of the place, but also of the fact that in a very short space several communities merge, each with its own unique requirements for life. On one side of the bog is a spruce forest, rising behind a line of bog laurel, leatherleaf, rosemary, and various other shrubs; on the other side are stands of red maples. You're also likely to see flagging, string and other markings next to the boardwalk—testimony to the fact that Hawley Bog is a hands-on learning site for students from five colleges in the region, who investigate such things as the interactions between the carnivorous pitcher plant and its insect dinner.

By taking the right-hand trail from the same parking lot, you can walk a system of old roadways through a beautiful slice of the **Kenneth Dubuque Memorial State Forest** *(4 miles W of Charlemont. 413-339-5504)*. This is a wonderland of woods, including yellow and white birch, red oak, sugar maple, hemlock, black cherry, beech, and moosewood.

There are plenty of stone fences and old foundation holes to poke around, remains of a rather sizable community that once existed here. This is also a perfect place to see and hear wood frogs, green frogs, and spring peepers. While you're nosing about for frogs, notice the beech trees with parallel scars on their trunks—claw marks from black bears. Other beeches may show a twisted, jumbled growth where bears have sat in a fork and pulled limbs full of nuts toward them, breaking off the branches in the process.

Mohawk Trail State Forest

After making your way back out to Mass. 2 and continuing west, your next best chance to soak up the outdoors comes in a couple of miles at beautiful **Mohawk Trail State Forest** (Charlemont. 413-339-5504. www.state.ma.us). The forest offers picnicking, camping, and thoroughly wonderful walking. You can put together a fine 3.5-mile-long trek by parking your car outside the campground entrance station and following the signs for the group camping area. Along the way you'll pass a boulevard of majestic white pines, interspersed with hemlocks and laurels. You'll also encounter the occasional maple, beech, and yellow birch. If you look carefully, you may also see the remains of broken pines and hemlocks here—victims of a thunderstorm's microburst that exploded overhead in 1988, snapping even the biggest trees.

A short distance past a faint road taking off to the left, make a left turn onto the forest nature trail, which is marked by either white or blue blazes. From here the walk becomes a lazy amble—first through a delightful mix of forest, fern, and club moss, then onto a small road leading into a meadow busy with hawkweed, pokeweed, milkweed, and yarrow. Bluebirds and song sparrows are in abundance here, the sparrows dancing between the edge of the forest and their grassy feeding areas.

Though not marked by trails, this meadow is framed by huge white pines on one side and the state's largest maple in another. (Mohawk is in general one of the best places in the state to see big trees; driving west again on a climbing portion of Mass. 2, you'll see off to your left hundreds of big white pines, although they are

Song Sparrows

There are few bird species as widely distributed—or as physically variable across its range—as the little song sparrow. The species is found from the Aleutian Islands off the coast of Alaska all the way to central Mexico, and in the East from Florida to Maine. When males first arrive on the breeding grounds, the air is thick with their flutey, warbling song. The male meets challenges from other males with a noticeable puffing out of feathers, sometimes a raising of the wings, and lots and lots of singing. If you're here when young are on the nest, which is often built right on the ground, count on the crafty song sparrow to go out of its way to avoid giving you any sign of where it has made its home.

rather inaccessible in a jumble of steep ravines.) After reaching the end of the first meadow, the path winds into the woods again, then enters yet another meadow down below. At the far side of this second clearing, the route veers right to join the Deerfield River. A short distance beyond the grave of Revolutionary War soldier John Wheeler and his wife Susannah is a Y-intersection, where you'll turn right, moving yet again through the shadows of forest back to the parking area.

Mount Greylock State Reservation

Continue driving west on Mass. 2 from Mohawk Trail State Forest to the town of North Adams. Just over a mile west of downtown, Notch Road will be on your left heading south. Follow this road for roughly 9 miles into the **Mount Greylock State Reservation** (*50 Rockwell Rd., Lanesborouogh. 413-499-4262. www.state.ma.us/dem/forparks.htm. Limited road access Nov.–early May*).

For much of your climb through the reservation, the land will be a portrait of the lilt and tumble of the northern Berkshires and southern Taconic Range. Here you will see great sweeps of beech, white ash, cherry, yellow, black and white birch, and sugar maples, their feet wrapped in striped maple and hobblebush. Keep in mind that by the middle 1800s much of this area had been nearly wiped clean of trees, cleared for agriculture as well as for lumber and charcoal production. The forest began taking hold again after the Civil War. By the time you reach the upper tier of **Mount Greylock,** however—at 3,487 feet, the highest point in Massachusetts—you'll be in a very different place indeed. Here lies a tattered sweep of red spruce and balsam fir seen nowhere in Massachusetts except on this cluster of high peaks. This is the southern edge of the boreal forest. Indeed, as far as plant communities are concerned (and, of course, as far as wildlife is concerned as well), your climb from the valleys below is the equivalent of traveling far to the north, well into Canada.

This diversity of habitat, combined with the sheer size of the reservation—roughly 12,500 acres—makes this one of the most intriguing natural areas in the state. Besides an abundance of hiking trails, as well as a wonderful lineup of nature walks, talks, and evening programs, this is a mecca for wildlife- and bird-watching. Deer, bobcats, fishers, and black bears are here, as are coyotes and snowshoe hare. Bird lovers will want to make for the high country, where they stand a chance of hearing and seeing blackpoll warblers (the only nesting populations in the state), as well as spotting mourning, yellow-rumped, and blackburnian warblers, white-throated sparrows, juncos, olive-sided flycatchers, and, if you're very lucky, Swainson's thrush and yellow-bellied flycatchers. This last bird is found most often in the stunted spruce along the upper stretches of Summit Road.

Whereas the southern Berkshires were fast favorites of artists of the Hudson River school, difficult access—and the rough world of the lumber camps—left few willing to turn their brushes to Greylock. For a great many years, in fact, this peak was cherished mostly by students and professors from nearby Williams College. It was they who pushed hard to change the name of the mountain from Mount Hoosac to Greylock (whether for its hoary appearance in winter, or for a Native American leader named Gray Lock, no one can say for sure). The mountain did fare better with writers, though, gaining visits from the likes of Thoreau, Melville, and Hawthorne.

While Mount Greylock is fairly close to the Green Mountains of Vermont, it is in fact part of a very different upland complex, known as the **Taconic Range.** Some geologists feel that the Taconics literally "slid off" the Greens, moving westward some 15 miles from their original location, but the details of their origins are still the subject of much scientific debate. However the Taconics got here, they are undeniably dramatic, at least in part because these uplands were deeply cut by rivers such as the Hoosic and Batten Kill.

There are number of good ways to get oriented at Greylock. You can begin with a walk along the summit trails and a quick visit to the taste-fully designed **Bascom Lodge,** built by the Civilian Conservation Corps in the 1930s for a mere $11,000. You'll find another fine view and a wonderful place for lunch at the **Stony Ledge Picnic Area,** located at the end of Sperry Road. The view is staggering, not for its vastness, but for the wild feeling it offers. This area of the reservation is a steep, tightly folded landscape, part of a 1,600-acre designated natural area and home to some of Greylock's only old-growth forest. This is an in-your-face kind of view. The steep-sided wall of a grand monadnock plunges into a remarkably narrow section of valley floor called **The Hopper,** so named by locals because it resembled the inside of a railroad coal hopper. A self-guided nature/historic trail takes off from the Sperry Campground area; also nearby is the **Hopper Trail,** which includes both dark woods and splendid overlooks.

Mount Greylock Visitor Center

Dropping south off the summit along Rockwell Road is the state-owned **Mount Greylock Visitor Center** *(Mass. 7 near Lanesborough. 413-443-0011),* which is run by the Appalachian Mountain Club. Besides an array of exhibits, the center keeps a naturalist on hand during the summer months, offering a fine variety of nature programs.

The visitor center is also the departure point for a 2.2-mile loop walk —first north along the **Brook and Berry Trail,** then across Rockwell Road to the **Cliff Loop Trail.** Heading south again toward the visitor center on the Cliff Loop trail, you'll find yourself wrapped not only in beautiful patches of mixed hardwood forest, but also in meadows stitched with plantain and timothy, as well as overgrown fields of blueberry and meadow-sweet. Near the trailhead you'll find spectacular views toward the south. Look for the blue waters of **Pontoosuc Lake** in the near distance and the southern Taconic Range rising from a dense cloak of forest far to the south. ■

Summit House, Mount Holyoke

Holyoke Range and Skinner State Parks

MASSACHUSETTS ■ 3,000 acres (Holyoke); 390 acres (Skinner) ■ Central Massachusetts, 5 miles north of South Hadley ■ Year-round. Road to Mount Holyoke summit closed mid-Nov.–mid-April ■ Camping, hiking, walking, bird-watching ■ Adm. fee to Summit House. Open Mem. Day–Labor Day ■ Contact the parks, P.O. Box 91, Hadley, MA 01035; phone 413-253-2883 (Holyoke), 413-586-0350 (Skinner). www.state.ma.us/dem/forparks.htm

ONE OF THE MOST ENCHANTING THINGS about New England is the way many of its residents build bridges between their culture and their natural surroundings. Take the **Summit House** *(reached by road or trail from Mass. 47)* on **Mount Holyoke,** for example, high above the Connecticut River Valley in Skinner State Park. Where other state park meeting centers might be content with offering the usual bevy of stargazing programs and bird walks, Skinner adds occasional summer music concerts, most of them breaking midway to let the audience soak up the views of the sun setting across a long sprawl of forest to the west. On a clear day you can see all the way to the foothills of the Berkshires, with Mount Greylock (see pp. 212-14) showing up in the distance as a tiny triangle above the horizon. In addition to offering interpretive programs and materials, Summit House also has a fine collection of videos available for viewing, highlighting the nature and history of the area.

In a way, such a marriage of art and nature makes perfect sense in this place, given the long history of visits here by writers and painters, from Nathaniel Hawthorne to the great landscape artist Thomas Cole. The lazy

Following pages: View from Mount Holyoke

twists and turns of the Connecticut River (the crescent-shape lake visible from the summit of Holyoke was in Cole's day an oxbow in the river) quickly became one of the most frequently painted landscapes in all of Massachusetts. Mount Holyoke vistas were especially popular with European artists, who considered the easy drape of green farms spreading out from the slow curve of the river to be the ultimate expression of pastoral bliss. Besides outstanding scenery, the Connecticut River is one of four major bird migration routes in the Northeast. It's a thrilling experience to stand on the summit of Holyoke in late fall, watching hawks flying south by the hundreds.

The **Holyoke Range,** along with the **Mount Tom Range,** visible just to the west across the Connecticut River, are the remnants of extinct volcanoes that arose some 200 million years ago. Indeed, many of the more distinctive cliffs you'll see during your treks are made up of flowing lava that hardened into basalt, or traprock. It's this basalt—hard and resistant to erosion—that has allowed the Holyoke Range to stand, while other mountains long ago weathered into plains. What is probably most unusual about these ranges is that they run not north and south, but east to west, twisted by a complex series of geological events.

Perhaps the best place to begin any visit to these side-by-side parks is at the **Notch Visitor Center** (*Mass. 116 NE of South Hadley. 413-253-2883*), which you'll find in a forested cradle between **Bare Mountain** and **Mount Norwottock.** Here you'll get the rundown on current activities, as well as a taste of what you'll be discovering along the roads and trails. Kids will find a number of things to their liking, from drawing activities to a "touch table" covered with bones and rocks. If time is limited, at least follow up your stop at the Notch with a walk around the **Laurel Loop Nature Trail,** which takes off from the visitor center.

These parks also have an abundance of longer hikes. If you have someone to pick you up at the other end, by all means consider a climb from the entrance to Skinner State Park to the summit of Holyoke (there's a road leading there as well). Once at the top, strike out for the backcountry on a 4.7-mile trek along the **Metcomet-Monadnock Trail.** Marked with white markers and blazes, the trail takes you across Seven Sisters, Mount Hitchcock, and magnificent Bare Mountain, descending down to the Granby Notch and the Notch Visitor Center. The entire M-M Trail is a 117-mile-long path from the Connecticut state line to Mount Monadnock in southern New Hampshire (see pp. 195-96). One of the most intriguing aspects of this hike is its surprising variety of habitats. The drier, south-facing slopes are stitched through with oak and hickory, basswood and butternut, while the north-facing slopes, a few feet away, are covered in more moisture-loving species such as hemlock, yellow birch, and black birch. If you still haven't had enough, consider a popular climb on the M-M Trail from the Notch Visitor Center through classic southern New England forest to the top of **Mount Norwottuck** (*1.1 miles one way*) and **Rattlesnake Knob** (*1.8 miles one way*), both offering commanding views of the surrounding countryside. ∎

Quabbin Park

Quabbin Park and Reservoir

MASSACHUSETTS ■ 3,200 acres ■ Central Massachusetts, 12 miles east of Amherst off Mass. 9 ■ Year-round ■ Hiking, walking, fishing, biking, bird-watching, wildlife viewing ■ Contact the park, P.O. Box 628, Belchertown, MA 01007; phone 413-323-7221. www.state.ma.us/mdc

QUABBIN, WHICH TAKES ITS NAME from a Nipmuc Indian word meaning "place of many waters," began turning into just one giant water in 1927. In that year, construction started on the Windsor Dam, an edifice that would ultimately back up some 412 billion gallons within a 121,000-acre watershed—at the time, the largest domestic water supply system in the world—all to satisfy the growing thirst of Boston. To give you a sense of the immensity of this reservoir, it contains a staggering 118 miles of shoreline, and another 63 miles if you throw in the islands. Every time it rains an inch, Quabbin Reservoir gains 1.6 billion gallons of water.

The impoundment actually protected the region, so that it came to be the largest tract of wild land in the state of Massachusetts. In fact, it's safe to say that this swath of southern New England is wilder today than it was 200, and quite possibly even 300, years ago. While the public park is 3,200 acres in size, the entire reservation, land and water combined, is a whopping 81,000 acres. Much of it is home for turkeys, red foxes, loons, great blue herons—even bobcats, moose, and fishers. Furthermore, there's an abundant variety of habitats at Quabbin, from swamp to pond to gardens of hay-scented, bracken, New York, and cinnamon ferns, as well as red pine stands, mixed hardwoods, and open clearings. This variety makes Quabbin a marvelous place for neotropical songbirds. Scientists from around the region have long turned to the park for wildlife research, as well as for studies on everything from forest productivity to acid rain. Quabbin is also an excellent place to watch bald eagles. Once gone from this area entirely, the eagles have been restored to the park over many years as biologists bring in young chicks and raise them on elevated platforms.

When you reach the park, stop at the visitor center, located on the right just before the dam. Pick up a copy of the "Quabbin Park Trail Guide," as well as an interpretive brochure of the Stewardship Demonstration Trail. There are more than 20 miles of trails and wood roads on the peninsula that are open to hiking. Of the nine trails described in the "Quabbin Park Trail Guide," the 3-mile round-trip walk from **Goodnough Dike** to **Pepper's Mill Pond** is a particularly good trip for those who are interested in spotting wildlife. Also good is the **Beaver Pond to Tower Trail,** similar in distance, taking off on the right side of the road across from Boat Cove.

If you're fond of cycling, you can make a nice loop on pavement via the U-shape park road around the peninsula (perhaps with a side trip to Goodnough Dike), connecting the two prongs with a roughly 3-mile ride along Mass. 9. However, note that mountain bikes are not allowed on the dirt forest roads that criss-cross the peninsula.

Finally, if you've brought the fly rod, the section of the **Swift River** downstream from Windsor Dam to Mass. 9 is open year-round for catch-and-release fishing. Only flyfishing is allowed, and a Massachusetts license is required. You can arrange for fishing permits and boat rentals at the visitor center. ■

Medicinal Plants

Quabbin's plants are well worth your attention. Various ferns, including sweet, maidenhair, and interrupted, grow in abundance along many of the trails, as does dogwood, huckleberry, and barberry. All of these plants were once valued for their medicinal properties: ferns for treating worms; huckleberry tea as a gargle for mouth sores; dogwood for treating recurring fevers; and barberry (recognized by its spiny-toothed leaves and drooping clusters of yellow flowers) as an antibacterial and antidiarrheal agent.

Mushroom on shady forest floor

Douglas State Forest

MASSACHUSETTS ■ 5,200 acres ■ South-central Massachusetts, 2 miles west of Douglas off Mass. 16 ■ Year-round ■ Hiking, walking, boating, swimming, mountain biking, bird-watching ■ Adm. fee Mem. Day–Labor Day. ■ Jet skis banned weekends and holidays ■ Contact the state forest, 107 Wallum Lake Rd., Douglas, MA 01516; phone 508-476-7872. www.state.ma.us/dem/parks/doug.htm

IT'S BEEN A LONG TIME since the Ringling Brothers showed up at Douglas State Forest to catch the rattlesnakes that they would use as attractions in their traveling circus. What's more, the great chestnuts of the past are gone, as they are throughout the East, victim of the great chestnut blight (see sidebar p. 199). What does remain in these 5,200 acres, though, is a wonderful network of motor-free hiking and biking trails winding through a beautiful southern New England forest, including 8 miles of the 91-mile-long **Midstate Trail,** which winds from Rhode Island all the way to New Hampshire. There's also a small but enjoyable bird blind and nature center in the preserve, as well as what has long been the key attraction for many visitors, **Wallum Lake**—an exceptionally clear body of water with a superb swimming beach. Speaking of clear water, many years ago some of what is now the Douglas State Forest was owned by the Providence Ice Company, which cut ice out of Wallum Lake and stored it in a six-story icehouse not far from the lake; it was then transported by railroad to Boston and Providence.

What to See and Do

Mountain bikers can enjoy a portion of the **Southern New England Trunkline Trail** through Douglas, accessed on Wallum Lake Road near forest headquarters, roughly a half mile north of the main entrance to the forest (maps are available at headquarters). This is a

Cedar Swamp Trail, Douglas State Forest

gravel ballast trail, running 55 miles between Franklin, Massachusetts, and Willamantic, Connecticut. For more information contact the Massachusetts Department of Environmental Management's Division of Resource Conservation (617-727-3160).

Cedar Swamp Trail

Of the many of trails available at Douglas, one of my favorites is the Cedar Swamp Trail, only a half mile in length, much of it along a boardwalk through an unforgettable slice of Atlantic white cedar swamp. The trail is marked by red diamond-shape blazes and begins at the preserve's nature center, located just south of the boat ramp on Wallum Lake. During my visit, I noticed a few numbers had been stolen from the posts linking this path to an interpretive brochure; at times I had to count posts to figure out where I was, but that hardly diminished the enchantment.

The story of this, and of thousands of other swamps and ponds throughout New England, began some 12,000 to 15,000 years ago, when glaciers began retreating northward. Chunks of ice from those mammoth ice sheets slowly melted away, often leaving sizable sinks, or depressions, in the ground; those deep enough to connect with the water table became ponds or swamps.

Given its rather bland crown, and the boggy, bug-ridden places where it grows, the Atlantic white cedar is a tree easily overlooked. And yet for centuries Americans counted on this cedar for everything from floorboards to organ pipes, log cabins to trolley-line ties. While the cedars you see today in New England are typically fairly modest in size (most are around 8 to 14 inches thick), early settlers in New England routinely found trees 5 and 6 feet thick. By the late 1700s, most of the big and small cedars had been thoroughly cut over. So valuable was the wood from this tree that beginning in the early 1800s, people began harvesting them from old swamps, retrieving trees that had died and toppled over—a supply that in some places ran 100 feet deep.

As well as admiring the cedar trees in the swamp portion of this walk, notice the abundance of sphagnum moss—an incredibly absorbent plant material often used by Native Americans as a diaperlike liner in baby cradles.

Those looking for a longer walk would do well to try the 2.2-mile **Coffeehouse Loop,** departing from the end of the road leading past the nature center and marked by blue dots. Named after a tavern that operated near here during the Revolutionary War, this path traverses an exquisite parcel of hemlock, white pine, and laurel woods, as well as an occasional open area where you may see white-tailed deer, ruffed grouse, or even an occasional red fox. In the more moist areas of the forest are large patches of sweet pepperbush, readily identified by its narrow, wedge-shape leaves. Walking clockwise around the Coffeehouse Loop, the latter portion rubs elbows with a pond and wetland area, filled with sedges and cattails and fragrant water lilies—the perfect place for an early morning session of bird-watching. ■

Rock House Reservation

MASSACHUSETTS ■ 750 acres ■ Central Massachusetts, 2 miles east of Ware on Mass. 9 ■ Year-round ■ Hiking, cross-country skiing, snowshoeing, bird-watching, archaeological items ■ Contact Trustees of Reservations, 572 Essex St., Beverly, MA 01915; phone **978-840-4446**. www.thetrustees.org

THE MASSIVE, CAVELIKE ROCK SHELTER from which this gem of a preserve takes its name is thought to have been exposed as the last glaciers retreated, some 12,000 to 15,000 years ago. Besides providing protection from the weather, the **Rock House** had the advantage of an opening that faces southeast, thus catching a fair amount of sun in the long months of winter. Not surprisingly, archaeologists have uncovered a vast treasure of artifacts from prehistoric people who used this spot as far back as 7,000 years ago. Among the researchers' finds are stone flakes, bone tools and pottery shards, as well as bones of deer, turkeys, and bears—even the tooth of a wolf.

With its museum, butterfly garden, and charming wooded pond, the Rock House Reservation provides a great walking experience for both adults and children. You can start your tour of the area with a fine loop walk of about 1.5 miles by following the **Inner Loop Trail** from the parking lot, bearing left at the pond, where you may see everything from flycatchers to green frogs, painted turtles to ribbon snakes. (Larger animals on the reservation include turkeys, white-tailed deer, and coyotes.) From here move along the west side of the pond past the Rock House to the fire road, and turn right. Follow the fire road to the intersection with the **Outer Loop Trail,** and turn right once again, making your way back to the pond. The wooded portions of this preserve are a beautiful mix of red oak, red maple, beech, spruce, hornbeam, sassafras, red pine, ash, black and gray birch, and hop hornbeam, with a soft, whispery understory of lady's slipper, club moss, and cinnamon, marsh, sensitive, and Christmas ferns. Open areas along the fire road, on the other hand, are awash with a different blend of plants: honeysuckle, dogwood, blackberry, blueberry, yarrow, and hawkweed.

The **Trailside Museum** is located in an open-air cottage just north of the pond and has a variety of displays about the natural history of the area, including illustrated displays of common birds, mammals, and trees. A porch on the back side of the museum is the perfect picnic spot, offering stunning views of the small pond below, broken here and there with large boulders deposited in exactly the right places by glaciers of the distant past. This is an incredibly peaceful place, wrapped in oak and maple trees, tossed with cattails and sedges, boneset, goldenrod, and wild mint. In the summer, the whole family will enjoy a visit to the **butterfly garden.** If birds are your pleasure, come early in the morning, bring along your life list, and see if you can check off wild turkey, great blue heron, turkey vulture, scarlet tanager, red-eyed vireo, winter wren, wood thrush, and eastern towhee. ■

In the Berkshires

Southern Berkshires Drive

MASSACHUSETTS ■ 10 miles ■ Western Massachusetts, Mount Everett State Reservation to Mount Washington State Forest ■ Year-round ■ Camping, hiking, canoeing, fishing, biking, bird-watching

THE BERKSHIRES, MUCH LIKE THE Taconic Range and Green Mountains to the north, were formed along ancient folds in the planet's crust. Long afterward, these twists of rock were uplifted into a large plateau. It has been the unyielding forces of erosion, however, that give the Berkshires their rounded, gentle appearance, turning them from what were once dramatic uplands into a cluster of welcoming hills. In the reaches of the Berkshires that occupy extreme southwest Massachusetts and northwest Connecticut, we find the southernmost outposts of the northern hardwood forest. Rather than the stands of oak and hickory so common to the surrounding lowlands, the quiet folds of the southern Berkshires hold instead a weave of beech, conifers, sugar maple, and yellow birch.

Perhaps no other region in America allows travelers to spend every single day deep in the woods with their hiking boots on and every single evening wrapped in exquisite cultural entertainment. Cultural fare in the Berkshires includes music with the Boston Symphony Orchestra at Tanglewood *(Lenox. 413-637-1940 July-Aug., 617-638-9267 rest of year. Adm. fee)* and an array of theater and dance, including the renowned Jacob's Pillow *(Becket. 413-243-0745. Adm. fee)*, Shakespeare & Company *(Lenox. 413-637-3353. Adm. fee)*, and the Berkshire Theater Festival *(Stockbridge. 413-298-5576. Adm. fee)*.

To the southwest and within easy striking distance of these evening treats are a number of small but splendid natural areas accessible along a 10-mile drive between Mount Everett State Reservation and Mount Washington State Forest. From the historic village of South Egremont on Mass. 23, take Mass. 41 south, turning west on Mount Washington Road. This roadway climbs through a beautiful mix of woods and fields before curving south to become East Street, the route of the drive. (If you wish, you can take this road all the way to Salisbury, Connecticut.)

Mount Everett State Reservation

Just over 7.5 miles from the junction of Mass. 41 and the Mount Washington Road is Mount Everett State Reservation *(413-528-0330. Limited road access Nov.-May)*, an 1,100-acre portected area with a paved road that takes you within a half mile of the summit of 2,602-foot **Mount Everett.** The gate from the parking area may be closed, but consider leaving the car and walking in. From the gate to the summit is 2 miles, with the road rising sharply enough to get your heart pumping —but the views at the end are well worth the effort. As you climb, the vegetation becomes increasingly scrubby, with patches of yellow birch, maple, beech, hemlock, red oak, and mountain laurel dwindling to scrub oak and pitch pine on the upper ridges, along with patchy quilts of fireweed, raspberry, and blueberry.

While the steps to an old fire tower have been removed, you can still walk along the edge of the bare rock summit and enjoy spectacular helpings of Berkshire scenery. To the south is **Mount Race,** 4 miles away and nearly 300 feet lower, and beyond that, **Bear Mountain,** which is the highest mountain in Connecticut (see p. 240). Also visible to the southeast are the shining waters of **Twin Lakes** near Salisbury, while to the

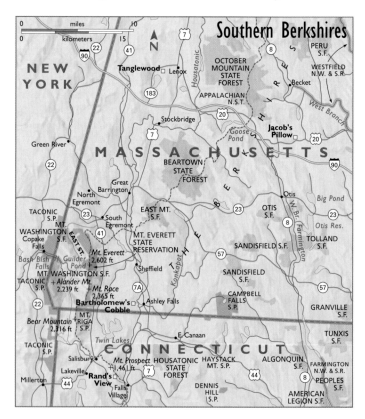

southwest you can see New York's **Catskill Mountains.** If you happen to be in the area from early September through the first part of November, keep in mind that this summit is a splendid place to watch migrating raptors. In the right conditions—which usually means cool weather and northwest winds—you can see literally hundreds of these travelers, including red-tailed, sharp-shinned, broad-winged, and Cooper's hawks, as well as turkey vultures, American kestrels, northern harriers, and even the occasional peregrine falcon.

Guilder Pond

The Appalachian Trail crosses the paved summit road and descends to a picnic area next to the lovely, but still rather wild-looking Guilder Pond, surrounded by a forest that in June is splashed with the beautiful blooms of mountain laurel. If you're here on a summer morning, you may notice white-flowered plants floating on the pond. These are the blooms of the fragrant water lily, which usually shows itself only in the daylight hours until about noon. A relative of the yellow pond lily, these water plants were long used by herbal healers to treat everything from diarrhea to sore throats.

If you've brought your canoe or kayak, the first or last order of business may be a slow float on Guilder, the highest freshwater pond in Massachusetts. One parking area is nearby, next to the Appalachian Trail, and another is a little farther up, along a narrow, steep, somewhat rocky road. From either location it's a fairly short walk to the summit of Mount Everett.

Mount Washington State Forest

Leaving Mount Everett State Reservation, turn left on East Street, then right in 0.3 mile at a white church. Turn right again at a T-junction with West Street and wind downhill. Turn left onto Falls Road and follow the signs to **Bash Bish Falls** in Mount Washington State Forest.

A waterfall has to work hard to earn the title of most beautiful in the Berkshires, but that's the accolade commonly applied to this one, located just inside the Massachusetts line. A parking area a mile farther down the road, in New York State, offers a much flatter approach to the falls. Families with small children should opt for this route. No matter how you get there, the walk is a delight, dropping from the Massachusetts access lot through a magnificent stand of yellow birch and hemlock. The falls themselves do in fact bash and bish a bit, splitting around a huge cleft in the rock before making a plunge of some 60 feet into an emerald pool. This is as close to paradise as one can probably get in a northern climate.

For a fine network of trails, head for an area just behind the Mount Washington State Forest headquarters *(East St., S of turnoff to Bash Bish Falls. 413-528-0330)*. A 5-mile round-trip walk from here up **Alander Mountain,** for example, affords some marvelous views from the mountain's summit—a fitting end to the Southern Berkshires drive. ■

Bartholomew's Cobble

MASSACHUSETTS ■ 278 acres ■ Southwest Massachusetts, 7 miles south of Sheffield off Mass. 7A ■ Year-round ■ Hiking, walking, canoeing, bird-watching, wildflower viewing ■ Adm. fee ■ Contact the preserve, P.O. Box 128, Ashley Falls, MA 01222; phone 413-229-8600. www.thetrustees.org

OF ALL THE EXTRAORDINARY PLACES in the Berkshire country, from dark, abrupt chasms where the hemlock huddle to the wind-blasted summits of Mount Everett and Mount Race, little Bartholomew's Cobble—all 278 acres of it—is a favorite of many travelers. For starters, it boasts a fine

Bartholomew's Cobble

little museum, the **Bailey Natural History Museum** (*Daily Mem. Day–Columbus Day, Wed.-Sun. rest of year*). This facility has the kind of clean, thoughtful displays that can be really helpful to budding naturalists: songbird mounts complete with nest and eggs, butterflies, and exhibits of local archaeology. The museum is also the meeting place for some excellent, if all too infrequent events, such as canoe trips with a naturalist on **Upper** and **Lower Goose Pond,** as well as trips on the **Housatonic River,** tree studies with a regional forester, wildflower slide shows, and bird walks.

The network of trails on the property, all of them fairly short, traverses many habitats; some trails, like the **Ledges Interpretive Trail,** are tied to interpretive pamphlets that are remarkably enlightening.

Go to **Half River Pond** and look for the painted, spotted, and the now-threatened wood turtle. Head to **Corbin's Neck** for a good view of grassland birds, including healthy populations of eastern bluebirds and bobolinks. Hop in your canoe for a float down a lazy stretch of the Housatonic River (see pp. 241-249).

The word "cobble" isn't given in honor of the local mender of shoes. Cobbles are rock outcrops of limestone and marble, laced with hard, erosion-resistant quartzite, formed hundreds of million years ago under an inland sea. Thanks to that quartzite, these outcrops have been able to resist the forces of water and ice that have turned many other features to rubble. On the other hand, the limestone and marble leach into the soil; both are highly alkaline, or "sweet," which tends to create the kind of soil that ferns and many other plants love. The Ledges Interpretive Trail is a great place for fern connoisseurs, offering the chance to see everything from maidenhair, spleenwort, ostrich, and bulbet ferns to wall rue and purple-stemmed cliffbrake. (Vegetation in general flourishes in Bartholomew's Cobble; the museum's current list of vascular plants is 15 pages long!)

Not that bird-watchers will be disappointed, mind you, what with the cobble being on a flyway for some 240 species. Besides those mentioned above, along the river during the summer you'll find herons and egrets, while the forest areas of the preserve are home to a great variety of neotropical songbirds, as well as to five different species of woodpecker.

The cobble, as the locals know it, is also home to a high concentration of bluebirds. This is thanks to strong management efforts, including the scattering of bluebird boxes throughout the preserve. (Bluebirds tend to lose nesting sites to more aggressive birds, such as the house sparrow and European starling.) The cobble is a great place to watch these beautiful fliers darting out from trees or fence posts, flying low across the fields to snatch insects or grasshoppers. Migrating bluebirds tend to return to their nesting grounds early in the spring—a habit that brings delight to people, but can put them at great risk if the weather turns sour. Little wonder that Bartholomew's Cobble is one of only two sites in Massachusetts to be listed by the park service as a national natural landmark.

If you're walking on your own, begin with the Ledges Interpretive Trail (pamphlet in hand, of course), then cut off to follow the **Bailey Trail** along the Housatonic to **Half River Pond.** From there walk back a few steps and catch the **Tulip Trail,** which climbs to the **Tractor Path.** At this juncture, you'll turn left and follow the trail to the overlook at **Hurlburt's Hill.**

At the end of the path, pull up a bench and enjoy one of the most pleasing views in all New England. Here the world falls gently away to the north and west in a quilt of forest and field, then rises with one mighty breath to become the high line of the southern Berkshires. It isn't exactly the backdrop from *The Sound of Music,* but don't be surprised if you find yourself heading down the Tractor Path humming a contented tune. ∎

Lyme Disease

Lyme disease was discovered in 1975, when researchers noticed unusually large numbers of children with arthritis in Lyme, Connecticut, and two nearby towns. The disease is caused by a spirochete bacterium and spread by a tick the size of a poppyseed—typically the deer tick in the East and the black-legged tick in the West. Lyme disease has spread throughout much of the Northeast, Midwest, and North-west, and is of increasing concern to people who spend time in the outdoors. (That said, it's important to realize that not all of these ticks carry Lyme disease, nor does every infected tick transmit it.)

The best plan, of course, is to plan ahead. When you're out hiking, try to stay in the center of the path and avoid brushing against trailside shrubs and grass. Wear a tucked-in shirt and long pants stuffed into socks. Tick repellent around the ankles and on exposed areas of skin may also help. When you come inside, inspect yourself and your children. Pay particular attention to armpits, groin, scalp, and belt line, as well as the neck and head of children. If you do find a tick, the best way to remove it is with a pair of precision tweezers, grasping it firmly where its mouth enters the skin. Keep in mind that the tick generally needs to be attached to a person's skin for about 36 to 48 hours before the infection can be transmitted.

The progression of Lyme dis-ease normally follows a set pattern, which for most people begins with a rash in the shape of a ring that expands outward from the bite, rather like a target. (If left untreated, the rash will expand for several weeks and then fade.) Other early symptoms, present even in those people who do not show the rash, may include flulike symptoms such as fatigue, mild headache, low-grade fever, stiffness of muscles and joints, and swollen glands. If treated early with anti-biotics, the disease is fairly easy to eradicate. If left untreated, however, later symptoms can include complications of the joints, nervous system, and heart. It's important, therefore, to visit a doctor as soon as you suspect the disease. He or she will evaluate your symptoms and may call for a blood test. Be aware, though, that the blood test is not completely reliable, especially in the disease's early stages.

While there is now a vaccine for Lyme disease, it's not without shortcomings. For one thing, it involves three shots given over the course of a year. The shots should be timed so that the last dose is given six to eight weeks before peak tick season (late May–late June). In addition, researchers do not yet know how long these shots will provide protection; booster shots may be required in the sec-ond and third years. Finally, there is as yet no data on the side effects of long exposure to this drug. People with a family history of arthritis, for example, or with heart conditions, are at this point being advised against taking it. For more informa-tion, contact the American Lyme Disease Foundation (914-277-6970. www.aldf.com).

Fanny Stebbins Memorial Wildlife Refuge

MASSACHUSETTS ■ 333 acres ■ South-central Massachusetts, near the intersection of US 5 and Mass. 192 ■ Year-round ■ Walking, bird-watching ■ Contact Allen Bird Club of Springfield, 14 Fernwood Rd., Longmeadow, MA 01106.

THESE 333 ACRES OF MARSH, field, forest, and meadow are all but unknown even to most residents of Massachusetts. Nevertheless, this is one of the finest floodplain environments to be found anywhere. The birds alone are enough to put a grin on your face: barred and great horned owls, ruffed grouse, titmice, and blue jays, and in the backwater of the cove, egrets, great blue herons, cormorants, sanderlings, teal, and so many more. Being a stopover on the Atlantic flyway, this is an especially fine place to come in the fall, when south-bound waterfowl are winging their way to winter grounds by the thousands. Wildlife in general—including the occasional moose and even black bear—use the cover provided by the forests and tangles of the Connecticut River corridor to move north and south, often passing unseen through fairly populated regions of Massachusetts and Connecticut.

Near the parking area at the corner of Bark Haul and Pond Side Roads is a large map of the refuge. For a rewarding 3-mile walk, head west from this point (in the same direction as Bark Haul Road) on a grassy walking path, where you'll soon pass a pond on the right. This is an excellent place to see kingfishers, a handsome, ragged-headed bird with a white belt around its neck. Look for it on tree branches overhanging the water; upon spotting a fish it will launch and perhaps hover for a few seconds, finally making a dramatic dive to nab it with its long, sharp bill. The species name of the belted kingfisher, by the way—*alcyon*—is a reference to the ancient Greek myth of Alcyone. Told that her seafaring husband had been killed in a shipwreck, Alcyone was consumed by grief, so much so that she went down to the ocean and threw herself in, hoping to end it all. Instead, the gods changed her into a kingfisher, and her husband with her, and in their honor forbade the winds to blow during the kingfisher's breeding season.

After crossing a railroad track at 0.1 mile, continue straight to an intersection of trails and turn left. As you make your way southward, you'll see side trails taking off to the right. These lead down to the river and make for some good exploring through trees so big, with an understory so rich, the place feels almost primeval. You can also reach the river by taking a right at the intersection of trails, and then a short distance later a left on the **Natti Trail,** running beside Longmeadow Brook. The summer air here is thick and damp with vegetation, sweet yet slightly acrid, as if you were smelling the very breath of the earth. On a hot day

Cabbage butterfly on purple loosestrife, Fanny Stebbins Memorial Wildlife Refuge

it's not all that hard to imagine this valley as it was long ago, in the Triassic period. Back then this was a lush tropical lowland. Giant ferns and enormous conifers were everywhere, as were dinosaurs, including the fast-running, meat-eating *Coelophysis.*

You may be surprised by the size of the **Connecticut River,** as well as by the way it is pocked with sandy beaches in many places. This is big water, full of silent currents and eddies, the kind of place where so many early explorers must have stood, awestruck, wondering what fantastic lands must lie upstream.

Back on the main trail again and heading south, you'll enter the **Elliot Section** at the end of a large field. Following trails to the southwest will take you to **Raspberry Cove,** which is a wonderful place to spot waterfowl. Alternatively, turn left here (east), keeping the fields on your left and the woods on your right. Just after crossing the railroad tracks again, you'll come to a large concrete piling and a boardwalk along the edge of a wetland, a favorite hangout for the local beavers. After this comes yet another field, which you'll once again keep on your left. At the southeast corner of the field turn left onto a path that leads back to the parking area.

Note that in the spring, as well as after heavy rains in any season, the hiking trails at the Fanny Stebbins refuge can become quite muddy. Be sure to bring the appropriate wet-weather footwear. ■

Cedar waxwing

Boardwalk, Peoples State Forest

Peoples State Forest

CONNECTICUT ■ 2,954 acres ■ Northwest Connecticut, 5 miles east of Winsted off US 44 ■ April–mid-Nov. ■ Camping, hiking, guided walks, wildlife viewing ■ Contact the state forest, P.O. Box 1, Pleasant Valley, CT 06063; phone 860-379-2469

IT WOULD BE HARD to imagine a clearer example of the power of the New England woods to rise again than in the lands making up the nearly 3,000-acre Peoples State Forest. In the late 1700s alone, the loud ring of axes was a nearly constant sound here, as settlers cut trees by the thousands to make charcoal for feeding the great iron foundries of northwest Connecticut. Not by accident did this part of the state became the principle location for manufacturing cannon during the Revolutionary War. At a single hearth site, workers would typically stack some 30 cords of wood, which would then be covered in dirt and burned; the resulting

Following pages: Autumn, Peoples State Forest

charcoal was then loaded into wagons and hauled to iron furnaces to the west. Foundries continued to operate near here until 1923, further depleting the trees.

In time people began to farm this area, which of course continued to keep the woods at bay. (Consider that besides keeping the fields clear, a single farm family might burn 25 cords of wood a year for cooking and heating.) As in other parts of New England, the forests you see here today have been growing only since the turn of the 20th century, when people left for the cities for better jobs and much of the nation's farming activity shifted to the Midwest. It was then that schoolchildren, Boy Scouts, and various individuals and civic groups launched a heroic effort to purchase portions of this land and donate them to the state, thus earning the preserve the name Peoples State Forest.

A number of fine hiking trails crisscross the reserve, including a good 2-mile round-trip to **Chaugham's Lookout.** This walk departs from the Big Springs Recreation Area, located on Greenwoods Road, 3 miles east of East River Road, along the **Jessie Gerard Trail.** The path winds though rich stands of hemlock, red oak, and white pine, as well as through gardens of hay-scented fern, Canada mayflower, laurel, and sarsaparilla. In just over a half mile is an impressive overlook of the **West Branch Farmington River;** Chaugham's Lookout, the destination viewpoint, is a 15-minute walk past that. The lookout was named for a man of Narragansett blood who arrived in this area in 1740. Shortly thereafter, and to the horror of some of the locals, he eloped with young Molly Barber to found a settlement just to the south known as Barkhamsted Lighthouse. (The Lighthouse refers simply to the lights shining through the Chaughams' log cabin, which stage drivers on the Farmington River Turnpike used as a reference point on their regular trips to Hartford.) Over time, Barkhamsted Lighthouse became one of the most ethnically diverse communities of its size in the nation, including men and women of various Native American tribes, freed slaves, Creoles, and many others.

Another, slightly longer walk at Peoples is the 3-mile-long **Beaver Swamp Loop Trail,** which begins on the **Charles Pack Trail,** 1.4 miles from the forest entrance at Greenwoods Road. This is a wonderful trail for spotting wildlife; of late there have been reports of bears, otters, northern harriers, great blue herons, and, in the past few years, the occasional moose. The rather extensive lowlands of the Peoples State Forest are the site of much activity from beavers: ambitious residents that allow other life to flourish. Willow and blue flag iris, cattail and red maple and buttonbush, swamp sparrows and red-winged blackbirds—all are here in large part because of wetlands created by the beaver.

If you're here on a weekend, by all means stop by the **Stone Museum** (*weekends Mem. Day–Columbus Day*) located on Greenwoods Road. Check out the exhibits there as well as any planned activities. Interpretive hikes, for example, are offered throughout the summer and fall, as are Saturday evening slide shows on a range of topics, including birds, trees, and geology. ■

White-water rafting

West Branch Farmington Wild and Scenic River

CONNECTICUT ■ 14 miles ■ Northwest Connecticut from Hartland to Cantos ■ Kayaking, canoeing, fishing, tubing ■ Contact Farmington River Watershed Association, 749 Hopmeadow St., Simsbury, CT 06070; phone 860-658-4442 for information and water release times. www.frwa.org

WHETHER YOU'VE COME with a fly rod or a paddle, the West Branch Farmington—so far the only river segment in Connecticut to be federally designated a Wild and Scenic River—offers no end of satisfaction. Experienced kayakers or white-water canoeists may want to investigate the 2.5-mile, Class I through III run from **Satan's Kingdom Recreation Area** *(New Hartford on US 44. 860-693-6465)* to a point just before the US 202 bridge near Canton. Another equally engaging paddle, though a longer one of 11 miles, is from the state picnic area in Riverton, below the US 20 bridge (and across from the Hitchcock Chair Factory Store), to Satan's Kingdom Recreation Area, on the right, just before the US 44 bridge. If you didn't bring your boat, rentals are available at Clare Outdoors *(860-672-6365)* on US 7 in West Cornwall, as well as at O'Hara's Landing Marina *(860-824-7583)* on Twin Lakes Road in Salisbury.

Tubing is also extremely popular on certain sections of the Farmington. You can rent tubes at Farmington River Tubing *(860-693-6465)*, located at Satan's Kingdom Recreation Area in New Hartford. When you're not busy navigating rapids, keep an eye out for a wonderful array of birdlife. Broad-winged hawks and bald eagles are sometimes seen along the river, as well as a variety of waterbirds, including mallards, black ducks, wood ducks, and great blue herons. ■

Bear Mountain

CONNECTICUT ■ Northwest Connecticut, 3 miles north of Salisbury on Conn. 41 ■ Year-round ■ Hiking; final portion of trail is steep and not for inexperienced hikers or children ■ Contact the Appalachian Mountain Club regional office, Mt. Greylock Visitor Center, P.O. Box 1800, Lanesborough, MA 01237; phone 413-443-0011. http://outdoors.org

MANY PEOPLE WHO HIKE the trails of New England think first of the great runs of forest, the dizzy heights of the White Mountains, and the wind-blasted coast of Maine. However, there is a long string of unforgettable places in southern New England, well wrapped in woodlands, dotted with quiet ponds and rivers, and laced with trails that will thoroughly untangle you from the noise and bustle of daily life. The **Litchfield Hills** and surrounding environs are perfect examples of such places. Whether dipping a fly rod in the Housatonic or floating a canoe on Wood Creek Pond, savoring the scent of autumn in the hardwoods of Topsmead or bird-watching at White Memorial, this part of New England can cast a spell every bit as unforgettable as the wider, wilder spaces to the north.

You could well begin your tour of northwest Connecticut with a visit to Bear Mountain, at 2,316 feet the highest peak entirely within the state. If there is one quintessential outdoor experience in the southern hardwoods, it has to be to climb for several hours in the thick of the forest, rubbing ankles with ginger and violets and Solomon's seal, finally coming to rest flushed and slightly out of breath on the crest of a soaring mountain, a choppy sea of tree-covered hills spreading out before you as far as the eye can see. Bear Mountain offers exactly that kind of experience. For those who are up to the challenge of a 7-mile round-trip walk, gaining a significant amount of elevation along the way, you could do no better than this trek, skirting one of the largest tracts of wild woodlands in either Connecticut or Massachusetts.

The walk begins on the **Undermountain Trail,** which leads off from the parking area on Conn. 41 north of Salisbury. Well-traveled and marked by blue blazes, the trail climbs for just over a mile to a right turn onto Paradise Lane. From here the path continues uphill for a while, skirts the dramatic chasm known as **Sage's Ravine,** and then drops to meet the **Appalachian Trail,** which is marked by white blazes. Make a left onto the AT. Shortly after this intersection begins the toughest part of the hike, a scramble up the face of Bear Mountain, 500 vertical feet over roughly 0.3 mile, requiring the careful use of handholds along the way.

Any second guesses you might have about this hike during this last steep blast will be quickly erased by the views from the summit. To the north is Mount Everett (see p. 226), marked by a tower on the peak, as well as Mount Greylock (see pp. 212-14) and Mount Race. The shimmering body of water to the east is Twin Lakes, near Salisbury, and rising to the southeast is the great green swell of Mohawk Mountain. Finally, to the west are Mount Frissell, Round Mountain, and the mighty Catskills. ■

Covered bridge over the Housatonic River

Housatonic River

CONNECTICUT ■ Northwest Connecticut, along US 7 near Kent ■ Year-round
■ Camping, hiking, walking, kayaking, canoeing, fishing, wildflower viewing
■ Contact Housatonic Valley Association, P.O. Box 28, Cornwall Bridge, CT
06754; phone 860-672-6678. www.hvathewatershedgroup.org

MANY CLAIM THERE are no more beautiful lands in all of southern New
England than those rising from the banks of the Housatonic River in
northwest Connecticut. The Housatonic begins well to the north, fed by
numerous small springs on the flank of Brodie Mountain, near the town
of New Ashford. While there are places where it flows quickly, for the
most part this is a quiet, winding river, dappled with oxbows and oxbow
ponds—perfect habitat for a wide variety of birds. In addition, the various reeds, arrowhead, and other aquatic plants that line much of the river
provide fine cover for toads, spring peepers, and treefrogs

What to See and Do
Bulls Bridge to Tenmile River
Besides offering striking views
of the Housatonic River, this
mellow stretch of pathway cuts
through a delightful blend of
southern New England vegetation.
To reach the trailhead, follow US 7
south from the town of Kent for
3 miles, turning right (west) at a
stoplight onto Bulls Bridge Road.

A short distance after passing
through a covered bridge, you'll
cross an open bridge across the
Housatonic. The trailhead and
parking area for this walk is on
the left, immediately after the
open bridge.

Along the trail you'll find the
usual players—hemlocks, sugar
maples, and red oaks—as well as a

wonderful mix of ground plants like Solomon's seal, hepatica, ginger, violet, and red columbine, as well as shrubs like witch hazel. For centuries witch hazel been the plant of choice in making divining rods, which some people believe can be used to find underground water. (Religious leaders have had other ideas. Martin Luther, for example, suggested that the tip of a witch hazel branch wasn't being pulled toward earth by water, but by the hand of Satan.) This is also a good place to watch for an orchid known as the pink lady's slipper; besides being beautiful, this plant has a long history of use as a medicine. Settlers in America found native people using it to calm nerves and quickly adopted it as their own, substituting it for valerian, which had been the sedative of choice across the Atlantic. To this day there are herbalists who continue to tout the plant as perfect for inducing sleep without the use of narcotics. That said, keep in mind that like most orchids, lady's slipper does not propagate well and, like other flowers, should not be picked.

When the trail forks in 0.4 mile, bear to the left, trading blue blazes for the white blazes of the **Appalachian Trail.** Shortly after this intersection is a wonderful view of the Housatonic. From here it's a 15-minute walk to the bridge at **Tenmile River,** fresh out of the hills of New York. Along the way you'll pass through lovely clusters of Japanese honeysuckle and dogwood. If you're feeling energetic, you can walk another mile of the Appalachian Trail, climbing steadily for much of the way, to the

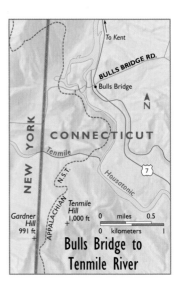

Bulls Bridge to Tenmile River

Tenmile Hill summit, where you'll find striking views of the surrounding uplands.

Pine Knob Loop Trail

About 15miles north of Kent on US 7 is a pleasant 2.5-mile walk that rises high above the **Housatonic Meadows State Park** campground (*Macedonia Brook SP. 860-927-3238. http://dep.state.ct.us*). to reveal an ocean of crumpled, wooded hills. There is something infinitely mysterious about these twisted runs of hardwood forest, cut here and there by breezy saddles and shaded brooks, the quiet land full of the secret lives of bear and deer and migrant songbirds.

From the junction of US 7 and Conn. 4 go north on US 7 a quarter mile to Housatonic Meadows State Park. You'll see a sign and parking area for Pine Knob Loop Trail .75 mile farther up the road on the left side. Begin the walk on a small road at the north end of the parking area. In 0.2 mile is a junction, where you'll keep straight, and in another 0.2 mile a second junction, where you'll bear to the left, making your way upward through oak and hemlock and chestnut saplings. The trail continues to climb steadily, traversing a series of rocky terraces before topping the first of two summits that make up **Pine Knob;** the best views, however, are on the second summit. Standing on that high point drinking in the tumble of land around you, keep in mind that it was not by accident that the Housatonic River flows through the valley directly below you.

The hills on either side of the river are underlaid with hard, erosion-resistant rock such as granite, while the land beneath the Housatonic contains softer rock, much of it marble, allowing the river an easier passage.

Falls Village to Housatonic Meadows State Park

Farther upriver is a 10-mile float that offers a wonderful variety of flat-water stretches, as well as Class II and Class III white water, all of it framed by enchanting forested hills. As an added bonus, in the early stretches of the trip you'll be passing a number of fine picnic

Rapids below Bulls Bridge, Housatonic River

Fly fishing, Housatonic River

areas in the **Housatonic State Forest** (*Mohawk SF, 860-491-3620*)—great places to pull out and grab a snack, or to trade the paddle for a shady spot and a good book.

Put in to the river at **Power Plant Park** in the town of Falls Village, on Conn. 126, 3 miles west of the intersection with US 7, just below the Great Falls. Take-out is at the picnic area for Housatonic Meadows State Park (*Macedonia Brook SP, 860-927-3238*). The most challenging section of this trip is the Class III water beneath the covered bridge in West Cornwall, but it is easily scouted by taking your boat out on the left just before the bridge. With time for an occasional stop, allow 5 hours to complete the run. For information on doing the trip with a commercial outfitter, call Clarke Outdoors (*860-672-4457*).

The waters of the Housatonic are among the best in the state for fly fishing. There are several access points to the river, including the Housatonic Meadows State Park campground and the Housatonic State Forest. If you've been meaning to try your hand at this sport, but just haven't gotten around to it, consider signing up for lessons and a little guiding from the Housatonic Anglers Flyfishing School (*West Cornwall. 860-672-4457*) or Housatonic River Outfitters (*West Cornwall. 860-672-1010*).

Housatonic Flatwater Upstream from Falls Village

Strange as it may seem, it's also possible to paddle upstream on the Housatonic for many miles from Falls Village, passing a restful

---

Boating the Housatonic

If you're a canoeist or kayaker fond of lake and pond travel, give the following places a try. **Burr Pond** (*85 acres. Conn. 8, Highland Lake Rd. exit. Left on Old Conn. 8 South, right on Burr Mountain Rd. Rentals available Mem. Day–Labor Day*) **Wood Creek Pond** (*151 acres. From the junction of US 44 and Conn. 272 in Norfolk, follow Conn. 272 north for 2 miles, then right onto Ashpohtag Rd. Launch is 0.3 mile on the left. Excellent birding*) **Mount Tom Pond** (*61.5 acres. The pond is located 10 miles west of Litchfield on US 202. No ramp*).

---

mix of corn and alfalfa fields, barns and cows, and wildflowers by the thousands.

Put in from Housatonic River Road west of Falls Village at a landing above the power dam. This is a wonderful stretch of water from which to catch glimpses of great blue herons winging silently on wide steel blue wings, as if just arrived from some far more ancient world. While these elegant birds feed mostly on fish and frogs, making quiet catches from along the banks, you may also see them on occasion take small mammals and even birds.

About a mile upstream from the put-in, on the right, is the mouth of the **Hollenbeck River,** a smaller, twisted run of pristine flat water simply teeming with birdlife. This is a delightful waterway to

Following pages: Sugar maples in autumn, Housatonic River Valley

Kent River Road

Bird enthusiasts may want to explore the Kent River Road *(near Kent, 0.5 mile N of Conn. 341),* a dirt lane that runs along the west side of the Housatonic. Small parking areas along the route will allow you to park and walk; in addition, a trail leads from a parking area at the end of the road. This is a fantastic place to spot vireos and flycatchers, as well as a wide variety of migrant warblers, including northern parula, yellow-throated, magnolia, Cape May, yellow-rumped, Nashville, black-and-white, cerulean, and blue-winged.

explore by canoe, and one of the finest places to catch dawn pouring new light onto the land. Bring your binoculars and bird books, and count on an unforgettable few hours in the wild.

Boaters can obtain water-release information from Northwest Utilities *(888-417-4837).* General information is also available from the Housatonic Valley Association.

Rand's View Trail

That you don't need to be down on the water to enjoy the environs of the Housatonic becomes wonderfully evident on the trail to **Rand's View** *(Appalachian Mountain Club regional office, 413-443-0011).* This moderate 1.2-mile climb winds along a stretch of what was formerly the Appalachian Trail, ending at a

wind-ruffled Nature Conservancy preserve that offers outstanding views. In fact, on a clear day you can see across a sea of tattered uplands all the way to Mount Greylock (see pp. 212-14) in northwest Massachusetts.

Leaving from Falls Village, you can reach the starting point for your walk by heading north on Conn. 126. From this turnoff, go 0.6 mile and turn left onto Point of Rocks Road, then 0.1 mile to Water Street on the right. In 0.4 mile, Water Street turns to the left, crossing the Housatonic River. Once across the bridge stay right, and in 0.4 mile, turn left onto Sugar Hill Road. The trailhead and the parking lot are at the end of Sugar Hill Road, 0.9 mile from this last turn.

The walk follows a dirt road along private property for 0.3 mile, then breaks off onto a blue-blazed trail through a forest of hickory, birch, hemlock, and the occasional white pine. Depending on the time of year, this is a good stretch of trail on which to find striking weaves of wildflowers: purple trillium and rue anemone, as well as the delicate white blossoms of miterwort.

You may also spot the soft, paperlike pink petals of wild geranium, or cranesbill, as it's sometimes called, for the shape of its fruits. The astringent qualities of this plant have been known by herbal healers for centuries, who use it to treat everything from open sores to diarrhea. Wild geranium has even been made into a poultice for swollen feet. Healers have also found that the stems of the plant act as a hemostatic, an agent that stops bleeding; thus the long-standing use of this geranium by Native Americans to treat cuts.

The Rand's View trail continues to climb, passing through stands of hemlock and yellow birch. This latter tree, recognized by its shiny yellow to silver bark and double-toothed leaves, has long been a favorite of furniture-makers. Eventually you will pass signs for the 310-acre **Patricia Winter Woodland—Hamlet Hill Preserve.** When you've gone 0.4 mile past the preserve boundary, you'll meet a fork in the trail. The right-hand trail leads 0.7 mile up **Mount Prospect,** while continuing straight—which puts you on the Appalachian Trail—brings you to the ragged, tumbling vistas of Rand's View. ■

Covered bridge, West Cornwall, Connecticut

Canada geese on Ongley Pond, White Memorial

White Memorial Foundation and Conservation Center

CONNECTICUT ■ 4,000 acres ■ Northwest Connecticut, 3 miles west of Litch-field on US 202 ■ Year-round ■ Camping, hiking, walking, kayaking, canoeing, bird-watching ■ Contact the center, 80 Whitehall Rd., Litchfield, CT 06759; phone 860-567-0857. www.whitememorialcc.org

YOU'LL DO A LOT OF SEARCHING before you find a natural history center anywhere in the country more engaging, or more thoughtfully managed, than the White Memorial Foundation and Conservation Center in Litchfield. Anyone planning to spend time in the outdoors of southern New England should plan at least one long day, if not two, here, in order to meet some of the native flora and fauna up close and personal.

In the kind of forward-thinking act that often goes uncelebrated, Connecticut resident Alain White and his sister May created the White Memorial Foundation in 1913, using as the centerpiece beautiful **Bantam Lake,** the largest freshwater lake in the state. Given the development that was sure to come, the Whites said they wanted to preserve the natural beauty and character of the place for future generations. In the years that followed, the foundation grounds would grow to some 4,000 acres, stretching from Bantam Lake up the lovely Bantam River to Little Pond.

Besides these foundation lands, in the course of their lives the Whites also donated thousands of acres to the state of Connecticut for parks and reserves, including portions of Peoples (see pp. 235-38) and Mohawk Trail State Forests (see pp. 211-12), and Macedonia Brook, Kent Falls, and Campbell Falls State Parks. Alain also spent a great deal of time studying and practicing wildlife conservation principles. In 1924, for example, he was instrumental in reviving populations of the nearly extinct wood duck, bringing in an English gamekeeper named Henry Bowden to raise the birds on one of the foundation's ponds; in the years that followed some thousand wood ducks were raised here, with several hundred trapped and held over each winter to provide breeding stock.

The first stop at White Memorial should be the **Nature Museum** *(Adm. fee)*, which offers a delightful excursion through 12,000 years of regional natural history. This is a facility that relies less on technical bells and whistles than on a simple but splendid use of imagination. No matter where you walk, where you turn, something will catch your eye: flashy colored leaves lining the walls, constellations painted on the ceiling, a life-size beaver lodge, stunning photos of the property as back-drops for the exhibits.

Beyond the museum are 35 miles of excellent hiking trails, canoe launch facilities, three campgrounds, an orienteering course, and outdoor education classrooms. The White Memorial offers an extensive lineup of programs for children *(enrollment required)*, as well as shorter inter-pretive programs for all ages on everything from dinosaurs to insects, bird-watching to stargazing.

Those in the mood for walking should consider an early morning or late evening walk on the **Lake Trail,** passing a fine observation platform on the north shore of Bantam Lake, where you're likely to spot a variety of ducks and gulls. The **Little Pond Boardwalk Trail** and the **Butternut Brook Trail,** for their part, traverse an exquisite area of open water and wetlands. This is a good place to see grebes, terns, and swallows, and, in the open marshes, swamp sparrows, rail, and red-winged blackbirds as well. The Little Pond trail is especially engaging, mostly because of the fantastic boardwalk system around the pond, skirting cloaks of cat-tails and swamp maple as well as captivating gardens of forget-me-nots and wild rose.

If you happen to be at White Memorial as a beginning bird-watcher— and that's an excellent reason to be here—keep in mind these sugges-tions. For starters, early morning and late evening are always the best times to see birds; the middle of the day is down time, and there's far less going on in the way of feeding or communicating. Secondly, experienced bird-watchers tend to make their way slowly down trails, breaking now and then to look around and listen before resuming their stroll. In many environments, simply being seated quietly in inconspicuous clothing is the best bird-watching strategy, as this makes it far less likely that birds will notice you. Also, if you're trying to identify a bird, if at all possible approach it with the sun at your back, so the bird will be well lit, and not just a darkened silhouette.

Finally, canoeists and kayakers should consider a paddle on the **Bantam River,** putting in where it crosses Whites Woods Road, which allows you to either go upstream for roughly 2 miles to Little Pond, or downstream for several miles through an area of wetlands to Bantam Lake. You can also put in at the bridge on High Bridge Road, near the western edge of the preserve, and follow the river downstream for 1.5 miles to the north shore of Bantam Lake. ∎

Understory of hay-scented ferns, Sharon Audubon Center

Sharon Audubon Center

CONNECTICUT ■ 890 acres ■ Northwest Connecticut, 3 miles west of Cornwall Bridge ■ Year-round ■ Walking, guided walks, bird-watching, wildflower viewing ■ Contact the center, 325 Cornwall Bridge Rd., Sharon, CT 06069; phone 860-364-0520. http://audubon.org/local/sanctuary/sharon/

SOME OF THE BEST PLACES to visit are the small, well-managed nature preserves—the kind filled not with multimillion-dollar museum displays, but rather with volunteers and patrons who stick by them season after season. These staffers gain in the process a certain level of native wisdom about what's going on in the back forty at any given moment: They know when to start looking for warblers in spring; how to gauge what time of year it is, even what week, based on the mat of wildflowers blooming along a woodland trail; how to become friends with a certain painted turtle who keeps showing up along the boardwalk, summer after summer. With such values in mind, no place hits the mark more often than the Audubon Society preserves, and of those, the Sharon Audubon Center is indeed a gem.

Like many such centers, Sharon has at the starting point of its trails a greaseboard for writing recent sightings and sounds, which for anyone trying to master local flora and fauna can be exactly the right start. (Your cause is further helped by illustrations, placed here by the staff, of some of the property's most common trees and plants.) Had you been here in August, for example, guidebooks in hand, you could have fashioned a daylong treasure hunt out of nothing more than trying to match the sightings on that greaseboard. Plants listed included moth mullein, nightshade, Indian pipe, blue vervain, wild leek, wintergreen, bergamot, fringed loosestrife, St. John'swort, motherwort, and steeplebush.

Depending on the season, you can find birds by the dozen, including wood thrush, ovenbird, eastern bluebird, veery, vireo, scarlet tanager, chimney swift, barred owl, red-tailed hawk, American goldfinch, various warblers, belted kingfisher, eastern kingbird, great blue heron, wood duck, song sparrow, eastern towhee, turkey vulture, and osprey. Rounding out the list were gray tree frogs and bullfrogs, painted turtles and snapping turtles, garter snakes, raccoons, little brown bats, big brown bats, beavers, and even cicadas.

The center itself, while not fancy, is wonderfully instructive. There are aquariums scattered about, mimicking pond life, as well as mounts of various local mammals. Cushioned chairs have been placed before large windows looking out on a line of bird feeders, creating an ideal place for beginning bird-watchers to sit back and learn the basics. Downstairs is an adventure room, which provides games as well as partitioned cubbyholes into which kids can crawl and listen to sounds of whales, birds, and rushing streams. The center's summer calendar includes weekend walks to watch birds, identify trees, and learn wildflowers. You can even stargaze or enjoy the woods under the full moon. If you can time your visit for the **Sharon Audubon Festival,** which typically happens over two days in July, by all means do so. In addition to the usual attractions you'll find live music at the site, as well as in-depth workshops on everything from birds to gardening.

Those looking for a moderate bit of walking would do well to set out on a 3.5-mile loop beginning with the **Hendrickson Bog Meadow Trail,** which traverses a forest rich with hemlock, birch, witch hazel, and hornbeam on the way to **Hendrickson Bog Meadow Pond.** This is a nearly perfect pond, by the way, right down to the boardwalks, the beaver runs, and the carefully placed benches on which you can sit and listen to a most enchanting concert featuring the musical talents of the local frogs. From the north shore of the pond, continue on the Hendrickson Bog Meadow Trail, which soon veers back into the woods and shortly thereafter joins the **Woodchuck Trail.** Follow the Woodchuck through a series of woodlands and open meadows, the latter providing gorgeous views to the west across green hills and wooded valleys. The Woodchuck eventually makes a loop and joins the Hendrickson Bog Meadow Trail, where you'll take a right, following it back to the nature center.

Besides offering an interpretive brochure full of useful and interesting plant information, the staff has also come up with another ingenious way to disseminate this kind of material. Along the path is a series of tall wooden stakes, atop which are mounted clear plastic tennis-ball containers. These are lined with sheets of paper, printed side facing out, offering descriptions of special attractions at that location. You lift the container from the post, read the message, replace it, and go on your way. ∎

Topsmead State Forest

CONNECTICUT ■ 514 acres ■ Northwest Connecticut, 2 miles east of Litchfield off Conn. 118 ■ Year-round ■ Walking, horseback riding, bird-watching ■ Contact the state forest, P.O. Box 108, Litchfield, CT 06759; phone 860-567-5694. http://dep.state.ct.us

NEAR THE TURN OF THE 20th century, Waterbury, Connecticut, was the brass capital of the world, and Henry Sabin Chase was a key member of its governing body. Needless to say, Henry was a wealthy man, and among the many gifts he bestowed on his daughter Edith was 16 acres on the top of Jefferson Hill. Here she built a rustic cabin, then replaced it years later with the striking summer home called **Chase Cottage** (*Guided tours June-Oct. 2nd and 4th weekend of each month*) that stands to this day. It is a beautiful cottage with an exterior trim of cypress wood, downspouts made of lead, and a slate roof. Its interior woodwork and flooring are of the finest oak.

As nice as the house was, however, Edith loved the outdoors, giving tremendous attention to flower gardens and other landscaping features, many of which are still maintained. Combine this with the great deal of additional acreage that now surrounds the house and is kept in natural condition for walking, horseback riding, and picnicking, and you have the kind of place that on any given afternoon can leave you feeling as if you were the guest of a wealthy friend, strolling the grounds waiting for her to return for afternoon tea.

Topsmead is not a particularly wild place, but it is uniquely satisfying. When I visited the 0.7-mile **Edith M. Chase Ecology Trail,** the bird blind was missing. What was left of the interpretive signs was reminiscent of what might be erected on a wood lot by caring students of the high school biology club: old signs on sheets of plywood telling about litter, about water pollution, and about the sun being the ultimate source of energy. If ever there was a place simply to ramble, be it along a mowed lane through mats of bladder campion, or through the dark reaches of the forest along the state forest's **Stairs Trail,** this is it. The wet, shady areas of the preserve are good places to find jewelweed, which in August will be hung with lovely orange, spur-shaped flowers. In the fall these blooms will be replaced by small green pods; at the slightest touch the pods pop open, firing their seeds in all directions—a trait that has earned the plant the alternate name of "spotted touch-me-not." The juice of jewelweed has long been used to relieve the itching of nettle stings and poison ivy.

Don't go to Topsmead to find the biggest, rarest, or wildest of anything. Come instead to feed all sides of your brain on a mix of exquisite lawns and gardens, the smell of a hay field, the promise of an unkempt slice of woods where the green frogs pluck the loose strings of their banjos, and in the distance the veery sings, its voice running down the scale like water in a nearby brook. ■

Devil's Hopyard State Park

CONNECTICUT ■ 860 acres ■ Central Connecticut, off Conn. 82 in East Haddam ■ Year-round ■ Camping, hiking ■ Contact the park, 366 Hopyard Rd., East Haddam, CT 06423; phone 860-873-8566. http://dep.state.ct.us

THE LANDS AROUND Devil's Hopyard, cut by the beautiful Eightmile River, are currently the site of intense conservation efforts. The idea behind these efforts is to link the protected lands in such a way that they do not become islands broken by development, but rather contiguous habitat, large enough to provide lasting homes for mammals, plants, and birds. It is to this effort that conservation biology is most dedicated, leaning on decades of research in order to identify— and ultimately, protect—those landscapes that are key to the survival of New England's flora and fauna.

Walking the Devil's Hopyard is a treat—in part because of the grand sight of the tannin-stained **Eightmile River,** which at one point makes a dramatic, 60-foot-long tumble over a series of basalt ledges—and also because many of the trees here are mature enough (and thus free of lower branches)

Waterfall, Devil's Hopyard State Park

to offer a parklike feel to many of the trails. In parts of New England, it was this kind of forest, only with far bigger trees and even more space between them, that greeted explorers in the 17th and 18th centuries. While there were plenty of tangled thickets to be found in wet areas, in many other locations it was possible to travel about quite easily by horseback, sometimes with a wagon in tow, because of the age of the woods.

One of the best ways to get your bearings here is to take a 3-mile, round-trip walk via the **Orange Trail** (blazed with orange dots on an ivory background) to a vista overlooking the Eightmile River. On the otherhand, if woods are the surroundings you enjoy most, try the peace and quiet of the 2.5-mile **Red and Green Trail,** which loops southwest from the parking area, marked by red and green blazes. ■

Pachaug State Forest

CONNECTICUT ■ 28,000 acres ■ Central Connecticut, 2 miles northeast of Voluntown via Conn. 138 and 49 ■ Year-round ■ Walking, bird-watching, wild-flower viewing ■ Contact the state forest, P.O. Box 5, Voluntown, CT 06384; phone 860-376-4075. http://dep.state.ct.us

AT NEARLY 28,000 ACRES, Pachaug (an Indian term, loosely translated as "bend in the river"), is the largest state forest complex in Connecticut. Yet what you see today as a beautiful woodland was not long ago nearly unbroken farms and pastures, a history revealed by miles of stone fence.

What to See and Do

Indeed, one of the best ways to appreciate the power of a New England forest to reclaim cleared land is to make the easy 2-mile round-trip to the summit of **Mount Misery.**

Nature's Forecasters

Long before weather forecasting was a science, people turned to nature to get a sense of what tomorrow might bring. A farmer might notice swallows flying low or spiders deserting their webs and know that rain was on the way. When it came to telling temperature, that same farmer might turn to the rhododendron. When the thermometer falls below roughly 60°F, the plant's leaves begin to droop. As the temperature drops, they continue to droop in obvious increments, moving another notch for about every ten degrees lost in temperature. Just above freezing, the leaves curl back on themselves.

Starting from the parking area on Cutoff Road, a dirt road north of the entrance, follow the blue-blazed **Pauchag Trail** to the left. From here the world falls away in a dense mass of trees—red maples, white and red oaks, hickories, hemlocks, and white ash. Many people find it surprising that Connecticut has one of the highest percentages of forested land of any state in America, bested only by New Hampshire and Maine. However, the view as you climb to the top of Mount Misery can go a long way toward convincing you of this fact. To add variety—and a little extra distance—to the walk, continue off the summit to the southwest and make a right onto the first dirt road you reach. Follow this to a T-intersection with another dirt lane and turn right, which will lead you back to the parking area.

Canoeing and Kayaking

Pachaug State Forest also offers venues for those who like the water. If you've brought a boat, or will rent one (*rental information 860-376-4075*), consider a launch at the **Pachaug River** near

Beachdale Pond, located near the park entrance. From the ramp you can head into Beachdale Pond, and from there either upstream (north) along **Mount Misery Brook** for roughly a mile, or downstream (south) along the same waterway, either of which offers fine wetland habitat.

In the Green Falls area of the forest, southeast of Voluntown, excellent paddling awaits you at **Green Falls Pond.** The boat launch can be reached either from Conn. 138, on a gravel route called East Road, or from Conn. 49, by traveling a gravel route known as Fish Road *(adm. fee weekends).* Rocky islands dot the water, and at the southern end the pond empties over the Green Falls Dam into a steep ravine.

Biking

Pachaug State Forest contains a web of dirt tote roads that are perfect for mountain bikes. **Firetower Road** and **Trail 1 Road** to Phillips Pond are especially good mountain-biking routes, and either can be linked with other tracks to make short but satisfying loop rides. You can pick up a map at forest headquarters.

Rhododendron Sanctuary

Of all the memorable vegetation of the southern New England forest, few species are more unforgettable than a full-blown

Understory of ferns, Pachaug State Forest

bloom of *Rhododendron maximum,* its pink and white flowers hovering overhead at the tips of long, corkscrew branches.

For all its beauty, though, this plant has earned mixed reviews from those who live, work, and travel outdoors. Beekeepers since ancient Greece have steered clear of the plant for fear of poisoned honey made from the plant's nectar (although the plant's toxins don't seem to harm the bees themselves). And modern-day hikers have sometimes been stopped in their tracks by dense rhododendron thickets.

The trail leading into the sanctuary takes off from the north side of the large playing field you will see when you arrive. Although the walk into the heart of the sanctuary is only a half mile long, en route you will encounter a wonderful garden of starflower, Canada mayflower, and highbush blueberry. As the ground grows wetter, this array yields to arrowleaf, sweet pepperbush, cinnamon fern, skunk cabbage, sweet gale, Atlantic white cedar, and insect-devouring pitcher plants.

If it's early morning or late in the day, keep your ears open for a fine medley of birdsong, including that of olive-sided flycatchers, brown creepers, redbreasted nuthatches, and Canada warblers. ∎

Riding a dirt trail, Myles Standish State Forest

Myles Standish State Forest

MASSACHUSETTS ■ 16,000 acres ■ Southeast Massachusetts, off Mass. 58 in South Carver ■ Trails closed Sat. and holidays mid-Oct.–Dec. and deer week, shotgun-hunting season ■ Camping, hiking, walking, boating, canoeing, swimming, fishing, mountain biking, horseback riding, cross-country skiing, bird-watching ■ Fee for swimming and picnic areas ■ Contact the state forest, P.O. Box 66, South Carver, MA 02366; phone 508-866-2526. www.state.ma.us/dem/parks/mssf.htm

HOW INTRIGUING THAT you would find one of the largest publicly owned outdoor areas in the state of Massachusetts only 40 miles from Boston. The state purchased these lands in 1916, after a group of wealthy Bostonians had used them for years as a sanctuary for game birds. Today (and thanks in no small part to the tireless tree planting and other improvements made in the 1930s by the Civilian Conservation Corps), the forest is a remarkably appealing place, highly cherished for its recreational opportunities. Standish has some 55 miles of trails that are ideal for horseback riding, mountain biking, hiking, and cross-country skiing. It also features ten freshwater ponds, some of which are perfect for launching your canoe or trying out your fishing rod. Rounding out the offerings are six camping areas with a whopping 400-plus sites, as well as a fairly decent schedule of interpretive programs offered by the state forest's staff throughout the summer.

Myles Standish, in case you were sleeping or otherwise distracted that day in history class, was a traveler on board the *Mayflower* who was eventually elected military captain of the Plymouth Colony. It was to Myles Standish that the job fell of poking around the cold, wind-blasted reaches of Cape Cod looking for a place to settle. Later, the soldier was enlisted to organize the Pilgrims' systems of defense. Standish was generally respected for the heroic way in which he served the colonists in the face of terrible privation and loss of life in the colony's early days. Not everyone was a fan, however. One contemporary, in a comment sounding like something out of Monty Python 350 years later, wrote in a letter that "Standish looks like a silly boy and is in utter contempt."

What makes Myles Standish State Forest interesting from an ecological perspective are the vast sprawls of pitch pine, making this the largest remaining pine barrens in all of New England. Because, like certain other conifers, pitch pine requires fire to regenerate, foresters conduct controlled burns to promote the health of the forest. This area is also not only a common stopover place for a many migrating birds, but provides nesting spots for prairie warblers, eastern bluebirds, common yellowthroats, common flickers, eastern towhees, brown thrashers, hermit thrushes, and whip-poor-wills.

If walking is on your mind, start out with a 3.1-mile trek over relatively flat ground around **East Head Reservoir.** The trail is blazed with blue triangular markers and begins a short walk from the headquarters parking area, on the other side of a small flowage. This is the only self-guided trail in the Myles Standish State Forest, and the 14 numbered posts keyed to an interpretive guide (available from the information center beside forest headquarters) serve as a great introduction to the natural areas through which you walk.

Mountain bikers, on the other hand, have a wide variety of routes to choose from, though the occasional patch of dry, loose soil may clue you in to the reason why some local riders refer to certain trails as "Miles of Sandish." **Charge** and **Fearing Ponds** both provide good rides for families, though you'll need to be mindful of your speed, given that these paved paths are also used by walkers.

Perhaps the biggest issue for riders to wrestle with in Myles Standish is the fact that there are a lot of trails here, and relatively few of them are marked very well. Anyone considering backcountry cycling here should stop by the park store near headquarters and purchase a map before setting out into the park. ■

Champlain
Lowlands

Missisquoi River, Vermont

ALTHOUGH THIS REGION makes up a relatively small portion of our book, the lowland valley that is today graced by beautiful Lake Champlain forms one of the most pleasing landscapes in all of America. To the east of this shimmering, 100-mile-long lake are rolling lands dappled with farms and fruit orchards, the apple trees planted in some of the best agricultural soil for 100 miles. Backing the farms are the lovely wooded uplands of the Green Mountains, a place of nooks and shaded ravines,

Burton Island State Park, Vermont

sending out braids of fast-stepping streams into the valley below. To the
west, on the other hand, are the equally beautiful Adirondack Mountains
of New York, bedecked each fall by a blanket of yellow, red, and russet
leaves. Along the margins of the lake itself are small villages, grassy
parks, sailboats lying at anchor, and canoeists just offshore, their paddles
flashing in the summer sun.

This sweep of lowlands is thought to have been created some 200
million years ago, when the area marked by this valley dropped along
a series of block faults at the eastern edge of the Adirondack margin.
For a long time afterward, the region drained not south to north toward
the St. Lawrence as it does today, but north to south. During the last of
the glacial epochs, often referred to as the Wisconsin period, a feature
known as the Champlain ice lobe—a mammoth plug of ice far thicker
and longer lasting than other ice flows in neighboring states—came to
the region. As the climate warmed and the glaciers began retreating,
water backed up behind the plug, eventually creating a massive body
of water known as Lake Vermont. Much bigger than Lake Champlain is
now, Lake Vermont changed many landlocked features, such as Mount
Philo, into little more than tiny islands. When the ice plug finally broke,
the waters of Lake Vermont flowed northward to the St. Lawrence,
lowering Lake Champlain to about the level we see today.

The Champlain lowlands have long appealed to humans, offering
what may be the longest record of occupation anywhere in Vermont.
Hunter-gatherers lived here as far back as 10,000 to 12,000 years ago.
When agriculture began taking hold some 3,000 years ago, hunting
remained important, but the cultivation of grains and other foodstuffs
pulled people into larger, more socially complex villages. European settlers, too, would eventually gain a foothold in places like the Champlain
Valley and Connecticut River Valley, quickly anchoring a web of small,
self-sufficient farms. In just 30 years, from 1760 to 1790, the population

of Vermont climbed from 300 to more than 85,000, much of it built on the back of farms.

A region of abundant groundwater, with a climate moderated by the lake and the surrounding mountains, the Champlain lowlands still possess a strong appeal. Outdoor lovers can enjoy both a variety and an abundance of life found almost nowhere else in northern New England. Like the Connecticut River Valley to the east, this is an especially fine mixing zone for trees. Members of the northern woods grow side by side with species typically found farther to the south or to the west, in New York State. Oaks and hickories are abundant, for example, as are swamp white oaks and silver maples, the last two trees gracing the lands just south of the Canadian border. Along the eastern shore of Lake Champlain, by contrast, are some of the finest marshlands in New England, many of them ideal for a day of slow, careful exploring by kayak or canoe.

The Champlain lowlands make a perfect base for a first glimpse of Vermont. A series of state parks and state and federal wildlife refuges on the east and north end of the lake offer wonderful opportunities for wildflower enthusiasts and bird-watchers. These areas, along with the forested uplands to the east and some extremely good interpretive stops, allow visitors to cultivate a thoroughly unforgettable sense of place. ∎

Nature trail at Missisquoi National Wildlife Refuge

Missisquoi National Wildlife Refuge

VERMONT ■ 6,338 acres ■ Northwest Vermont, off Vt. 78 ■ Best months May-Oct. ■ Camping, hiking, kayaking, canoeing, bird-watching ■ Contact the refuge, 371 N. River St., Swanton, VT 05488; phone 802-868-4781

IF YOU WANT A SENSE of how incredibly rich the Champlain lowlands can be, look no farther than the Missisquoi National Wildlife Refuge, green and watery and chock-full of life, lying at the head of the great Champlain Valley. Not only do some common creatures of the lowlands thrive in this refuge, but so do many animals who are all but absent elsewhere in New England, such as the Eastern spiny soft-shell turtle and American woodcock.

Refuge headquarters is the starting point for the enchanting **Black Creek** and **Maquam Creek interpretive trails** *(trail guides available on-site),* which will introduce you to a variety of intriguing habitats. There's also fine flat-water canoeing or kayaking on both **Dead Creek** and the **Missisquoi River,** either of which will carry you past wild rice, arrow-head, and bulrush along a delta rich in birdlife to Lake Champlain's **Missisquoi Bay.** *(Note that some areas of the refuge are closed at times to protect wildlife; check with staff before you go.)*

Missisquoi is one of a chain of refuges along the Atlantic flyway serving birds traveling between summer nesting grounds and wintering areas far to the south. Though the refuge is worth a visit any time of the year, fall is unforgettable, as thousands of ring-necked ducks settle in to feed there, along with mallard, black ducks, and green-winged teal. Missisquoi lands are also home to the **Shad Island great blue heron rookery,** the largest such colony in New England.

What to See and Do

Boaters simply carry their craft across Vt. 78 to a common put-in point. Those going to Dead Creek paddle right, toward Swanton, and then make a left at the first channel. Walkers head out from a set of interpretive panels next to the small gravel parking area behind headquarters.

The roughly 1 mile of flat walking described here begins in a meadow of cow vetch, milkweed, tall meadow rue, and a variety of grasses. Overhead you're likely to catch glimpses of red-tailed or rough-legged hawks tracing circles in the sky; closer to the ground, look for bobolinks and bluebirds, as well as the occasional eastern garter snake. This open, expansive feeling ends abruptly after about 200 yards, shortly after you cross a set of railroad tracks. From here on you'll find yourself wrapped in tangles of vines and thickets and sensitive fern, as well as alders and poplars, red and silver maples, and elms. Not long after this railroad crossing, a trail comes in from the right. This is the return path—for now, though, continue straight.

Adding to the junglelike feel of this place is a generous helping of marsh and standing water, as well as beautiful Black Creek, running dark and quiet through the woods, dappled with pond lilies and water lilies beyond the counting. At times the banks of the creek are flush with northern leopard frogs, plopping into the water by the dozen just ahead of you. Several years ago biologists grew concerned when a large number of Champlain Valley leopard frogs began showing deformities, just as they had in other states around the country. Although researchers suspect a number of environmental causes, from water pollution to ozone depletion (perhaps acting collectively), the problem remains a mystery.

The trail loop runs along Black Creek, makes a right turn, crosses a boardwalk over a fine little wetland, then makes one final right turn at a T-intersection, at which point Maquam Creek will be on your left. ■

Red-tailed Hawk

Keep your eyes to the sky, and you may spot this powerful raptor circling high above an open pasture, searching for mice. At other times you might find it sitting in a tree beside a meadow, watching for the smallest movements in the grass below.

The best clue to identifying a red-tailed hawk in flight is the tail, reddish brown above and pale underneath; also visible will be white underparts, as well as a band of dark streaks across the abdomen. Its cry is a high, descending *keeeeer*.

The red-tailed is not only one of the largest in the hawk family (these birds are typically just under 2 feet long), but also one of the most widespread, thriving from Nova Scotia to Alaska, Florida to Arizona, and beyond.

Burton Island State Park

VERMONT ■ 253 acres ■ Northwest Vermont off Vt. 36, following signs for Kill Kare State Park ■ Mid-May–Labor Day. Boat access only; a ferry runs from Kill Kare to Burton Island ■ Camping, hiking, boating, kayaking, canoeing, swimming ■ Adm. fee ■ Contact the park, P.O. Box 123, St. Albans Bay, VT 05481; phone 802-524-6353 (summer), 802-879-5674 (winter), or 800-252-2363. www.vtstateparks.com/burton

TRUE ENOUGH, it's a beautiful place. Fine stands of white cedar and white pine grow here, with spruces and sumacs and alders. Through the warm months long tosses of wildflowers are framed by the blue, blue shimmer of Lake Champlain. But Burton Island's main attraction is what it doesn't have—and that's cars. Not that there aren't plenty of people here on summer weekends. But somehow 253 acres of beach and grassland and forest seem to grow to many times that size when you're not surrounded by the honking of horns and the smell of exhaust. (When the state first acquired the park in 1960, there were plans to build a causeway from the mainland to accommodate vehicles; fortunately, the plans were scrapped.) Walking the trails of the park, you may notice stone piles or fence lines, even old foundations and farm implements, reminders that before this island was a park, it was a farm—at least since the 1840s, when farmer C.C. Burton used it as pasturage for his cows.

What to See and Do

One of the best ways to savor **Burton Island** is to take a walk on the **North Shore Trail**—an easy path, with numbers linked to an interpretive brochure, that crosses many of the island's habitats. The theme in the early part of the walk is clearly **Lake Champlain,** which takes its name from that intrepid French explorer, Samuel de Champlain. Four years after he'd finished mapping the upper coast of New England, Champlain agreed to lead an expedition into this area with an Algonquian chief, with plans to help the chief win a victory over his enemies, the Iroquois. As darkness lifted from the land on that long ago morning, Champlain saw that he was utterly outnumbered. But in true Champlain style, he led the Algonquian on a slow march into what must have seemed certain suicide. At 30 yards, Champlain later reported, he saw an Iroquois leader begin to draw his bow, at which point he raised his gun and fired it, killing two of the Iroquois and mortally wounding another. Despite the odds, the Algonquian managed to win that particular battle. And yet the war itself only got hotter, ultimately fueled by even stronger enemies, the English and the French—the former taking sides with the Iroquois, the latter with the Algonquian.

After nudging the lakeshore for less than a mile, you'll reach **Eagle**

Bull Island, Burton Island State Park

Following pages: Lightning storm over Vermont

Bay. On most summer days, this is a good place to spot ring-billed gulls circling low over the inlet, casting an eye for something to eat. While we usually think of gulls feeding on the bounty of seashores and lakes, they will in fact eat virtually any kind of food imaginable, including insects, berries, grasshoppers, and worms.

From a point just west of here, you can pick up the **West Shore Trail,** which runs south for 1 mile to the tip of the island (a perfect place to swim and picnic), or reach the same place by continuing along the cobbly shore of the lake. If you opt for the West Shore Trail, you'll be passing through an area full of young white cedars, poplars, and especially staghorn sumacs— all pioneer players in the game of turning this former pasture into a full-blown woods.

Staghorn sumac takes its name from the fact that the plant's hairy, branched twigs resemble deer antlers. Both staghorn and smooth sumac were used extensively by native peoples. In late summer or early autumn they soaked the hairy fruits in water to make a refreshing drink that tastes somewhat like unsweetened lemonade (settlers sometimes referred to sumac as lemonade tree or vinegar tree). From the bark they also made a tea for sore throats.

For the return trip from the tip of the island, you can either follow the **Southern Tip Trail,** which is a wide mowed path leading through yet more groves of sumac, or join up with the **Island Farm Trail,** which will land you at the nature center. Don't leave the island without a stop at this nature center; in the summer months a naturalist will be on duty to answer questions, as well as to offer programs on the natural and cultural history of the island. ■

Fallen leaf at Burton Island State Park

Hawley House, Kingsland Bay State Park

Kingsland Bay State Park

VERMONT ■ 264 acres ■ Northwest Vermont, south of Burlington off US 7 near Ferrisburg ■ Mid-May–Labor Day ■ Hiking, kayaking, canoeing ■ Adm. fee ■ Contact the park, 787 Kingsland Bay State Park Rd., Ferrisburg, VT 05456; phone 802-877-3445 (summer), 802-483-2001 (winter), or 800-658-1622. www.vtstateparks.com/kingland

THIS SMALL PARK on the eastern shore of Lake Champlain is anything but fancy: a pleasant lakeside lawn, a place to launch a sea kayak or a canoe, and a fine little 1-mile round-trip walk to a striking headland. Then again, what more could you possibly need?

When you arrive at Kingsland Bay, park in the large lot just past the fee station. The **Red Trail** begins at the edge of the bay near the tennis courts. It winds through woods of hemlocks, white oaks, shagbark hickories, and rather stately stands of red pines. Throughout your treks in central New England, you'll see red pine growing just like this, in pure stands. When blister rust attacked and killed millions of white pines in the early 1900s, the task of replanting was almost always accomplished with red pine. It's a tree that grows very fast (2 feet in a single year is not unusual), and it does so in soils that other trees wouldn't tolerate.

Among these trees you'll find a variety of large stumps—remnants of the magnificent old-growth white pine forest that stood until roughly 1900. Also here are many interesting woodland plants, including shadbush, false Solomon's seal, and the beautiful white trillium. The white trillium, in fact, is found in greater numbers in the lime-rich soils along Lake Champlain than anywhere else in New England. Native peoples used trilliums in general for many medicinal purposes; the red trillium, common throughout Vermont, was especially celebrated as a means of controlling bleeding after childbirth. To this day many people refer to the plant as birthroot.

After rounding the headland, the trail makes a short climb, then begins the return trip through clusters of honeysuckle, passing a spur trail on the left heading to the lakeshore. The final stretches of forest are rich with white oaks, hobblebushes, and basswoods. This last tree is recognized by its broad, saw-toothed leaves, uneven at the base. In some places basswood is referred to as bee tree, since in early summer its canopy of yellow to white flowers is tended by thousands of bees.

The beautiful old stone house graced with shady porches that you'll pass next to the parking area is known as the **Hawley House.** Built in 1790, it was part of an exclusive girls' camp named École Champlain until the 1960s.

Canoeing and Kayaking

On Hawkins Road, approximately 2 miles before the park entrance, is a bridge crossing **Little Otter Creek.** This is a wonderful put-in spot, allowing paddlers to head either north or south through the **Little Otter Creek Wildlife Management Area** (802-878-1564), a preserve of more than 1,000 acres.

Downstream (northbound) paddlers can follow **Little Otter Creek's** gentle flow for less than 2 miles until they reach the waters of Lake Champlain, coming out just east of **McDonough Point.**

If you're looking for kayak instruction or guided trips on Lake Champlain, you might contact PaddleWays Sea Kayak Adventures (Burlington. 802-660-8606. www .paddleways.com). ■

Nearby
Although the forests on **Mount Philo State Park** (Mt. Philo Rd. off US 7 near Charlotte, VT. 802-425-2390 summer, 802-483-2001 winter. Mid-May–mid-Oct.) suffered significant damage during the ice storms of 1998 (see sidebar p. 193), Vermont's first state park remains a great spot from which to enjoy the beauty of the Champlain Valley and the Adirondack Mountains. There is a small, ten-unit campground here and a wonderful picnic area— probably one of the best places in the state from which to watch the sunset. Travelers should note that the road to the summit and campground is not recommended for trailers; a steep hiking trail also leads to the top.

Goldenrod

Beached canoe at Button Bay State Park

Button Bay State Park

VERMONT ■ 253 acres ■ Northwest Vermont, west of Vergennes off Vt. 22A ■ Mid-May–Columbus Day ■ Camping, hiking, canoeing, swimming, wildflower viewing ■ Adm. fee ■ Contact the park, 5 Button Bay State Park Rd., Vergennes, VT 05491; phone 802-475-2377 (summer), 802-483-2001 (winter), or 800-658-1622. www.vtstateparks.com/button

BESIDES BEING JUST PLAIN BEAUTIFUL, the slice of land that cradles Button Bay State Park has seen its share of notable historical figures, from Samuel de Champlain in 1609 to Benjamin Franklin and Ethan Allen in 1776, and a year after that, Benedict Arnold. Actually, when you're visiting this park, it's hard not to think of the past in one form or another: rum-runners paddling back and forth to Canada under the cover of darkness; the British heading south down the lake to invade the rebellious colonists.

For many decades Button Bay was in private hands. In the late 1800s it was a summer home for Samuel Putnam Avery, whose family was the first to import European art masterpieces into the United States. And long before any of that, the park had a geologic history that still shows itself at every turn. Even the name of the park, Button Bay, refers to a time thousands of years ago, when clay deposited by glaciers settled around the stems of various aquatic plants. When the plants died, they left holes in the clay mounds where their stems had been; these mounds were later compressed under the weight of sediments, creating small doughnuts, or buttons. (The term "button," used as a name for the bay, was first applied by British soldiers, who thought the clay pieces looked like button molds used in England.)

Button Bay is a fantastic place in which to see meadow flowers such as daisies and Queen Anne's lace. That, too, is thanks to conditions established a long, long time ago, when shells, the remains of various sea creatures, and clay were cemented together to form the limestone that underlies much of this park. Limestone soils tend to be free of acid and thus favor the growth of many plants.

Next to the park's swimming pool, a half-mile trail takes off for the **Button Bay Nature Center,** first traversing a wild mix of sumac, birdsfoot trefoil, and flowering raspberry, then a lovely, somewhat unusual mix of mature forest, including maples, white and redcedars, white pines, hemlocks, red and white oaks, basswoods, and shagbark hickories. The nature center itself is a thoroughly inviting little cottage stuffed with information about the park's cultural and natural history; a park naturalist is on hand from June to Labor Day to answer questions and lead outings.

After orienting yourself at the nature center, walk out to the point and enjoy a wonderful view of the lake, then return to the parking area via **Champlain Trail,** which leaves from behind the nature center. This path winds through a mature forest—an unusual feature, given that nearly all of the land in this area was cleared for farming. There are some interesting plants to be found along this trail, as well as some nice white cedar trees, hanging on among the moss-covered rocks of the lakeshore. ■

Nearby
For those who want to know more about the region or learn regional crafts, just a few miles north of Button Bay State Park is the **Lake Champlain Maritime Museum** (W of Vergennes, off Vt. 22A. 802-475-2022. www.lcmm.org). This excellent museum offers not only big helpings of history but also a variety of workshops—from marine photography and coastal kayaking to making traditional paddles, watercraft, and brown-ash pack baskets.

Resources

The following is a select list of resources. Contact state and local associations for additional information. Note that most campsites operate seasonally. Plan ahead. For chain hotels and motels operating in New England, see p. 283.

MAINE

Federal and State Agencies

Bureau of Parks and Lands
22 State House Station
Augusta, ME 04333
207-287-3821
www.state.me.us/doc/
prkslnds/reserve.htm
Parks and public reserve lands, boat access sites, ATV and snowmobile trails, etc. Campground reservations.

Department of Inland Fisheries and Wildlife
284 State Street
41 State House Station
Augusta, ME 04333
207-287-8000
or 800-287-8003
General information and licenses.

Office of Tourism
888-MAINE-45
800-533-9595
Tourist information, updates on cross-country skiing, snow-mobiling, and fall foliage.

Outfitters and Activities

Maine Wilderness Tours
RR1, Box 462
Belgrade, ME 04917
207-495-7729
Sporting vacations with information on the best outfitters and guides throughout Maine.

Acadia National Park and Vicinity

Acadia Bike and
Coastal Kayaking
Tours
48 Cottage Street
Bar Harbor, ME 04609
207-288-9605

Sea kayaking tours and bike rentals.

Bold Coast Charter Company
P.O. Box 364
Cutler, ME 04626
207-259-4484
www.boldcoast.com
Puffin-watching and other coastal excursions from Cutler.

Crab Apple Whitewater, Inc.
HC 63, Box 25
The Forks, ME 04985
207-663-4491
or 800-553-7238
Scenic float-trips to Class IV to V white-water on the Kennebec and Dead Rivers.

Katahdin Outfitters
P.O. Box 34
Millinocket, ME 04462
800-862-2663
Canoe rentals and more.

Southwestern Maine

Bethel Outdoor Adventures
121 Mayville Road
Bethel, ME 04217
207-824-4224
or 800-533-3607
Canoe, kayak, and bicycle rentals; hiking and mountain biking trail maps.

Lodgings

Acadia National Park and Vicinity

Asticou Inn
Route 3
Northeast Harbor, ME 04662
207-276-3344
Exclusive hotel offering garden strolling, harbor views, and a fine restaurant.

Bar Harbo Chamber of Commerce
P.O. Box 158
Bar Harbor, ME 04609
207-288-5103
www.barharborinfo.com
For complete listings of lodgings in Bar Harbor.

Claremont Hotel
P.O. Box 137
Southwest Harbor, ME 04679
207-244-5036
or 800-244-5036

A resort with croquet, rocking chairs, rowboats, and more.

Baxter State Park and Vicinity

Hotel Terrace
52 Medway Road
Millinocket, ME 04462
207-723-4525
Quiet, relaxed family-style atmosphere with 11 rooms and restaurant.

The Big Moose Inn
Baxter State Park Road
P.O. Box 98
Millinocket, ME 04462
207-723-8391
A restaurant, cabins overlooking Millinocket Lake, campground, and old inn.

Southwestern Maine

The Captain Lord Mansion
P.O. Box 800
Kennebunkport, ME 04046
207-967-3141
The comforts of home in a federal-style inn.

Camping

For state parks campsite reservations, call 207-287-3824 (or 800-332-1501 in state) at least three days in advance, or write to the Bureau of Parks and Lands.

Acadia National Park and Vicinity

Mount Desert Narrows
Camping Resort
RR1, P.O. Box 2045
Bar Harbor, ME 04609
207-288-4782
Full camping resources.

The Seaview
16 Norwood Road
Eastport, ME 04631
207-853-4471
74 sites with views of the Atlantic Ocean.

Baxter State Park and Vicinity

Cathedral Pines
Campground
P.O. Box 146
Eustis, ME 04936
207-246-3491
Sites among the trees on the shores of Flagstaff Lake.

Mattawamkeag Wilderness
Park
P.O. Box 5
Mattawamkeag, ME 04459
207-736-2465
or 888-724-2465
52 sites on 1,000 acres by
the Mattawamkeag River.

Moosehead Family
Campground
P.O. Box 307
Greenville, ME 04441
207-695-2210
35 sites in town.

NEW HAMPSHIRE

Federal and
State Agencies

Fish and Game Department
2 Hazen Drive
Concord, NH 03301-1856
603-271-3421
For licensing, season dates,
and information on
educational courses.

New Hampshire Division of
Parks & Recreation
P.O. Box 1856
Concord, NH 03302-1856
603-271-3556
or 603-271-3628 (camping
reservations)
Park locations, facilities, and
activities information.

New Hampshire Division
of Travel and Tourism
Development
P.O. Box 1856
Concord, NH 03302
603-271-2343
or 800 FUN-IN-NH
Events, attractions, dining,
lodging, and more.

Outdoor Education
and Resources

Vermont Institute
of Natural Science
27023 Church Hill Road
Woodstock, NH 05091
802-457-2779
Programs, talks, and
a rehabilitation center
for raptors.

Outfitters
and Activities

Great Glen Trails
Outdoor Center
P.O. Box 300
Gorham, NH 03581
603-466-2333

www.mt-washington.com
40 miles of mountain
trails, fly-fishing school,
and a full paddling school
offering touring, kayaking,
and canoeing.

Mountain Bike and Nature
Center at The Balsams
RR1, Box 1000
Dixville Notch, NH 03576
603-255-3921
www.thebalsams.com
For trails and nearby
flat- and white-water
activities.

Saco Bound and
Rapid River Company
P.O. Box 119, US 302
Center Conway, NH 03813
603-447-2177
www.sacobound.com
Canoe rentals and kayak
touring on Lake Umbagog.

Lodgings

Appalachian Mountain Club
Pinkham Notch Visitor
Center
P.O. Box 298
Gorham, NH 03581
603-466-2727
Back-country huts along
the Appalachian Trail staffed
by AMC members; natural
history programs; dinner
and breakfast included.

Home Hill Country Inn
and French Restaurant
703 River Road
Plainfield, NH 03781
603-675-6165
The 1818 inn offers
haute cuisine dining and
seasonal activities.

Mount Washington Hotel
and Resort
US 302
Bretton Woods, NH
03575
603-278-1000
or 800-258-0330
A grand hotel offering a
wide range of rooms.

Notchland Inn
US 302
Hart's Location, NH 03812
603-374-6131
or 800-866-6131
www.notchland.com
Idyllic location with wood-
burning fire-places and an
outdoor hot tub.

Camping

For statewide camping,

contact the New Hampshire
Division of Parks & Recreation for state park
reservations or check out
more campsites at
www.ucampnh.com.

Northern New Hampshire

White Mountains
and Vicinity

In the White Mountain
National Forest, reserva-
tions for the following
campgrounds can be made
at 877-444-6777: Barnes
Field, Basin, Compton,
Covered Bridge, Dolly
Copp Big Meadow,
Hancock, Osceala Vista,
Sugarloaf, Waterville, and
White Lodge. For all
others, call one the visitor
information center on the
day. Make reservations at
www.reserveusa.com.

There are campgrounds
at Franconia Notch State
Park, Crawford Notch
State Park, and Moose
Brook State Park.
Reservations for the
state parks can be made
at 603-271-3628.

Log Haven Campground
and Restaurant
P.O. Box 239
Errol, NH 03579
603-482-3294
www.loghaven.com
Woodland location with 77
sites and a pool.

Squam Lake
and Vicinity

Hack-Ma-Tack Campground
713 Endicott Street
Laconia, NH 03246
603-366-5977
150 sites on 30 acres
in the woods, all with
electricity and water.

Pine Hollow Camping World
US 3
Weirs Beach, NH 03247
603-366-2222
or 508-647-1966 (winter)
100 sites, 1 mile from the
main beach at Laconia.

Silver Lake Park Campground
P.O. Box 7
Lochmere, NH 03252
603-524-6289
Quiet, landscaped family
campground with 76 sites
along the lakeshore.

Southern New Hampshire

Ferndale Acres Campground
132 Wednesday Hill Road
Lee, NH 03824
603-659-5082
or 603-623-2351 (winter)
150 sites. Near both sea
and mountains.

Forest Glen Campground
73 Mast Road
Lee, NH 03824
603-659-3416
100 lakeside sites near
Hampton Beach.

Hampton Beach State
RV Park
2 Ocean Boulevard
Hampton Beach, NH 03842
603-926-8990
All 28 sites are for fully
self-contained RVs and
overlook the ocean inlet.

Monadnock State Park
P.O. Box 181
Jaffrey, NH 03452
603-532-8862
21 family sites in the woods;
hiking and nature observation; pets prohibited.

VERMONT

Federal and
State Agencies

State agency and tourist
information is available at the
Vermont state government's
webpage at www.state.vt.us./

Vermont Department
of Fish & Wildlife
103 South Main Street
Waterbury, VT 05671
802-241-3700
Hunting, fishing, and
trapping information.

Vermont Department of
Forests, Parks & Recreation
103 South Main Street
Waterbury, VT 05671
802-241-3655
Seasonal tourist packages
and information on
camping and skiing.

Vermont Department of
Tourism and Marketing
6 Baldwin Street
Montpelier, VT 05633
802-828-3236
or 800-VERMONT
www.1-800-vermont.com
Sights, events and destina-
tions throughout Vermont.

Outdoor Education
and Resources

Vermont Outdoor Guide
Association
P.O. Box 10
North Ferrisburg, VT 05473
800-425-8747
www.voga.org
Over 70 environmental
education programs and
over 80 guide services with
low-impact activities on
the environment through-
out the state of Vermont.

Outfitters
and Activities

See the Vermont Outdoor
Guide Association above.

Lodgings

Inns and Bed and
Breakfast Association
802-223-3443
www.vtchamber.com
Call the Vermont State
Chamber of Commerce
for more information.

Vermont Lodging and
Restaurants Association
802-660-9001
Complete listings throughout Vermont.

Vermont Ski Areas
Association
802-223-2439
www.skivermont.com
Places to stay around the
slopes and more.

Camping

In season, call the state parks
directly for reservations
and a "Vermont Campground
Guide," which covers both
state and private grounds.
www.vtstateparks.com.

Northern Vermont

For northeastern state parks
call 800-658-6934 in winter
for reservations. In summer,
call the following parks for
information: Brighton State
Park 802-723-4360 for campground reservations, or 802-
479-4280 for headquarters;
Ricker Pond State Park at
802-584-3821 for camp-
ground reservations or 802-
479-4280 for headquarters;
Smugglers Notch State Park
at 802-253-4014 for camp-
ground reservations or 802-

479-4280 for headquarters;
Stillwater State Park at 802-
584-3822 for campground
reservations or 802-479-
4280 for headquarters.

For northwestern state parks
in winter, call 800-252-2363
for reservations. Call the following parks directly in summer: Burton Island State Park
at 802-524-6353 for camp-
ground reservations; Underhill
State Park at 802-899-3022.

Green Mountains and
Central Vermont

A complete listing of Green
Mountain National Forest
campgrounds can be found
at www.gorp.com/dow/
eastern/gmcmp.htm.

For southeastern state parks,
call 800-299-3071 in winter,
or directly in summer
as follows: Jamaica State
Park at 802-874-4600 for
campground reservations
or 802-886-8838
for park headquarters;
Quechee Gorge State Park
at 802-295-2990 for camp-
ground reservations or 802-
886-8838 for headquarters.

For camping information on
state parks in the southwest,
call 800-658-1622 in winter
or directly in summer as follows: Branbury State Park at
802-247-5925 for camp-
ground reservations or 802-
483-2001 for headquarters;
Emerald Lake State Park at
802-362-1655 for reserva-
tions or 802-483-2001 for
headquarters.

MASSACHUSETTS

Federal and
State Agencies

Division of Fisheries
and Wildlife
Richard Cronin Field
Headquarters
1 Rabbit Hill Road
Westbourgh, MA 01581
508-792-7270
Fishing and hunting information, general inquiries.

Massachusetts Office of
Travel and Tourism
10 Park Plaza, Suite 4510
Boston, MA 02116

617-727-3201
or 800-227-MASS
www.massvacation.com
Updates on fall foliage and
skiing, calendar of events.

Ferry Services to Martha's Vineyard and Nantucket Island

Cape Island Express Lines
508-997-1688
www.mvferry.com
From New Bedford to
Vineyard Haven.

Hy-Line Cruises
508-778-2600
www.hy-linecruises.com
From Hyannis to Oak Bluffs
and Nantucket.

The Steamship Authority
508-477-8600
www.islandferry.com
From Woods Hole, serving
Vineyard Haven and Oak
Bluffs and also Nantucket.

Outdoor Education and Resources

Northfield Mountain
Recreation and
Environmental Center
99 Millers Falls Road
Northfield, MA 01360
413-659-3714
or 800-859-2960
Recreational courses from
edible plants to star-gazing.

Outfitters and Activities

The Berkshires and Vicinity

Crab Apple Whitewater, Inc.
P.O. Box 295
Charlemont, MA 01339
413-625-2288
or 800-553-7238
Scenic float-trips on Class
III and IV white water on
the Deerfield River.

Dick Moon's Sporting Goods
114 Fenn Street
Pittsfield, MA 01201
413-442-8281
Fly-fishing trips, biking, bird-
watching, photography, and
canoe tours.

Smith & Morey Fly Fishing
Outfitters & Guide Services
36 Church Street
Shelburne Falls, MA

01370
413-625-6279
Guide services on the
Deerfield River

Zoar Outdoor
7 Main Street
P.O. Box 245
Charlemont, MA 01339
413-339-4010
or 800-532-7483
Guided trips and canoes
and sit-on-top kayak
rentals for use on the
Deerfield River.

Cape Cod and the East

Martha's Vineyard Kayak
Company
P.O. Box 4114
Tisbury, MA 02568
508-693-0895
www.menemsha.com
Kayak rentals and scenic
tours on Martha's Vineyard.

Young's Bicycle Shop
6 Broad Street
on Steamboat Wharf
Nantucket, MA 02554
508-228-1151
www.youngsbicycleshop
.com
Bicycle sales and service
and car rentals on the
island.

Lodgings

For extensive accomodation
information throughout
Massachusetts, contact the
Office of Travel and Tourism
(see above)

Berkshires Visitor Bureau
Berkshire Common
Plaza Level
Pittsfield, MA 01201
413-443-9186
or 800-237-5747
www.berkshires.org
Full lodging information
for the Berkshires.

Martha's Vineyard
Chamber of Commerce
P.O. Box 1698
Vineyard Haven, MA
02568
508-693-0085
www.mvy.com
Lodging information plus
free vacation kit on events,
ferries, sights, etc. on
Martha's Vineyard.

Nantucket Visitor Service
25 Federal Street
Nantucket, MA 02554

508-228-0925
Listings of licensed hotels
and lodgings on Nantucket.

Camping

For campsite reservations
in state forests and parks, call
toll-free 877-I-CAMP-MA
or visit www.reserveamerica
.com.

The Berkshires and Vicinity

D.A.R. State Forest
555 East Street
Williamsburg, MA 01096
413-268-7098
50 sites and many trails,
one wheelchair accessible.

Mohawk Trail State Forest
P.O. Box 7
Charlemont, MA 01339
413-339-5504
56 campsites and 6 cabins
with hiking trails, trout
fishing, and swimming.

Mount Greylock State Reservation
3 Rockwell Road
Lanesborough, MA 01237
413-449-9426.
Limited services at camp-
ground. Hike to the summit
for a panoramic view of
5 states.

Pittsfield State Forest
1041 Cascade Street
Pittsfield, MA 01201
413-442-8992
Two camping areas with
31 sites and a beach.

Cape Cod and the East

Nickerson State Park
3488 Main Street
Brewster, MA 02631
508-896-3491
420 wooded sites on
1,900 acres with swimming,
boating, and biking.

Myles Standish State Forest
Cranberry Road
P.O. Box 66
South Carver, MA 02366
508-866-2526
45 campsites located
in the trees or pondside.

Shawme-Crowell
State Forest
42 Main Rte 130
Sandwich, MA 02563
508-888-0351
Over 700 acres of wood-
land with 285 sites and hiking and horse trails.

Scusset Beach State
Reservation
    140 Scusset Beach Road
    Buzzards Bay, MA 02532
    508-888-0859
    Year-round camping for
    tents and RVs, located
    at the east end of the
    Cape Cod Canal.

RHODE ISLAND

Federal and
State Agencies

Department of
Environmental Management
    Foundry Complex
    235 Promenade Complex
    Providence, RI 02908
    401-222-3576
    Provides information on
    regulations and locations
    for purchasing licenses.

Division of
Parks & Recreation
    2321 Hartford Avenue
    Johnston, RI 02919
    401-222-2632
    www.riparks.com
    Information on state
    parks, beaches, and more.

Rhode Island Tourism
    1 West Exchange Street
    Providence, RI 02903
    401-222-2601
    or 800-556-2484
    www.visitrhodeisland.com
    Provides lists of lodging
    and campsites.

Ferry Services
to Block Island

Interstate Navigation
Company
    401-783-4613
    From Point Judith and
    New London.

Nelseco
    860-442-7891
    From New London.

Viking Fleet
    613-668-5700
    Seasonal transportation
    from Montauk, N.Y.

Lodgings

Bed and Breakfasts
of Rhode Island
    P.O. Box 3291
    Newport, RI 02840
    800-828-0000
    www.visitnewport.com/

bedandbreakfasts
    Reservations service
    for the entire state.

Block Island Holidays
    P.O. Box 803
    Block Island, RI 02807
    800-905-0590
    www.blockisland.com
    Provides accommodations
    for Block Island.

Camping

There are no campgrounds
on Block Island, but nearby
campsites on the mainland
include Burlingame
State Park, Charles Town
Breachway and Ninigret
Conservation Area.
Make reservations through
the Division of Parks &
Recreation.

CONNECTICUT

Federal and
State Agencies

Connecticut Department of
Environmental Protection
    79 Elm Street
    Hartford, CT 06106-5127
    860-424-3200 (State
    Parks and Recreation
    Division)
    860-434-8638 (Boating
    Division)
    860-424-3474 (Fisheries
    Division)
    860-424-3630 (Forestry
    Division).

Connecticut Department
of Tourism
    505 Hudson Street
    Hartford, CT 06106
    860-270-8080
    or 800-CT-BOUND
    www.ctbound.org
    General queries and
    what to see and do
    in the state.

Outfitters
and Activities

Backcountry Outfitters
    P.O. Box 70
    Kent, CT 06757
    860-927-3377
    Cross-country skis and
    snowshoe rentals for the
    Litchfields.

Clarke Outdoors
    163 US 7
    West Cornwall, CT 06796

860-672-6365
    Rafting, canoeing, and
    kayaking along the
    Housatonic; Bulls
    Bridge Gorge white-
    water trips.

Lodgings

1890 Colonial Bed
and Breakfast
    P.O. Box 25, Conn. 41
    Sharon, CT 06069
    860 364 0436
    Spacious, luxury rooms
    with breakfast included.

Chaucer House
    88 North Main Street
    Kent, CT 06757
    860-927-4858
    Romantic, colonial bed
    and breakfast getaway
    with a gourmet breakfast.

Fife and Drum Restaurant
and Inn
    53 N. Main Street
    Kent, CT 06757
    860-927-3509
    8 private rooms, one
    handicapped accessible,
    many with four-poster
    or brass beds.

Mayflower Inn
    Conn. 47
    Washington, CT
    860-868-9466
    28 acres of gardens, 25
    luxury rooms and
    gourmet restaurant.

Saybrook Point Inn and Spa
    2 Bridge Street
    Old Saybrook, CT 06475
    860-395-2000
    or 800-243-0212
    62 rooms and a psa
    at the mouth of the
    Connecticut River.

Camping

For reservations at
state park campgrounds,
call 877-668-2267 or the
park directly (see below).
Check www.reserveamerica
.com for online information.
Also check out the
following webpage:
http://dep.state
.ct.us/rec/camping.htm.

Devil's Hopyard State Park
    366 Hopyard Road
    East Haddam, CT 06423
    860-873-8566
    21 sites in the woods
    near a beautiful waterfall.

Swimming prohibited.

Hammonasset Beach
State Park
  Box 271
  Madison, CT 06443
  203-245-1817
  or 203-245-2785
  560 sites with salt-water
  fishing.

Housatonic Meadows
State Park
  Cornwall Bridge, CT
  06754
  860-672-6772
  95 rustic sites. Swimming
  prohibited.

Lake Waramaug State Park
  30 Lake Waramaug Road
  New Preston, CT 06777
  (860) 868-0220
  or 860 868 2592
  78 wooded and open sites.

Macedonia Brook
State Park
  159 Macedonia Brook
  Road
  Kent, CT 06757
  860-927-4100
  or 860-927-3238
  80 sites with excellent
  hiking and stream fishing.

Rocky Neck State Park
  P.O. Box 676
  Niantic, CT 06357
  860-739-5471
  Over 150 sites with

swimming and fishing.

William F. Miller
Campground
  Hammonasset Beach
  State Park,
  Box 271
  Madison, CT 06443
  203-245-1817
  or 203-245-2785
  560 sites with salt-water
  fishing.

Hotel & Motel Chains

(In Maine, New Hampshire,
Vermont, Massachusetts,
Rhode Island, Connecticut)

Best Western International
  800-528-1234

Budget Host
  800-BUD-HOST

Choice Hotels
  800-4-CHOICE

Clarion Hotels
  800-CLARION

Comfort Inns
  800-228-5150

Days Inn
  800-325-2525

Doubletree Hotels and
Guest Suites
  800-222-TREE

Econolodge
  800-446-6900

Embassy Suites
  800-362-2779

Fairfield Inn by Marriott

  800-228-2800

Friendship Inns Hotel
  800-453-4511

Hampton Inns
  800-HAMPTON

Hilton Hotels
  800-HILTONS

Holiday Inns
  800-HOLIDAY

Howard Johnson
  800-654-2000

Motel 6
  00-466-8356

Quality Inns and Suites
  800-228-5151

Radisson Hotels
International
  800-333-3333

Ramada Inns
  800-2-RAMADA

Red Roof Inns
  800-843-7663

Ritz-Carlton
  800-241-3333

Sheraton Hotels and Inns
  800-325-3535

Super 8 Motels
  800-843-1991

Travelodge
  800-255-3050
  (Maine, CT and RI only)

Utell International
  800-223-9868

Westin Hotels and Resorts
  800-228-3000

About the Author and Photographer

Before **Gary Ferguson** began his writing career, he worked as a U.S. Forest Service interpretive naturalist in Idaho's Sawtooth National Recreation Area. He is the author of 13 books on nature and science, including *Through the Woods: A Journey Through America's Forests,* which won the prestigious Lowell Thomas Award. Gary has appeared on more than 100 radio and television programs across the country; his essays on nature can be heard on National Public Radio.

Michael Melford is a renowned photograher whose assignments include both travel and editorial photography. His award-winning work has appeared in many major U.S. publications, including *National Geographic Traveler, Travel and Leisure, Life, Fortune,* and *Newsweek.* He lives with his family in Mystic, Connecticut.

Illustrations Credits

Photographs in this book are by Michael Melford except for the following:

Cover - Larry Ulrich
p. 75 - George Grall/NGS Image Collection
p. 163 - David L. Arnold
p.213 - Phil Schermeister

Index

Abbreviations

A

B

C

D

E

F

National Geographic Guide to America's Outdoors: New England
by Gary Ferguson
Photographed by Michael Melford

Published by the National Geographic Society
John M. Fahey, Jr., *President and Chief Executive Officer*
Gilbert M. Grosvenor, *Chairman of the Board*
Nina D. Hoffman, *Senior Vice President*

Prepared by the Book Division
William R. Gray, *Vice President and Director*
Charles Kogod, *Assistant Director*
Barbara A. Payne, *Editorial Director and Managing Editor*
David Griffin, *Design Director*

Guides to America's Outdoors
Elizabeth L. Newhouse, *Director of Travel Books*
Cinda Rose, *Art Director*
Barbara A. Noe, *Associate Editor*
Caroline Hickey, *Senior Researcher*
Carl Mehler, *Director of Maps*
Roberta Conlan, *Project Director*

Staff for this Book
Patricia Daniels, *Editor*
Dorrit Green, *Designer*
Molly Roberts, *Illustrations Editor*
Caroline J. Dean, Victoria Garrett Jones, Keith R. Moore,
  Jane Sunderland, *Researchers*
Lise Sajewski, *Editorial Consultant*
Thomas L. Gray, *Map Editor*
Jerome N. Cookson, Thomas L. Gray, Nicholas P. Rosenbach,
  Gregory Ugiansky, National Geographic Maps,
  Mapping Specialists, *Map Research and Production*
Tibor G. Tóth, *Map Relief*
R. Gary Colbert, *Production Director*
Gillian Carol Dean, *Assistant Designer*
Janet Dustin, *Illustrations Assistant*
Deborah E. Patton, *Indexer*
Angela George, *Project Assistant*

Charles W. Johnson, Vermont State Naturalist, *Consultant*

Manufacturing and Quality Control
George V. White, *Director*; John T. Dunn, *Associate Director*; Vincent P. Ryan, *Manager;*
Phillip L. Schlosser, *Financial Analyst*

Copyright © 2000 National Geographic Society. All rights reserved.
Reproduction of the whole or any part of the contents without permission
is prohibited. Library of Congress Cataloging-in-Publication Data

The information in this book has been carefully checked and is accurate as of press date.
However, details are subject to change, and the National Geographic Society cannot be
responsible for such changes, or for errors or omissions. Assessments of sites are based on
the authors' subjective opinions, which do not necessarily reflect the publisher's opinion.
The publisher cannot be responsible for any consequences arising from the use of this book.